BEHOLD YOUR
MOTHER

A Biblical and Historical Defense
of the Marian Doctrines

TIM STAPLES

Catholic
Answers
Press

Unless otherwise noted, biblical citations are taken from the Revised Standard Version Bible, Catholic Edition

(© 1965, 1966, Division of Christian Education of the National Council of the Churches of Christ in the United States of America).

Published by Catholic Answers, Inc.
2020 Gillespie Way
El Cajon, California 92020
1-888-291-8000 orders
619-387-0042 fax
catholic.com

Jacket and book design by Claudine Mansour Design
Jacket painting, *Madonna of Humility,* by Fra Angelico
Printed in the United States of America

ISBN 978-1-938983-80-1 hardcover
ISBN 978-1-938983-91-7 paperback
ISBN 978-1-938983-85-6 Kindle
ISBN 978-1-938983-86-3 ePub

All italics added for emphasis in citations from Scripture and ancient texts are the author's.

For Valerie

CONTENTS

INTRODUCTION
WHY MARY MATTERS

When I was on the outside looking in at the Catholic Church, I truly believed the emphasis on Mary in Catholic theology led to a loss of focus on Jesus. My aim, in speaking with Catholics, was not only to debunk Catholic theology's many myths about Mary, but also to point them back to what really matters for salvation: *Jesus Christ.*

Often I would say to them words that I have since heard many times from scores of well-meaning Protestant Christians: "We can agree to disagree about Mary. After all, Mary is hardly ever mentioned in the Bible. And when it comes down to it, *all that really matters is Jesus* anyway." In my mind, *at best,* the Marian dogmas really didn't matter. *At worst,* they led poor souls away from salvation in Jesus Christ, who said so plainly, "I am the way, and the truth, and the life: no one comes to the Father, but by me" (John 14:6).

Now, the Catholic Church agrees with all Christians on the centrality of the person of Jesus Christ in the proclamation of the Christian faith.[1] Its dogmas—*all of them*—are essential to the Christian life precisely because they have as their source and end *the person of Jesus Christ.* If this is true, then disagreement about a matter of faith and morals represents much more than a quarrel about some abstract concept; it is a disagreement about the very person of Jesus.

Many Protestants would actually agree with the Catholic Church here, at least in part. They would agree that a proper understanding of, for example, trinitarian theology, Christology, or even soteriology to be essential for salvation. However, where we generally part company is when we speak of the Marian doc-

---

1. "The transmission of the Christian faith consists primarily in proclaiming Jesus Christ in order to lead others to faith in him," *Catechism of the Catholic Church* (CCC) 425.

trines in this context. Are Catholics saying that missing the mark on Mary can distort our theology? Yes. The Church asks us to consider an "organic connection" (CCC 89) among *all* of the essential truths of the Faith, including the Mariological ones. *Lumen Gentium* 65 says it well:

> For Mary, who has entered deeply into the history of salvation, in a certain way unites within herself the greatest truths of the faith and echoes them; and when she is preached about and honored she calls believers to her son, to his sacrifice and to the love of the Father.[2]

For millions who claim Christ as their Lord and savior, this is far too much emphasis on Mary. Yet, a careful reading of this text from Vatican II reveals Mary to be not so much an object of faith as an instrument. Her divine Son is the terminus of faith; Mary leads the faithful efficaciously to him. Like the moon in relation to the sun, Mary is not the light; she is the most perfect reflection of that light to we who walk "through the valley of the shadow of death," as the psalmist says.

Mary prompts us to come to her Son. This truth will reappear throughout the pages of this book. In her life and being, the Mother of God will teach us who God the Father, the Son, and the Holy Spirit are in their eternal divine relations. She will teach us who her incarnate divine Son is. And so, not only does understanding the truth of Mary as Mother of God help us hit the mark of true biblical theology and true Christology, but denying its truth makes us miss that mark. As the saying attributed (falsely) to Mother Teresa puts it:

No Mary, No Jesus
Know Mary, Know Jesus

---

2. Tanner, *Vatican Council II*, 65.

We will see just how profoundly true this saying is.

In seeing the truth about Mary's Immaculate Conception and Assumption, we will not only see *the glory of Mary*, but we will see the immeasurable dignity and calling of all Christians *in her*. At the same time, we will see God's glory and faithfulness to his promises concretized—his grace perfected—in the life of a real human person. It is in this sense that true Mariology serves to keep the dogmas of our faith from becoming mere abstractions. We see completed in her what awaits the entire body of the faithful who "endure until the end" (Matt. 10:22)—complete victory over sin and the effects of sin. And in the Perpetual Virginity of Mary we will see the truth with regard to the nature of *the sacred*. Our Lady will teach us of the holiness of marriage, the sacraments, and in particular, the nature and meaning of *a life consecrated to God*.

On the flip side of this, we will also see that getting wrong Mary's Immaculate Conception and Assumption means getting wrong who we are as Christians and the "hope" that serves as "a sure and steadfast anchor of the soul" (Heb. 6:19). Missing the mark on Mary's Perpetual Virginity harms our understanding of the nature of marriage, the sacraments, and consecrated life. All of these truths and more are "re-echoed" in the life of the Blessed Virgin. The stakes are high here, folks.

Finally, in seeing Mary's role in God's plan of salvation and her queenship, we will glimpse our own calling to cooperate with God in saving souls and in helping all the world to see their call to become members of not just a family of God, but a *royal family*. To the degree we miss these truths we will miss the urgency of God's call to evangelize.

Why does Mary matter? In answering this question we would do well to consider the exhortation from our Lord Jesus Christ himself to St. John, who was then gazing up at his dying savior and Lord from the foot of the cross. Jesus' words to the youngest apostle, and to each of us, were few yet profound: "Behold, your mother" (John 19:27).

Considering the context, this exhortation could hardly have been more urgent. Our Lord was in the midst of unimaginable suffering in order to redeem the entire world when he uttered these words that have echoed down through the centuries. Was Jesus exhorting John to "lose his focus" on *him*? Hardly! Our Lord understood—as the Catholic Church has continued to proclaim these last 2,000 years in imitation of her divine spouse—that Mariology is not a nice but optional addition to the Faith. It is in truly beholding the Mother of God that one sees her divine Son. Mary was chosen by God to be his most perfect creation to bring Jesus to the world and to bring the world to Jesus.

PART I

MOTHER OF GOD

I

THE GREATEST OF ALL
MARIAN TITLES

Theotokos, Greek for *God-bearer,* is the first and greatest of all Mary's titles and God's supreme gift to her—the foundation in the order of grace of all other Marian dogmas and doctrines. As the Council of Ephesus declared in 431:

> If anyone does not confess that God is truly Emmanuel, and that on this account the Holy Virgin is the Mother of God (for according to the flesh she gave birth to the Word of God become flesh by birth), let him be anathema."[3]

According to the council fathers, this Marian dogma presupposes what all Christians believe: Jesus Christ is God. Indeed, it is from this foundational truth that the *Theotokos* necessarily follows. If Jesus Christ is truly a divine person, then Mary, the Mother of Jesus, is the *Mother of God.*

This seems simple enough. And we should note here that for many in the more traditional Protestant communities, believing Mary to be the *Theotokos* is an area of *agreement* with Catholics. They may not see all of the theological implications involved, but they believe the basic truth that Mary truly is the Mother of God. Yet, for millions in Fundamentalist and Evangelical communities, it is a different story. Especially among Fundamentalists, this ancient teaching places Catholics in the same league with polytheists and idolaters.

---

3. Tanner, *The Decrees of the Ecumenical Councils,* 59.

The objections most often come in two basic forms. First, we hear words to the effect that: "Nowhere in Sacred Scripture do we find the words 'Mother of God' used to describe Mary. If this doctrine were as important as Catholics claim, would not at least one of the inspired writers have used it?" Or, we hear: "It is impossible for God to have a mother. The very claim is blasphemy. If a dog gives birth to a dog, a cat to a cat, and a human to a human, Mary would have to be God in order to give birth to God!"

The Catholic Answer

In saying Mary cannot be the Mother of God because Scripture never explicitly describes her in those terms, Fundamentalists set a trap for themselves and their own beliefs. Where does the Bible say "all doctrines must be explicitly stated in the Bible?" Nowhere. And this is just the beginning of the difficulties. We would have to rule out a host of essential Christian doctrines that are also not declared in Scripture.

For example, all Christians believe in the Trinity. Yet, the word *Trinity* is not found in the Bible. The term *homoousios,* used by the Council of Nicaea to define Christ's shared divinity with the Father—and used by Catholics and non-Catholics alike—is not a biblical term. Christian theology concerning holy matrimony is not found explicit in Scripture, either. Is a couple married by the minister, or do they confect the sacrament between themselves in the presence of the minister? Is marriage a sacrament at all? Is a minister even necessary? Is the couple truly married at church, at the consummation, or could it be done in their living room with only God as their witness? These and other questions require more than the Bible to answer.

Ironically, even the canon of Scripture itself would also go up in smoke if we were to truly rely on Scripture alone. Where does Scripture tell us non-apostles like St. Luke, St. Mark or perhaps the inspired author of Hebrews could write inspired and inerrant Scripture? Where does the Bible tell us who wrote the Gospels, the Acts of the Apostles, Hebrews, Revelation, etc.? Or, as the saying goes, "There is no divinely inspired table of contents *for* the Bible *in* the Bible."

The truth is, all Christians rely upon Church Tradition as well as upon Scripture in order to articulate core Christian teachings. Indeed, the Bible itself tells us that we ought to do just that: "So then, brethren, stand firm and hold to the traditions which you were taught by us, either by word of mouth or by letter" (2 Thess. 2:15). Oral Tradition can never *contradict* Scripture. Indeed, one can argue that all dogma is found at least *implicitly* in Scripture. But to require Scripture alone as the sole rule of faith is not a historically Christian doctrine at all.

The real questions we need to ask are: 1. Does Scripture *contradict* the teaching that Mary is the Mother of God? 2. Is the *concept* or *the essential truth* of Mary as Mother of God found in Sacred Scripture? And so we proceed . . .

What the Bible Says

Granted, the phrase "Mother of God" is not in Scripture, but we do have something synonymous in Luke 1:43, in the account of the Visitation of Mary to her much older relative Elizabeth. When Mary entered Elizabeth's home and greeted her, Elizabeth "exclaimed with a loud cry: 'Blessed are you among women, and blessed is the fruit of your womb! And why is this granted me, that the *mother of my Lord* should come to me?'" The *Catechism of the Catholic Church* (CCC) explains:

> Called in the Gospels "the mother of Jesus," Mary is acclaimed by Elizabeth, at the prompting of the Spirit and even before the birth of her son, as "the mother of my Lord." In fact, the One whom she conceived as man by the Holy Spirit, who truly became her Son according to the flesh, was none other than the Father's eternal Son, the second person of the Holy Trinity. Hence, the Church confesses that Mary is truly "Mother of God" (495).

Biblical evidence for this dogma is not limited to the New Testament. St. Cyril of Jerusalem and the fathers of the Council of Ephesus referred to an intriguing prophecy from Isaiah 7:14 in their own exposition of both Jesus' divinity and Mary's divine maternity.

> For the holy prophet Isaiah does not lie when he says, "Behold a virgin shall conceive and bear a son and they shall call his name Emmanuel, which is interpreted God with us."[4]

The Messiah was to be born of a woman, and yet he was to be called *Immanuel*, which means *God with us*. According to the council fathers, *God with us* means what it says: Jesus is God; so this prophetic virgin, Mary, would then be the Mother of God. Thus we have a text from the Old Testament that prophesied the mother of the Messiah was indeed to be the Mother of God. Add to that the text of Luke 1:43 and we have both the Old and New Testaments revealing the "Catholic" truth about Mary.

Lord vs. God

"Not so fast," say many among our Protestant friends. Jimmy Swaggart represents one among a chorus of voices who object to this historical Christian understanding. He presents quite a different take on Luke 1:43:

> Here Elisabeth called Jesus "Lord" . . . *But once again it must be emphasized that it was not God that was born of Mary, it was the human child—the Lord Jesus Christ.*[5]

To be fair to Swaggart, the New Testament does use the term *lord* to denote authority figures or even things—e.g., idols that are obviously *not* the one, true God. In 1 Corinthians 8:5, for example,

---

4. Ibid., 71. This quote is taken from St. Cyril of Alexandria's "Letter to John of Antioch," which was incorporated into the "Formula of Union" adopted by the council fathers and ratified by the pope.

5. Swaggart, *Catholicism and Christianity*, 101.

St. Paul writes, "Indeed there are many gods and many lords." This would indeed refer to some*thing* other than almighty God—*a lord*, instead of *the Lord*, if you will.[6] Does Jimmy Swaggart have an argument here? Could *lord* here in Luke 1:43 refer to *humanity* rather than divinity with regard to Christ? This is not a point to dismiss lightly.

So how are we to know whether *lord* (Gr., *kurios*) refers to divinity or not? As is the case with all of biblical exegesis, *context* is key. And we need not go beyond the above-quoted 1 Corinthians 8:5 to find an excellent example of this truth. Paul's words, "Indeed there are many gods and many lords," are immediately followed by: "Yet to us there is one God, the Father, from whom are all things, and for whom we exist, and *one Lord, Jesus Christ, through whom are all things and through whom we exist.*"

Both the pagan and Jewish converts in Corinth would have immediately understood Paul's carefully crafted words. Jesus is *the one Lord* in contrast to the "many [false] lords" worshipped in the surrounding pagan world. Thus, to these pagan converts, these words could hardly be plainer: Jesus is God. And his Jewish Christian readers would have been familiar with the great *sh'ma* of Deuteronomy 6:4: "Hear, therefore, O Israel, the Lord our God *is one Lord.*" When Paul refers to Jesus as *the one Lord*, his Jewish readers and listeners could have only one interpretation: Jesus is the one, almighty God of the *sh'ma*.

Moreover, considering that the Greek translation of the Hebrew Scriptures—the Septuagint—used *kurios* in place of the unmentionable divine name YHWH throughout, the Jews were well accustomed to the usage of *lord* for divinity. Thus, when the context is understood, Paul is unequivocal: Jesus is *the one Lord, God almighty.*[7]

---

6. Cf. Liddel and Scott, *A Greek-English Lexicon*, 1013. The authors list numerous examples of *lord* (Gr., *kurios*) used in the sense of an earthly potentate, master, owner, or even *sir*. Cf. 1 Tim. 6:15, Matt. 21:40, Mark 6:21, John 12:21, etc.

7. We also note the definite connection between Jesus being "Lord" and his being creator as we also see in John 1:1–3. When 1 Corinthians 8:6 says "through whom all things exist," or when John 1:3 tells us, "without him was not anything made that was made,"

Mother of the Lord God

The key to our discussion, then, is to ascertain how *kurios* is being used of Christ in Luke 1:43. Is it being used to describe Jesus with regard to his humanity alone, or with regard to his divinity? Let's take a look again at the text. When Elizabeth exclaims, "Why is this granted to me that the mother of my Lord should come to me?," she refers to Jesus as Lord within a specific context. On the literal level, she calls Mary "*the mother* of my Lord." Mothers give birth to *persons*, not natures. This alone would lead us to conclude Mary to be the Mother of God if we understand properly Jesus to be one, divine person. We will come back and speak more to this point below.

When we examine the spiritual sense of Elizabeth's usage of *mother of my Lord* there is even more reason to believe she is referring to Christ as a divine person. In declaring, "And why is this granted me, that the mother of my Lord should come to me?," Elizabeth was referencing, almost verbatim, a text from 2 Samuel 6 in which we discover the Ark of the Covenant being brought into the newly conquered city of Jerusalem in triumphant procession. After having experienced a dramatic manifestation of the power of God at work in and through the ark, King David exclaimed, "How can the ark of the Lord come to me?" (2 Sam. 6:9).

With this reference, Elizabeth—*under the inspiration of the Holy Spirit*—suggests Mary is the *Ark of the New Covenant*. In Chapter 4 we will discuss this in more detail, but for now consider these parallels:

> 2 Samuel 6:16 presents King David *leaping* in the presence of *the ark*. Luke 1:41 tells how St. John the Baptist *leapt* in the womb of Elizabeth when *Mary* greeted her upon entering into her home.

---

we know we are talking about God, who in Scripture is revealed to be the creator of all things. Cf. Gen. 1:1, Isa. 44:24, 45:8, 12, etc.

2 Samuel 6:11 records that "the ark of the Lord abode in the house of Obededom the Gethite *three months.*" Luke 1:56 reveals that Mary "remained in the house of Elizabeth about *three months.*"

Further, recall the reason the Ark of the Covenant was believed to be surpassingly holy. It carried inside of it three holy objects:

1. A sample of the *manna,* the miraculous bread from heaven (Ex. 16).
2. The *Ten Commandments* (Ex. 20).
3. *Aaron's rod* that miraculously sprouted blossoms (Num. 17).[8]

All three of these gifts given by God to Israel were *types* of Jesus Christ. Mary carried within her womb:

The *true bread from heaven* (John 6:32).
The Word made flesh (John 1:14).
Our true *High Priest* (Heb. 3:1).

The parallels are unmistakable. Mary is revealed to have been graced by God to be the New Covenant Ark of the Covenant. And there is much that is revealed to us about Mary through this august title.[9] But from the clear revelation here of Mary being *Mother of my Lord,* in the context of her being revealed to be the *Ark of the Lord God of Israel,* it necessarily follows that Mary is *Mother of God.*

---

8. Cf. Heb. 9:4.
9. It should be noted that titles like this carry with them well-known connotations from the Old Testament. Take Jesus' statement in Mark 2:28, for example: "So the Son of man is Lord even of the Sabbath." This title was packed with meaning for his first-century Jewish audience. "Lord of the Sabbath?" In Scripture, almighty God alone is revealed to be the *Lord of the Sabbath* (cf. Ex. 16:23, 25; 20:10; Deut. 5:14, etc.). Thus, Jesus reveals his divinity. As we will see here and in chapters to come, "Ark of the Covenant" is similarly packed with meaning.

The Decisive Question: Who Is Jesus?

For those who would deny that Mary is the Mother of God there is one devastating question: "Who is Jesus Christ?" If Mary is not the Mother of God, then to whom did she give birth? For Jimmy Swaggart, the answer is to say Mary gave birth to an earthly and human "lord" rather than God. Thus, we must again ask the question: "Who, then, is Jesus Christ?"

This discussion reminds me of a debate I had years ago with a "nondenominational" minister where the topics were diverse, but eventually got around to Mary. When I mentioned Mary as "Mother of God," his face lit up and he vehemently objected. "God has no mother!" In front of the about 500 people in attendance, we had a dialogue that went something like this:

> TIM: "So, you reject the doctrine of Mary as Mother of God?"
>
> PASTOR BOB: "Absolutely, God has no mother!"
>
> TIM: "Well, let me ask you this question, then. Is Jesus God?"
>
> PASTOR BOB: "Absolutely, he is 100 percent God and 100 percent man!"
>
> TIM: "Okay, good. Let me ask you another question. Was he God when he was a little boy, let's say, of two years?"
>
> PASTOR BOB: "Absolutely!"
>
> TIM: "Good. We agree. Was he God when Mary was six months pregnant with him and he was living in her womb?"
>
> PASTOR BOB: "Yes, he was God from the moment of his conception!"
>
> TIM: "Was he God when he was coming out of the womb of Mary at his birth?"
>
> PASTOR BOB: He responded a bit slower and softer at this point, but after a brief pause he said, "Yes, he was God then, too."
>
> TIM: "Was Mary, then, the Mother of God?"

At this point there was a long and deafening silence, which Pastor Bob broke by exclaiming, "No, she is not the Mother of God! She is the mother of the man, Jesus Christ!"

A New Nestorianism

Pastor Bob's rejection of Mary as Mother of God was rooted, as was my own when I was Protestant, in a lot of misunderstanding and anti-Catholic bias built up over years. But rejecting Mary as *Theotokos* inevitably results in one of three serious Christological errors:

1. Denial of the divinity of Christ.
2. Creation of two persons to represent Jesus Christ, one human and one divine.
3. The "unintelligible Christology" of which Fr. John Hardon, S.J., wrote.

If Mary didn't give birth to God, she must have given birth to *a mere human person,* as the first two of the above-mentioned errors claim. The first is the error of Arianism, named after its fourth-century Alexandrian founder, the infamous priest and archheretic Arius. He and all who follow in his footsteps deny Jesus is God and thus cease to be Christian at all. This error lives today in quasi-Christian sects such as the Jehovah's Witnesses and the Iglesia Ni Cristo, among others. We have already presented an antidote, albeit briefly, to this false teaching when we demonstrated the truth concerning Christ's divinity.

The second position is where we want to focus our attention now, because it represents a rebirth of the ancient heresy of Nestorianism, and is, unfortunately, alive and well in popular Evangelical and Fundamentalist Christianity today.

Nestorius, the patriarch of Constantinople from 428 to 431, was excommunicated by Pope Celestine and the Council of Ephesus for denying that Mary was the Mother of God. The crux of his error is found in his claim that in Christ there are *two persons* with a *moral union* rather than *two natures* with a *hypostatic union.*[10]

---

10. There is a real question among theologians today as to whether Nestorius actually taught "Nestorianism." We would argue he did, but the point is both debatable and beyond the scope of this book. From here forward I will refer to the teaching condemned by

This view radically divides Christ's humanity and divinity to the point of presenting an all-but-incoherent Christology. When we speak to Jesus are we speaking to *two subjects*? Would Jesus speak to himself as two subjects? "Good morning, divine Jesus, how are you?" "I'm well, thank you human Jesus . . . "

The Catholic and biblical position teaches Jesus Christ to be one person—*one subject*—to whom two natures both distinctly belong: one divine and one human. The natures of Christ are joined in his one, divine *hypostasis,* or *person,* without being co-mingled or divided. This union is thus called the *hypostatic union.*[11] It is the same divine person, Jesus Christ, who speaks and acts as both God and man.

In denying Mary to be the true Mother of God, millions of our Protestant friends who believe Mary gave birth to the *man,* Jesus Christ, and not God, end up in agreement—though often unwit-tingly—with the Nestorian heresy. Some will proceed to divide the events in Christ's life, claiming the *divine* Christ did some of his acts and the *human* Christ did others. Very commonly, we find the claim among Fundamentalists that the *human* Christ died, not the *divine.* Some will even claim only the *divine* Christ healed; or that we worship the *divine* Jesus but never the *man* Jesus.[12]

Cyril and the fathers of the Council of Ephesus referred to a host of scriptures to demonstrate the error of the Nestorians and all those who radically divide the actions and person of Christ.

---

the Church proposing there to be two persons in Christ as Nestorianism. We will not attempt to deal with the question of Nestorius himself.

11. The term *hypostatic* is rooted in the Greek word *hypostasis,* which means *nature* or *being.* It came to be used as *person. Persona,* in Latin, is a more precise word for *person* because *hypostasis,* in its original and ancient usage, could refer to the nature of a dog or cat as well as man. It did not have the connotation of an *individual substance of a rational nature* that *persona* does. That is why St. Jerome was not comfortable with its use as a reference to the *persons* of the Trinity or the *person* of Christ. However, *hypostatic union* came to be defined as the union of the two natures of Christ *in the one person* or *hypostasis* of Christ. And *hypostasis* came to be understood and used as synonymous with the Latin *persona.*

12. This is a minority opinion that I encountered in my days in the Assemblies of God. You will find it among a smattering of folks in Evangelical, Fundamentalist, and Pentecostal circles.

Fr. Valentine Long, O.F.M., sums up nicely what one finds in the conciliar decrees:

> St. Cyril had a wide choice of utterances from our blessed Lord to rely upon. Never once in the Gospels did Christ, who in word and deed revealed his two natures, speak as two persons. It was "Young man, I say to you, arise," and not "the God in me" says so. He did not ask the blind men before their instantaneous cure, "Do you believe my divine omnipotence can do this?" No, it was simply; "Do you believe that I am able to do this?" Dying on the cross, the Savior did not cry out that his human nature thirsted. His words were, "I thirst." His divinity worked miracles; his humanity needed to eat and drink and sleep, but the "I" of his assertions, which admitted both natures, allowed no duality of person. "The Father and I are one" and "The Father is greater than I" are expressions of the same undivided person.[13]

Anyone who maintains belief in the divinity of Christ and yet attempts to say Mary is the mother of the man Jesus but not the divine Jesus creates two persons in Christ. And this simply cannot be. The Bible says, "*In him* the whole fullness of deity dwells bodily" (Col. 2:9) and "*in him* all things were created, in heaven and on earth, visible and invisible" (Col.1:16). There is never a case of *in them* with reference to Christ. The subject of both the human and divine natures is always the same "he."

The seriousness of this error cannot be overstated because, between these two positions, we are ultimately talking about *different Christs*. Paul's words to the Corinthians come to mind:

> For if someone comes and preaches another Jesus than the one we preached, or if you receive a different spirit from the one you received, or if you accept a different gospel from the one you accepted, you submit to it readily enough (2 Cor. 11:4).

13. Long, *The Mother of God,* 25.

Imagine if someone were to come up to you and excitedly exclaim, "I've met Jesus, and he's changed my life. I want you to meet him, too!" "Great!" you respond. "I would like to meet him as well!" Suppose this someone were then to say, "He's right down the street over here. He's a Hispanic fellow, so be sure to pronounce his name *Hey-soos* when you speak to him." Folks, no matter how excited someone may be about meeting this man named Jesus, *this* Jesus would not have the power to save anyone. He is the wrong Jesus! Only the true Jesus has the power to save. That is why it is crucial for us to get the *right* Jesus in our Christology. And getting the right Mary helps us to get the right Jesus.

A Faulty Syllogism

But what about the oft-posed objection presented at the beginning of this chapter: "If a dog gives birth to a dog, a cat to a cat, a human to a human, Mary would have to be God in order to give birth to God!" How do we respond?

This question always brings to mind a debate I watched back in the eighties on the *John Ankerberg Show,* a Protestant television broadcast, between Walter Martin and Fr. Mitch Pacwa. Still a Protestant at the time, I was rooting for Martin—then one of the leading Evangelical apologists in the world and a mentor of mine.

During the debate Martin made the classic blunder of claiming that Mary was the mother of Jesus' human nature only, and so could not be called *Mother of God.* As part of his argument he presented the classic syllogism used by the Church for well over a millennium and a half:

Major premise: Jesus is God
Minor premise: Mary is the mother of Jesus
Conclusion: Mary is the Mother of God

But then he presented another syllogism that in his mind followed *necessarily* from the first, and one that if held would prove devastating to New Testament theology:

Major premise: God is Trinity
Minor premise: Mary is the mother of God
Conclusion: Mary is the mother of the Trinity

I can remember thinking, as I watched the debate, "Yeah, Pacwa, explain that one away!"

In his response, Fr. Pacwa explained that Mary is only the mother of the *second person* of the Blessed Trinity incarnate, because the Father and the Holy Spirit did not become incarnate. In his syllogism, Martin had fallen prey to the logical fallacy of the *undistributed middle term*. The term "God" in the title "Mother of God" must be clarified—distributed properly—as referring *only* to the second person of the Blessed Trinity, who *is* God but who *isn't* the Trinity.

When we say *God*, we may be referring to all three persons of the Blessed Trinity, but not necessarily so. The three persons in the Trinity are distinct within the eternal relations, so we can speak of them individually. Thus, we can say Mary is only the Mother of the *second person* of the Trinity. But we must also remember that the three persons share the same divine nature; hence, they are each fully God. There are not three Gods, nor are there "parts" with God. He is absolutely one in essence or nature. Thus, we can say Mary is simply the *Mother of God*.

This point of confusion is relatively simple to clear up, but our Protestant friends might still perceive an apparent weakness in our argument, as Walter Martin did during the debate. Even if Mary is only the mother of the second person of the Blessed Trinity, he (the second person of the Trinity) is just as eternal as the other two divine persons. Mary, Protestants might say, would still have to be eternal in order to be his mother. Thus, we really haven't answered the objection that in order to give birth to God, Mary would have to *be* God.

Yet the Catholic Church does not say Mary is the source of the divine nature of the second person of the Blessed Trinity. That would be both heretical and absurd. But it does not then follow that she cannot be his mother.

We can use the example of normal human reproduction to help clarify this point. When a man and wife have a child, they are not the source of the child's immortal soul. God, the source of all life, directly creates each individual soul.[14] However, we do not conclude from this that the mother is merely the mother of the *body* of the child. Instead she is the mother of a whole *person* who is a body/soul composite.

Analogously, though Mary did not provide Jesus with either his divine nature or his immortal human soul, she was more than the mother of a body. Mary, like any other mother, gave birth to a person; and that person is God.

So What?

The Martin/Pacwa debate took an unexpected turn when John Ankerberg actually *agreed* with Fr. Pacwa that Mary was the Mother of God. This made for interesting television! In reply Ankerberg said words to the effect of: "So, she's the Mother of God, so what?" What, he wanted to know, was the big deal?

Ankerberg came to acknowledge the truth that Mary is the Mother of God, but like so many Protestants, did not recognize the biblical implications that flow from this essential Christian teaching. He objected to what he perceived as the "Mary worship" that flows from the Catholic understanding of Mary's divine maternity; he objected to Catholics' calling Mary the "Mother of the Church."

Of course, Catholics do not adore Mary as if she were God, but we *do* believe that being the Mother of God entitles Mary to a unique place of honor in the Church. In the next chapter we'll see why the title of *Theotokos* is such a big deal when we examine the problems inherent in its rejection.

14. Cf. Eccles. 12:7.

2

TRUTH AND CONSEQUENCES
WHAT HAPPENS WHEN
THEOTOKOS *IS REJECTED*

The fathers of Vatican Council II tell us:

> Mary . . . shines forth to the whole community of the elect . . .
> Devoutly meditating upon her and contemplating her in the
> light of the Word made man, the Church reverently penetrates
> more deeply into the great mystery of the Incarnation . . .
> Having entered deeply into the history of salvation, Mary, in
> a way, unites in her person and re-echoes the most important
> doctrines of the faith.[15]

Put simply: the truth about Mary is inextricably bound up with
the truth about her divine Son. One of the great minds of recent
memory, Fr. John Hardon, said it this way: "Christology is unintelligible without knowing the role of Christ's mother."[16] But the
opposite is equally as true. If we meditate "more deeply into the
great mystery of the Incarnation," we will also come to know the
Mother of God in a deeper way as well.

Indeed, the *Catechism of the Catholic Church* tells us there are
"mutual connections between [all of] the dogmas" and an intrinsic "coherence" between them precisely because all of the truths
of the Faith are ultimately unified and vivified in the one person

---

15. *Lumen Gentium* 65.
16. Hardon, *The Catholic Catechism*, 150.

of Jesus Christ who *is* the truth.[17] But the "organic connection" between Mariology and Christology can be seen in a most particular way, revealing the most grave of consequences where there are *disconnects.*[18]

Eric Svendsen will serve as our modern example of how *Mariological* error so often leads to *christological* error. And Walter Martin will show us how errors about Christ lead to errors about Mary. Both will hopefully help us to see the inseparable relationship between *Theotokos* and *Son.*

Walter Martin

In his classic apologetics work, *Kingdom of the Cults,* Martin gives us insight into why the dogma of the *Theotokos* is such a "big deal." As we saw in Chapter 1, Martin denied Mary is the Mother of God. This is somewhat well-known in apologetic circles. But what is perhaps lesser-known is that it was Martin's faulty *Christology* that appears to have led to his faulty *Mariology.*

You'll recall that Martin claimed Mary was "the mother of Jesus' body," and not the Mother of God, and that Mary "gave him his human nature alone," so that we cannot say she is the Mother of God; she is the *mother of the man,* Jesus Christ. This radical division of humanity and divinity was rooted in his claim that "sonship" in Christ has nothing at all to do with God in his eternal relations within the Blessed Trinity. In Martin's Christology, divinity and humanity are so sharply divided that he concluded "eternal sonship" to be an unbiblical Catholic invention:

> [T]here cannot be any such thing as eternal Sonship, for there is a logical contradiction of terminology due to the fact that the word "Son" predicates time and the involvement of creativity.

17. Cf. CCC 90.
18. Ibid., 89.

Christ, the Scripture tells us, as the Logos, is timeless, ". . . the Word *was* in the beginning" *not* the Son![19]

From Martin's perspective then, Mary as "Mother of God" is a nonstarter. If "Son of God" refers to Christ as the *eternal* Son, then there would be no denying that Mary is the mother of the Son of God, who is God; hence, Mother of God would be an inescapable conclusion. But if sonship only applies to "time and creativity," then references to Mary's "son" would not refer to divinity at all.

But there is just a little problem here. Beyond the fact that John 1:14 tells us "the Word was made flesh," and John 1:1 tells us "the Word was God"—thus, Mary is the mother of the Word and so she is the Mother of God anyway—the sad fact is that in the process of Martin's theologizing he ended up losing the real Jesus. Notice, the second person of the Blessed Trinity is no longer the eternal Son![20] And it gets worse from here, if that is possible! Martin goes on:

> The term "Son" itself is a functional term, as is the term "Father" and has no meaning apart from time. The term "Father" incidentally never carries the descriptive adjective "eternal" in Scripture; as a matter of fact, only the Spirit is called eternal ("the eternal Spirit"—Hebrews 9:14), emphasizing the fact that the words Father and Son are purely functional as previously stated.[21]

It would be difficult to overstate the importance of what we are saying here. Jesus revealed to us the essential truth that God exists *eternally* as Father, Son, and Holy Spirit in his inner life. For Martin, God would be father by analogy in relation to the humanity of Christ, but not in the eternal divine relations; hence, he is not the eternal Father. So, not only has Martin lost Jesus, the eternal Son; now he has lost the Father! This compels us to ask the ques-

19. Martin, *The Kingdom of the Cults*, 103.
20. The Eternal Sonship of Christ is revealed in multiple biblical texts including Colossians 1:15–16; John 3:16, 5:17–18, 17:5, etc.
21. Martin, *The Kingdom of the Cults*, 103.

tion: Who then is God, the Blessed Trinity, in eternity, according to Walter Martin and all those who agree with his theology? He is *not Father, Son,* and Holy Spirit. He must be the eternal . . . *Blah . . . the Word,* and the Holy Spirit. He would *become* a father *by analogy* when he created the universe and again *by analogy* at the Incarnation of the Word and through the adoption of all Christians as "sons of God." But he would not be the *eternal* Father. The metaphysical problems begin here and continue to eternity . . . literally. Let us now summarize Martin's teaching and some of the problems it presents:

1. Fatherhood and sonship would not be intrinsic to God. The Catholic Church understands that an essential aspect of Christ's mission was to reveal God to us *as he is* in his inner life as Father, Son, and Holy Spirit.[22] The Jews already understood God to be father by *analogy,* but they had no knowledge of God as *Eternal Father* in relation to the *Eternal Son.*[23] In Jesus' great high priestly prayer in John 17, he declared his Father was Father "before the world was made" (v. 5) and thus, to quote the *Catechism of the Catholic Church,* in "an unheard-of sense."[24] In fact, Christ revealed God's *name* as Father.[25] Names in Hebrew culture reveal something about the character of the one named.

---

22. Cf. Matt. 11:27–28: "All things have been delivered to me by my Father; and no one knows the Son except the Father, and no one knows the Father except the Son and any one to whom the Son chooses to reveal him."

23. CCC 238 cites Deuteronomy 32:6 and Malachi 2:10 as examples of how God is referred to as *father* by analogy in the Old Testament in the context of God being the *creator.* However, the Jews had no concept of God as Eternal Father in relation to the Eternal Son. They could not because the truth of the Trinity was revealed through Jesus Christ.

24. CCC 239–240: By calling God "Father, the language of faith indicates two main things: that God is the first origin of everything and transcendent authority; and that he is at the same time goodness and loving care for all his children . . . Jesus revealed that God is Father in an unheard-of sense; he is Father not only in being creator; he is eternally Father in relation to his only Son, who is eternally Son only in relation to his Father."

25. Cf. John 17:6, 11, 12, 26.

Thus, he reveals God to *be* Father, not just that he is *like* a father. Thus, God never *becomes* Father; he *is* the Eternal Father.[26]

2. If Sonship applies *only* to humanity and time, then "the Son" would also be extrinsic, or outside, if you will, of the second person of the Blessed Trinity. Thus, as much as he would have denied it, Martin effectively creates two persons to represent Christ—one divine and one human. This theology leads to the logical conclusion that the *person* who died on the cross 2,000 years ago would have been merely a man. If that were so, he would have no power to save us. Scripture reveals Christ as *the savior*, not *merely* a delegate of God the savior.[27] He was fully man in order to make fitting atonement for us. He was fully God in order to have the power to save us.

3. This theology completely reduces the revelation of God in the New Covenant that separates Christianity from all other religions in the world. Jesus revealed God as he is from all eternity as Father, Son and Holy Spirit. Martin reduces this to mere function. Thus, "Father" does not tell us who God *is*, only what God *does*. Radical feminists do something similar when they refuse to acknowledge God as "Father." God becomes reduced to that which he *does* as "Creator, Redeemer, and Sanctifier" and in the process there is a truly tragic loss of the knowledge of who God *is*. In the case of Walter Martin, it was bad theology that led to a similar loss.

---

26. Among Martin's errors is a misunderstanding of the term "begotten." To be begotten is not the same as to come into existence. St. Thomas Aquinas points out that this is true even when applied to human beings. We commonly say a newborn child was "born today," even though we know he has already been in existence for nine months. Thus, "born" does not strictly mean "came to be." Christ is "*eternally* begotten of the Father . . . begotten, not made, consubstantial with the Father." Thus, "begotten" does not imply "came to be" just as in the case of childbirth.

27. It is true that Jesus was a delegate of God as fully man, the Messiah, the anointed one of God (1 Tim. 2:5), but he was also God himself. Titus 2:13 refers to Christ as "the great God and our savior." That is why we said he was and is not *merely* a delegate of God, the savior. He *is* also God, our savior.

4. There is a basic metaphysical principle found, for example, in Malachi 3:6, that comes into play here as well: "For I the Lord do not change." In defense of Martin, he did seem to realize that one cannot posit change in the divine persons. As stated above, "fatherhood" and "sonship" would not relate to divinity at all in his way of thinking. Thus, he became a proper Nestorian (though he would never admit that) who divides Christ into two persons. And that is bad enough. However, one must be very careful here because when one posits the first person of the Blessed Trinity *became* the Father and the second person of the Blessed Trinity *became* the Son, it becomes very easy to slip into another heresy that would admit change into the divine persons. Below, we will discover Eric Svendsen to be a contemporary example of a Protestant apologist who regrettably takes that next step.

Walter Martin's bad Christology led to a bad Mariology. But he wouldn't have lost his Christological bearings if he had correctly understood Mary as *Theotokos*. The moment the thought arose in his mind that *Sonship* only applied to Christ's humanity, Martin could have reminded himself that Mary is the Mother of God. He would have lost neither the eternal Son nor the eternal Father because *Theotokos* would have guarded him from error. The prophetic words of the council come to mind once again: "Mary . . . unites in her person and re-echoes the most important doctrines of the faith."[28]

The Problem Continues

Unfortunately, many years after Walter Martin's death, the denial of Mary's divine maternity continues in Evangelical and especially Fundamentalist circles. In Eric Svendsen's book, *Evangelical Answers: A Critique of Current Roman Catholic Apologists*, we find just such an example. Svendsen gives four objections to the doctrine

---

28. *Lumen Gentium* 65.

of Mary as Mother of God, ranging from the novel (and bizarre) to the more traditional Protestant objections, that lead to *multiple errors in Christology,* and in the process gives us a good sampling of the confusion that persists today among many Protestants. Whereas Martin's bad Christology led to errant Mariology, Svendsen's bad Mariology led to errant Christology. We will begin with his fourth and strangest objection and then move to his first three:[29]

OBJECTION 1: Severed ties.

This claim, which denies Mary's *ongoing* maternal relationship with Christ, will sound absolutely crazy to my Catholic readers:

> The fourth and final objection to the title "Mother of God" is that such a title implies an on-going relationship . . . It is evident from the New Testament that Jesus effectively severed all biological ties with Mary before he went to the cross.[30]

He "severed all biological ties?" When did this happen?

Svendsen never really says. But he asserts that evidence for the so-called "severing" is found in Matthew 12:46–50:

> While he was still speaking to the people, behold, his mother and his brethren stood outside, asking to speak to him. But he replied to the man who told him, "Who is my mother, and who are my brethren?" And stretching out his hand toward his disciples, he said, "Here are my mother and my brethren! For whoever does the will of my Father in heaven is my brother, and sister, and mother."[31]

Because Jesus' biological ties with Mary were "severed"—probably when he began his public ministry—Svendsen can even allow,

---

29. Svendsen, *Evangelical Answers,* 127–136.
30. Ibid., 132.
31. Ibid.

for argument's sake, that Mary could have been the Mother of God for a time, but isn't any more:

> Let us assume for the moment that we agree on the title "Mother of God." It is one thing to affirm that Mary gave birth to Jesus, and hence *was* the Mother of God. It is another thing entirely to postulate that there is an on-going relationship . . . it does not thereby follow that she retains title or status as the "Mother of God." It is evident from many New Testament passages that Jesus effectively severed all biological ties with Mary before he went to the cross.[32]

The Catholic Answer

1. It is absurd to say that Mary ceased to be Jesus' mother.

Not only is Scripture silent about this alleged "severing," but the concept itself is farcical. Biological ties reach down to the level of DNA and to the essence of what it means to be human, including "the man Christ Jesus" (1 Tim. 2:5). To say those ties are "severable," to say that to the point that Mary would not be Jesus' mother any longer, is tantamount to denying his full humanity.[33]

2. In John 19:26–27, John says that Mary is Jesus' mother.

---

32. Ibid.

33. Though Svendsen leaves the discussion on the surface, the idea that Mary could cease being Jesus' mother leads dangerously to positing an "accidental" union of natures, which would deny the hypostatic union. In the *Summa Theologiae* (III, Q. 2, Art. 6) Thomas Aquinas rightly says theologies that posit "an accidental union [of Christ's human and divine natures] are not to be styled opinions but heresies condemned by the Church in councils." 2 Constantinople, *Anathemas Against the Three Chapters*, 4, 5, 8, confirms a "union of subsistence" that is indivisible in the hypostatic union. In simple terms: For Mary to cease being the Mother of God there would have to be a change in the unchangeable human nature of Christ in its union with the divine nature in the person of the second person of the Blessed Trinity. That can't happen.

When Jesus saw his mother, and the disciple whom he loved standing near, he said to his mother, "Woman, behold your son!" Then he said to the disciple, "Behold, your mother!" And from that hour the disciple took her to his own home. After this Jesus, knowing that all was now finished, said (to fulfill the Scripture), "I thirst."

If Jesus had "severed all biological ties" to Mary before he went to the cross, it is odd that John, under inerrant divine inspiration, would call her Jesus' mother right at the foot of the cross.

3. Even after the resurrection, Mary is referred to as the *Mother of Jesus* in Acts 1:14.

All these with one accord devoted themselves to prayer, together with the women and Mary the mother of Jesus, and with his brethren.

No evidence of any "severing" here, but there *is* evidence of an ongoing maternal relationship.

4. The biblical foundation for Svendsen's claim crumbles under the weight of serious scrutiny.
Once again, we read:

"Who is my mother, and who are my brethren?" And stretching out his hand toward his disciples, he said, "Here are my mother and my brethren! For whoever does the will of my Father in heaven is my brother, and sister, and mother" (Matt. 12:48–50).

In his encyclical *Redemptoris Mater,* Pope St. John Paul II explains in simple terms the proper interpretation of this text:

He [Jesus] wishes to divert attention from motherhood understood only as a fleshly bond, in order to direct it toward those mysterious bonds of the spirit which develop from hearing and keeping God's word.[34]

Jesus was not denying that Mary was his mother; rather, he was teaching us the most important aspect of Mary's divine maternity and, indeed, of all human motherhood: that it is first and foremost spiritual. Mary is both the mother of Jesus on the biological level and the ultimate example of spiritual motherhood in the order of grace.

OBJECTION 2: Original intent.

Svendsen claims "Mother of God" is an illegitimate title because, "The original intent for the title changed from one that upheld the deity of Christ to one that honors Mary."[35] No matter its original Christological meaning, today it's just an excuse for Catholics to worship Mary.

The Catholic Answer

Svendsen presents a false "either/or" proposition, for *Theotokos* upholds the truth about Christ as one divine person, which is first and foremost in importance, *and* honors Mary by association.

Fathers of the Church such as Cyril of Alexandria, as well as the Council of Ephesus, recorded for us "the original intent for the title," showing us its twofold purpose from the start. In fact, the very first canon approved and promulgated by the council acknowledges the title Mother of God was proper to "the holy virgin."[36] Pope Sixtus III, who ratified the Council of Ephesus in 432, certainly honored Mary when he built the magnificent Basilica of St. Mary Major immediately after the council—a majestic church

---

34. *Redemptoris Mater* 20.3–4.
35. Svendsen, *Evangelical Answers*, 128.
36. The first canon from the Council of Ephesus reads: "If anyone does not confess that Emmanuel is God in truth, and therefore that the holy virgin is the Mother of God (for she bore in a fleshly way the Word of God become flesh), let him be anathema."

still standing to this day, in which Mary is depicted as a queen sitting on a throne with her divine son, surrounded by angels.

Cyril of Alexandria, who was the prime mover at the council before the arrival of the papal legates, preached a now-famous sermon at the council titled "Theotokos, Cause of Joy for the Whole World." Let's see if we can find any "honor" proffered to Mary in this ancient sermon:

> I see the assembly of the saints, all zealously gathered together, invited by the holy Mother of God, Mary, ever-virgin . . . Hail, we say, O holy and mystic Trinity, who have called us together in this church dedicated to Mary, Mother of God. We hail you, O Mary Mother of God, venerable treasure of the entire world, inextinguishable lamp, crown of virginity, scepter of orthodoxy, imperishable temple, container of him who cannot be contained . . .
>
> Hail, you who held the Uncontainable One in your holy and virginal womb! Through you, the Holy Trinity is glorified; the precious cross is celebrated and adored throughout the whole world; heaven exults, the angels and archangels rejoice, the demons are put to flight, the devil, the tempter, falls from heaven, the fallen creation is brought back to paradise, all creatures trapped in idolatry come to know of the truth . . .
>
> But who among men is capable of celebrating Mary most glorious? The virginal womb: such a great wonder![37]

This sounds a lot like honor, coming from the very man who penned the canon declaring Mary to be Mother of God.

---

37. Cited in Gambero, *Mary and the Fathers of the Church*, 247–248.

OBJECTION 3: Breaking Jesus into parts.

Svendsen claims the title "Mother of God" is illogical. First, he offers the same syllogism we saw from Walter Martin before him; however, he adds an extra little twist we would do well to examine:

> (1) Some of Jesus is God, (2) Mary is the mother of some of Jesus; for Mary could very well be (and indeed is) mother of only the non-God part of Jesus.[38]

He then goes on to say:

> The person of Jesus isn't merely God, any more than the person of Jesus is merely man . . . Mary gave birth to a person who is *both* God and man. She did not give birth to the pre-incarnate form of the *Logos*.[39]

The Catholic Answer

There are two problems in Svendsen's assertions.

Problem 1: He claims Mary gave birth to part of Jesus: the human, or "non-God" part. Yet, there is nothing, not even a hint, in Scripture that would suggest Mary is mother only to "part of Jesus." In fact, not only does the Bible never say, "Mary is the mother of part of Jesus," but one has to ask how someone gives birth to "part" of a person in the first place.[40] And though Svendsen will claim he is not dividing the person of Christ—which the Council of Ephesus expressly forbade—the conclusion from his reasoning is inescapable. We're reminded of St. Irenaeus's dealings with the second-century Gnostics, who "with their tongue confess one Jesus Christ," but in reality "divide up Christ."[41]

---

38. Svendsen, *Evangelical Answers,* 130.
39. Ibid., 131.
40. Mary is called "the mother of [the] Lord" (Luke 1:43) and "the mother of Jesus" (John 2:1), but she is never called "Mother of part of Jesus," or anything like it.
41. *Against Heresies* III, 16, 6–8.

Svendsen does not go any deeper in the discussion, but I wonder if he would go on to say that "part of Jesus died" or "part of Jesus is worshipped," and so on. Be that as it may, he does say enough for us to know he *effectively* divides Christ into two persons. If the *subject* Mary gave birth to was not God, then he would have to be a man.

In reading Svendsen's theological maneuvering one cannot help but note how remarkable is the profusion of errors about Christ that stem from denying the essential role of his mother. Fr. Hardon's prophetic words—"Christology is unintelligible without knowing the role of Christ's mother"—come to mind once more.[42] And this leads us to the second problem with his above-cited statements.

Problem 2: Immediately after having effectively divided Christ into two persons, Svendsen then claims that Jesus is both a human and divine person. And by this, he does *not* mean that the one, divine person of Christ possesses two distinct natures—he explicitly rejects this; rather, he claims *the person* of Christ is both a divine and human person simultaneously.

The problem with this position can be further broken down into two points.

1. Although a person can possess two distinct natures (though this occurs only in Christ), a person cannot be one person and two persons *simultaneously*. That is akin to positing square circles, a logical impossibility.

2. In claiming that Mary "did not give birth to the pre-incarnate form of the Logos," Svendsen introduces change into the eternal, divine person of the Logos. Not only is there no pre- or post-incarnate form of the Logos revealed in Scripture, but there cannot be, because there can be no change in the eternal Word of God. This is heresy. "Change" is something God simply cannot do. Malachi 3:6 tells us, "For I the Lord do not change."[43]

Some may wonder if the Word's becoming flesh implies that

---

42. Hardon, *The Catholic Catechism*, 150.
43. See also James 1:17; Heb. 6:17–18.

the Word underwent change. The answer is no. As Thomas Aquinas explains:

> Since the Divine Person is infinite, no addition can be made to it: Hence Cyril says [Council of Ephesus, Part I, ch. 26]: "We do not conceive the mode of conjunction to be according to addition"; just as in the union of man with God, nothing is added to God by the grace of adoption, but what is Divine is united to man; hence, not God but man is perfected.[44]

When we speak of the hypostatic union of the divine and human natures of Christ in the one divine Person, we have to qualify what we mean by the union being "in the Person" of Christ. St. Thomas explains that inasmuch as the hypostatic union is a created union, it cannot be "in God" in the sense that there could be change in God.

> [E]very relation which we consider between God and the creature is really in the creature, by whose change the relation is brought into being; whereas it is not really in God, but only in our way of thinking, since it does not arise from any change in God. And hence we must say that the union of which we are speaking is not really in God, except only in our way of thinking; but in the human nature, which is a creature . . . Therefore we must say it [the hypostatic union] is something created.[45]

When the Councils of Ephesus and Chalcedon speak of the hypostatic union being "in the Person of Christ," it is so inasmuch as the human nature assumed by Christ now has as its subject the divine Person of Christ. But inasmuch as that union is a created union, it is not "in God." That is why Thomas says it is "not really in God, except in our way of thinking." The human nature has

---

44. *Summa Theologiae* III, Q. 3, Art. 1, Reply Obj. 1.
45. Ibid., Q. 2, Art. 7.

as its subject the divine Person. Therefore, it is "in God," in that qualified sense. But inasmuch as this involves change, it is not "in God" because God cannot change.

"But wait a minute," someone might say. "Didn't you just say Svendsen *divided* Christ into two persons? How can he now claim a divine/human mesh?" Please understand, we are not attempting to claim Svendsen *makes sense*. We are simply taking him at his word. He says that the second person of the Blessed Trinity *used to be God alone*, but at the Incarnation he became a God/man mixture. In contrast, the orthodox Christian position preserves the basic metaphysical principle that is rooted in reason and in Scripture we mentioned above: "For I the Lord do not change" (Mal. 3:6).

At the Incarnation, the second person of the Blessed Trinity added a human nature, but *he* did not change. The human nature of Christ received infinite dignity in and through the hypostatic union—hence, we can worship the man, Jesus Christ,[46] but God did not change in the process. Neither did Christ's human nature become a divine nature. But because of the hypostatic union, when one refers to the human nature of Christ, the subject is the divine person. This is why we can affirm that God, the second person of the Blessed Trinity, was born, suffered, died and was resurrected. Even though the divine nature cannot die, the divine person *did*, because of the hypostatic union. We say "he" died because whatever is attributed to each nature must ultimately be attributed to the subject—*the person*. Thus, we also worship the whole Christ, not part of him. And thus, Mary gave birth to the whole Christ, not part of him.

This is a great mystery, and we should not shy away from admitting it. 1 Timothy 3:16 says, "Great is the mystery of godliness. He [God] was manifest in the flesh, seen of angels preached on unto the gentiles and received up into glory." The truth of

---

46. From the third letter of Cyril of Alexandria to Nestorius, read at the Council of Ephesus: "Jesus Christ is considered as one, the only-begotten Son, honored with one worship, together with his own flesh." The council here condemns claiming "one [nature] is not worshipped alongside the other," because that would be to divide Christ into two persons.

the hypostatic union is beyond our ability to comprehend fully, but there is nothing about it that is *contrary* to reason. Svendsen's allowing for change in one of the three divine persons of the Blessed Trinity *is* contrary to reason; it is irrational. The Council of Ephesus, affirmed by the Council of Chalcedon, says quite succinctly and accurately:

> He did not cast aside what he was, but although he assumed flesh and blood, he remained what he was, God in nature and truth. We do not say that his flesh was turned into the nature of the godhead or that the unspeakable Word of God was changed into the nature of the flesh. For he (the Word) is unalterable and absolutely unchangeable and remains always the same as the scriptures say (Mal. 3:6).[47]

Take note of the emphasis that the person of the eternal Word of God does not and *cannot* change. Even the heretical Nestorians did not make a mistake as obvious as Svendsen's attempt to posit change in the Trinity. The Nestorians were at least clear that they were separating divine and human persons, which eliminates any chance of implying change in the divine person.

Svendsen's muddled reasoning seems to be rooted in a lack of understanding of the difference between "person" (*who* someone is) and "nature" (*what* someone is). Svendsen seems to fail to understand this distinction when he claims Mary gave birth to a nature, or to "part of Jesus." Mothers do not give birth to *natures*; they give birth to *persons*. This lack of understanding leads to an incoherent Christology as well as to Svendsen's last argument.

OBJECTION 4: The Council of Ephesus denies Christ's full humanity.

This is Svendsen's claim: When Cyril and the Council of Ephesus claimed Mary to be the Mother of God, this assertion did

---

47. Ibid., 51.

not properly distinguish between the natures of Christ. By calling Mary "Mother of God," and not "Mother of man," there is an implicit denial of the humanity of Christ; or a divinization of his humanity . . . it affirms that Mary gave birth to *one* nature, namely deity—stripped of all humanity.[48]

In making his argument, Svendsen does something truly novel. He not only claims the Council of Ephesus and its definition of Mary as Mother of God to be theologically incorrect, but he then asserts the Council of Chalcedon, just twenty years after the Council of Ephesus, in its "Definition of the Faith," *agrees with him, "Evangelicals, Chalcedon, and Nestorius" against the Council of Ephesus* by actually rejecting Mary as Mother of God.[49] This is quite a claim. So just what did the Council of Chalcedon say that would separate its theology from the Council of Ephesus? According to Eric Svendsen, here it is:

> The text of the document states, "as regards [Jesus'] manhood, begotten . . . of Mary the virgin, the Theotokos," hence being very careful not to ascribe birth to Christ's deity.[50]

That's it!

Now, in defense of Svendsen, if the council really was "careful not to ascribe birth to Christ's deity" we *would* have the Council of Chalcedon rejecting Mary as *Theotokos*, a title infallibly defined at the Council of Ephesus just twenty years before. But rest assured, folks, that is simply not true.

The Catholic Answer

Svendsen here produces a *most selective* quotation from the Council of Chalcedon, with a carefully placed ellipsis, in order to insert

---

48. Svendsen, *Evangelical Answers*, 131.
49. Ibid.
50. Ibid.

an assertion into the council that is simply not there. But his attempt fails. Just using his truncated quotation alone one can see
the council clearly used the title *Theotokos* for Mary, which is a
synonym for *Mother of God*. By using the term, the council plainly "ascribes birth to Christ's deity" in the very words Svendsen
quoted![51] But a simple reading of the entire text from the council,
without ellipsis, leaves no doubt as to its meaning. It very clearly
says Jesus was

> begotten before the ages from the Father as regards his divinity,
> and in the last days the same for us and for our salvation from
> Mary, the virgin God-bearer, as regards his humanity.[52]

These words simply distinguish the Word's eternal generation in
the Blessed Trinity, as the eternally begotten and fully divine Son
of the Father, from *his* (the Eternal Word's) temporal generation as
the fully human son of Mary. His divinity comes from the Father
(not in time, but eternally) and his humanity from Mary. But the
council was careful to call Mary "God-bearer" and not "man-bear-
er" precisely because they were defending the truth that Mary
gave birth to *one divine person*. Thus, contrary to what Svendsen
claimed, Chalcedon's "Definition of Faith" *does* ascribe birth—
being "begotten"—to Christ's deity, both in eternity and in time.

   Moreover, the claim that Chalcedon disagreed with Ephesus is
shown to be patently false when we consider that the Council of
Chalcedon declared *in this same* "Definition of Faith":

---

51. On pages 127–128 of *Evangelical Answers*, Svendsen makes the claim that both Ephesus
   and Chalcedon used *Theotokos* (*God-bearer*), rather than *mater theou* (*Mother of God*),
   claiming they did not want to call Mary the Mother of God. But the two terms are
   synonyms.

52. Both the Greek (which is the more authoritative original) and Latin manuscripts of the
   council make very clear that Mary begets God: *ek Marias tes parthenou tes Theotokou kata
   ten anthropoteta* and *ex Maria virgine Dei genetrice secundum humanitatem* both translate as
   "from Mary the virgin God-bearer according to humanity," meaning she gave birth
   to God, whose humanity requires the cooperation of a mother, as is the case in all
   childbirth.

And because of those who are . . . shamelessly and foolishly
asserting that he who was born of the holy virgin Mary was a
mere man, it has accepted the synodical letters of the blessed
Cyril, pastor of the church in Alexandria, to Nestorius and to
the Orientals, as being well-suited to refuting Nestorius' mad
folly . . .

The council also added "the letter of the primate of greatest and
older Rome, the most blessed and most saintly Archbishop Leo,
written to the sainted Archbishop Flavian to put down Eutyches'
evil-mindedness . . . ," which explicitly states, "Thus was true God
born in the undiminished and perfect nature of a true man." Thus,
the Council of Chalcedon agrees, contrary to Svendsen's claim,
"God [was] born . . ."

What about Svendsen's claim that the title *Mother of God* denies humanity in Christ? The fact that Mary—who is human—is
Christ's true mother implies a human nature already. To deny this
is to fall into a Manicheanism that denies Mary's true motherhood as well as a true Incarnation. Both councils made clear that
Christ's humanity was, in fact, received from Mary. But at the
same time, the councils do not call Mary *Mother of Man*, but *Mother of God* (*Theotokos*), as mentioned above, in order to preserve
the unity of the one divine person. Svendsen is clearly missing
what the Council of Ephesus declared so plainly and Chalcedon
affirmed: "For Scripture does not say that the Word united the
person of a man to himself, but that he became flesh."[53]

In Summary

What Eric Svendsen misses is, unfortunately, what millions of
Evangelical and Fundamentalist Christians get wrong as well. And
these just happen to be the central purposes of both the Council
of Ephesus and the Council of Chalcedon in defending a true
Christology while, at the same time, defending Mary's title *Mother*

53. Tanner, *Decrees of the Ecumenical Councils*, 43.

of God, or *Theotokos*: The fathers of *both* ecumenical councils preserved and defended the very biblical and foundational truth that there *is but one divine person in Christ*, while affirming that *he has two natures*, one divine and one human.

Ephesus emphasized the one person of Christ and that Christ's human nature does not equal a human person, because it dealt with the Nestorians, who taught there were two persons in Christ. Chalcedon emphasized the truth that there are two natures in Christ because it specifically dealt with heretics who denied Christ had a truly human nature (Monophysites, referring to those who taught Christ has "one nature"). Both councils affirm that these two natures can never be intermingled as too often Protestants intermingle them today, or divided as they are too often divided today. Indeed, in Svendsen's case, we saw both the division and intermingling of natures from the very same pen!

The answer comes clearly and succinctly from the Church Jesus Christ established on this earth to be his voice, which speaks with both authority and lucidity to the world via the Council of Chalcedon—and in agreement with the Council of Ephesus—in its "Definition of Faith":

> [T]he property of both natures is preserved and comes together into a single person and a single subsistent being; He is not parted or divided into two persons, but is one and the same only-begotten Son, God, Word, Lord Jesus Christ.[54]

In the final analysis, the manifold Protestant errors today, like those of the Nestorians before them, serve as yet another reminder that we cannot separate Mariology from Christology without distorting essential truths related to both.

54. Ibid., 86.

PART II

FULL OF GRACE

3
WHAT'S IN A NAME?

In his Apostolic Constitution of December 8, 1854, *Ineffabilis Deus*, Pope Blessed Pius IX declared:

> By the inspiration of the Holy Spirit, for the honor of the Holy and undivided Trinity, for the glory and adornment of the Virgin Mother of God, for the exaltation of the Catholic Faith, and for the furtherance of the Catholic religion, by the authority of Jesus Christ our Lord, of the Blessed Apostles Peter and Paul, and by our own: "We declare, pronounce, and define that the doctrine which holds that the most Blessed Virgin Mary, in the first instance of her conception, by a singular grace and privilege granted by Almighty God, in view of the merits of Jesus Christ, the Savior of the human race, was preserved free from all stain of original sin, is a doctrine revealed by God and therefore to be believed firmly and constantly by all the faithful."

It would be difficult to even estimate how many times we have heard the claim made: "There is not a single shred of biblical evidence for this you say Pope Pius IX defined *infallibly*." Responding to an argument made by Karl Keating, in his classic, *Catholicism and Fundamentalism*, Protestant apologist Robert Zins writes:

> What can we say to this other than it is not in the least given to us by anything remotely scriptural . . . What is to stop Rome

from declaring other dogmas and doctrines that have nothing to do with the revelation of God?[55]

I can hardly slight Zins for his comment, as I would have said it almost verbatim when I was Protestant. But this was before I studied the teachings of the Catholic Church on this matter from Catholic sources. I found the Immaculate Conception of Mary to have everything "to do with the revelation of God."

And I would also have to add that just as it would be difficult to estimate how many times I've heard similar claims to Zins' above, it would be equally difficult to recount how many times I have heard, "I've never heard that before," when I have presented even a few of the seven biblical and historical reasons for what Wordsworth referred to as "tainted nature's solitary boast" that we will examine over our next three chapters.[56]

We will reserve an eighth reason, deeply rooted in the history of the Church, for Appendix IV. But please note: This is certainly not intended to be an exhaustive list. There are other biblical and historical reasons for Mary's Immaculate Conception; nevertheless, we believe the reasons we will present here to be sufficient to convince the most skeptical among skeptics.

REASON 1: The angel Gabriel calls Mary "full of grace."

The Annunciation, in which an angelic messenger appears to Mary to reveal God's plan for the birth of the savior, begins with Luke 1:28–30:

> And [the angel Gabriel] came to [Mary] and said, "Hail, full of grace, the Lord is with you!" But she was greatly troubled at the saying, and considered in her mind what sort of greeting this might be. And the angel said to her, "Do not be afraid, Mary, for you have found favor with God."

55. Zins, *Romanism,* 154.
56. Wordsworth, "The Virgin," *Complete Works,* 7:316.

In his 1987 encyclical *Redemptoris Mater*, Pope St. John Paul II ponders this text:

> [W]hat could those extraordinary words mean, and in particular the expression "full of grace" [*kecharitomene*]? . . . For the messenger greets Mary as "full of grace"; he calls her thus as if it were her real name. He does not call her by her proper earthly name: Miryam [= Mary], but by this new name: "full of grace." What does this new name mean?

He continues by noting that

> the Gospel context, which mingles revelations and ancient promises, enables us to understand that among all the "spiritual blessings in Christ" this is a special "blessing" . . . the greeting and the name "full of grace" . . . in the context of the angel's announcement ["full of grace"] refer[s] first of all to the election of Mary as Mother of the Son of God. But at the same time the "fullness of grace" indicates all the supernatural munificence from which Mary benefits by being chosen and destined to be the Mother of Christ.[57]

His Holiness explains beautifully and succinctly what we will flesh out in more detail throughout this chapter and beyond. First, he notes that the angel actually gives Mary a new name. And I should add here the importance of understanding the role of the angel. The word *angelos* in Greek means "messenger." Angels are generally called to disappear into the message they are sent by God to communicate. Thus, this name does not have its origin in Gabriel. It comes from God.[58] Secondly, he calls our attention

---

57. *Redemptoris Mater* 8.1, 8.3, 8.5, 9.1.

58. Angels are, at times, so intertwined with the message they have come to bring that they can be mistaken for God himself, such as we see with St. John falling down in adoration before the angel who was bringing him a message from God in both Revelation 19:10 and 22:8. In fact, exegetes are sometimes at odds as to when it is the angel and when it is almighty God who is speaking, such as in Genesis 18. Fr. E.F. Sutcliffe comments, "It

to the importance of the new name—"full of grace" (Gr., *ke-charitomene*). And finally, he emphasizes the context of the passage, "which mingles revelations and ancient promises" in presenting us the truth about Mary immaculate.

Just a Name?

Living in a Western culture that has lost a sense of the significance of names, we might pass over the "naming" of Mary without a second glance. But this can lead to us missing the deeper meaning of the text.

The New Testament was written from the perspective of an ancient oriental people who understood God-given names to reveal something that is *permanent* about the nature or character of the one named. Isaiah 7:14—a prophetic text that speaks of the then-future Messiah—is just one example among many of the importance of names in the Old Testament:

> Therefore the Lord himself will give you a sign. Behold, a [virgin] shall conceive and bear a son, and shall call *his name* Immanuel [emphasis added].

Isaiah 9:6–7 reveals multiple more "names" for the coming Messiah:

> For to us a child is born, to us a son is given; and the government will be upon his shoulder, and *his name* shall be called "Wonderful Counselor, Mighty God, Everlasting Father, Prince of Peace [emphasis added]."

As an apologist, I have been asked the question many times, "Why didn't Joseph and Mary name Jesus 'Immanuel' in fulfillment of

is difficult to know whether Yahweh appeared in person or through the intermediary of an angel," referring to the first fifteen verses of the chapter (*A Catholic Commentary on Sacred Scripture*, 195).

Isaiah 7?" Our second text, from Isaiah 9, helps supply the answer. The messiah was never intended to be *addressed* by all of these names. These "names" revealed the Christ was *to be* the Wonderful Counselor who brings the fullness of the revelation of God to all of humanity. He was *to be* "the Mighty God," literally "God with us," through the great mystery of the Incarnation. And he was *to be* both a Prince who brings peace and reconciliation with God and at the same time the "source" of creation—a "father" by analogy. In simple terms, the messiah was to be both God and man.

If these names *were* intended to be given names, it would have created a bit of a problem. Can you imagine Joseph and Mary raising Jesus with all those names? "Good morning, Immanuel, Wonderful Counselor, Mighty God, Everlasting Father, Prince of Peace!" The name "Jesus" certainly made conversation with the anointed one a lot easier!

And yet, to say that these "names" were to represent *descriptions* rather than *appellations* does not fully grasp what Scripture reveals either. A description may represent something fleeting, whereas in the Bible a "name" reveals something that gets to one's very core or essence—something *permanent*.

Perhaps the best example of this is found in God's revelation of his own name in Exodus 3:14—*I AM*. Christians and Jews have understood for thousands of years this "name" to be much more than a mere title or even a description; it reveals volumes about God's very nature. Through this name, God is revealed to be the one absolutely *necessary* being who alone does not receive his being from any other. There is no *potentiality* in him. He is *pure actuality*. He has no beginning and no end. He alone possesses all perfection. He is omnipotent, omnipresent, and omniscient. He simply *IS WHO IS*.

Thus, we see revealed through the ministry of the angel that Mary, the prophetic Mother of the Messiah, was not merely to be *addressed* as "full of grace" but rather was called by God to *be* "full of grace." Having been *named* "full of grace," Mary was and is for all-time free from all sin.

Change We Can Believe In

In all of Scripture we find only seven examples of God com-
manding name changes. And there seems to be three key com-
ponents involved in each. Each of these name changes represents
a particular *calling* in the life of the one named. Five of the seven
represent a calling to be a *patriarch* or *matriarch* over God's family
on earth. And in each of these examples God uses these chosen
few to be signs of hope and promise for his people at crucial times
in salvation history. Here is a quick rundown of all seven:

1. "Lo-Ammi" (Heb., *Not My People*) becomes "Ammi" (Heb.,
   My People), Hosea 2:23.
2. "Lo-Ruhanah" (Heb., *Not My Beloved*) becomes "Ruhanah"
   (Heb., *My Beloved*), Hosea 2:23.
3. "Abram" (Heb., *Exalted Father*) becomes "Abraham" (Heb.,
   Father of the Multitudes), Genesis 17:5.
4. "Sarai" (Heb., *My Princess*) becomes "Sarah" (Heb., *Princess* or
   Mother of Multitudes), Genesis 17:15.
5. "Jacob" (Heb., *Supplanter*) becomes "Israel" (Heb., *He Who
   Prevails with God*), Genesis 32:28.
6. "Simon" (from Heb., *Hearing*) becomes "Peter" (Gr., *Rock*).
7. "Mary" (from Aram., *Lady*) becomes "*Kecharitomene*" (Gr., *Full
   of Grace*).[59]

In the cases of Abraham, Sarah, and Israel, these name changes reveal something permanent about the calling as well as the
character of the one named. Abraham and Sarah transition from
being a *father* and *princess* of one family to being *father* and *princess*
or *mother of nations and kings*, for the entire people of God.[60] They

---

59. Some may object that the other six examples were name changes in which the new
    names were actually used as appellations rather than mere descriptors. But we argue
    that the "name" that is used as a descriptor is just as much a name—as we saw with
    Isaiah 7:14 and 9:6–7 in relation to our Lord—as is a name that is used in everyday
    conversation.
60. The people of God are referred to as a family and a "priestly *kingdom*" in both the Old
    Testament (Ex. 19:6) and the New Testament (1 Pet. 5:9 and Eph. 3:15). Hence, Sarah,

become patriarch and matriarch of God's people forever.[61] Israel becomes the patriarch whose name—*he who prevails with God*—continues in the Church, which in the New Testament is called *the Israel of God* (see Gal. 6:16). Both Jacob and the Church are not merely *named* Israel, but they truly are, by God's grace, forever destined to prevail with God.

Just as St. Peter was made patriarch over the universal people of God with his name change in Matthew 16, by her name change Mary is being revealed as the matriarch—called here in Luke 1 to bring Christ to the whole world through a nuptial union with the Holy Spirit—of the people of God.

We could and we will discover much more meaning in this text as we plumb its depths in coming chapters, but perhaps we should slow down at this point before drawing any more conclusions and consider some objections to this train of thought.

A Common Greeting?

We often hear Protestant apologists object, "How does Luke 1 have anything to do with Mary being without sin? It says nothing of the sort! This was just a simple greeting."[62]

Yet, according to Mary herself, this was no simple greeting. She was *greatly troubled* by it, and wondered what sort of greeting it could be. You couldn't imagine your neighbor being greatly troubled if you said "hello" to him, could you? Neither would Mary have been greatly troubled if the angel's greeting had been simply that.[63]

---

the principle matriarch of the Old Covenant, is referred to as "mother" in Isaiah 51:1–2 and in royal terms here in Genesis 17. Abraham is also referred to as "father" in Isaiah 51, and many times in the New Testament (Rom. 4:1–18; Jas. 2:21; Luke 16:24, etc.).

61. Sarah's calling as matriarch continues after death, according to Isaiah 51:1–2. And Abraham's patriarchy also continues after death, according to Romans 4:11–12.

62. On page 28 of *Mary: Another Redeemer?*, James White refers to Luke 1:28 as "such a simple greeting, easily understood in its context."

63. Some may say that Mary was startled because an angel was speaking to her. The text indicates something different. It says she was "greatly troubled at the saying, and considered in her mind what sort of greeting this might be." It was not the fact that an angel was speaking to her, but the greeting itself that troubled her.

The angel's greeting, *Kaire, kecharitomene* ("Hail, full of grace"), has multiple levels of meaning that will necessitate our revisiting Luke 1:28, but for now we will focus on St. Luke's use of the perfect passive participle to represent this new name for Mary. *Kecharitomene* signifies not simply *full of grace*, but *she who has been filled with grace*. This invokes the context of the revelation of her definite and specific vocation to be the Mother of God. As Scripture scholar Carroll Stuhlmueller explains:

> In regard to Mary, therefore, [Luke] points out that she is the object of God's grace and favor. Because the verb is also a participle, Mary is shown to have been chosen for a long time past; God's full flow of favor has already been concentrating upon her.[64]

In what many consider the best Greek grammar in the English language, H. W. Smyth defines the perfect tense as "completed action with permanent result."[65] A participle is a verbal adjective, a descriptive term. In the perfect tense it normally represents a past, completed action that has resulted in a present state of being.[66] It carries a sense of *completion*; thus, Mary *was* graced and now *is* perfectly *full* of grace.[67] The Greek verb is remarkably precise compared to most languages. If Mary had been anything less than perfectly filled with grace, there would have been multiple ways for Luke to have expressed it.[68]

---

64. Stuhlmueller, *Jerome Biblical Commentary,* 44:31.

65. Smyth, *Greek Grammar,* 413.

66. Hewett, *New Testament Greek,* 76. Hewett says the perfect expresses "a completed action . . . The action itself does not continue; the effects of the now past action continue . . . [it] is an accomplished act that has present consequences."

67. Robertson, *Word Pictures in the New Testament,* vol. 2, 14: "'Highly favored' (*kecharitomene*). The perfect passive participle of *charitoo*, it means 'endowed with grace' (*charis*), enriched with grace as in Ephesians 1:6. The Vulgate *gratia plena* [full of grace] is right, if it means 'full of grace which thou hast received,' wrong, if it means 'full of grace which thou hast to bestow.'"

68. A contemporary example: If I say "I washed my car" using the perfect tense in Koine Greek, that would mean that the car was washed completely and is in a state of having been washed. If the job was not completed ("perfected") in the past, I would not

Thus, if Mary were revealed to have simply been "graced" as any other Christian, or even if she were greatly but less-than-perfectly graced, it would be very strange that she would have been named "full of grace." But she was so named.

And so, as Mariologist and Greek scholar Fr. Mateo put it so well, "[I]t is correct to paraphrase *kecharitomene* as "completely, perfectly, enduringly endowed with grace."[69]

Kecharitomene, then, becomes more than just a description of a gift of grace given to Mary in the past. It gets to the core of Mary's being: a permanent state that is wholly incompatible with the presence of sin. Mary has been and always will be "full of grace."

History Repeats the Refrain

In the modern era, attempts to understand Luke 1:28 apart from its linguistic, prophetic, and historical setting tend to reduce it to the mundane, missing the splendor of the text. Even Martin Luther stated in his *Personal Prayer Book* (1522):

> [Mary] is full of grace, proclaimed to be entirely without sin
> . . . God's grace fills her with everything good and makes her
> devoid of all evil . . . God is with her, meaning all she did or
> left undone is divine and the action of God in her. Moreover,
> God protected her from all that might be hurtful to her.[70]

Luther, at least in this case, was not presenting anything novel. A fourth-century homily, *On the Annunciation to the Mother of God*

---

normally use the perfect. I could use the imperfect, "I was washing my car," but the job was not completed. The imperfect represents a past ongoing action that may or may not have been completed. If I completed the job, but the car is now in need of another washing, I would use the aorist, which means a past action with no necessary connection to the present. The perfect tense gets at the sense of completion without a need for the action to be repeated or completed (unless further information is provided in the context to indicate as much). The car has been and is in a completed state of having been washed.

69. Fr. Mateo, *Refuting the Attack on Mary,* 21.
70. Ibid., 23, cf. Pelikan, *Luther's Works,* 40.

and *Against the Impious Arius*, most likely written by an unknown monk and disciple of St. Basil named John around the year 370, gives us insight into the early Church's understanding of the angel's greeting. This ancient homily begins with a discussion between God and the archangel Gabriel in heaven:

> At this time, then, the angel Gabriel was sent by the Sun of justice. Go—he told him—to the city of Nazareth, in Galilee, to the Virgin Mary, espoused to Joseph the builder, for I, the Builder of all creation, will espouse myself to this Virgin, for the salvation of men . . . I wish to be born of her as man.

God then explains to Gabriel how he will restore the world through a new Adam and a new Eve:

> For by her virginal womb, I plan to renew the human race; by my condescension, I want to reestablish the image I molded; I want to restore the ancient image, reshaping it. I formed the first man from a virgin earth, but the devil, making himself master, plundered him as an enemy and threw him to the earth, thus mocking my fallen image. Now I want to remold a new Adam for myself from the virgin earth, so that nature might prepare a beautiful defense and receive the just crown against him who conquered her.

Then, Gabriel is sent by God to Mary:

> And so the angel arrived at the Virgin Mary's home and, having entered, said to her: *Rejoice, full of grace!* He greeted her, his fellow servant, as if she were a great lady . . . you have been made worthy to provide a dwelling for such a Lord . . . you have become the most pure workshop of the divine economy; you have appeared as the worthy chariot for our King's entrance into life; you have been proclaimed the treasure, the spiritual pearl. *Blessed are you among women!*

Ponder Mary's response from the perspective of this fourth-century writer:

> The all-holy Virgin, hearing these words . . . asked herself what manner of greeting this might be. Where might this discourse lead? What do these words mean for me? It was the angel who greeted me first. Who am I? What dignity have I achieved? I, full of grace? But how and why? The Lord is with me? But is the Lord not with anyone who fears his name? I am blessed among women? On what basis and why and how? What gift does this foretell for me? What miracle do these words speak of?

> The angel, seeing her so troubled, said to her . . . *Do not fear, Mary, for you have found favor with God.* You have been made the most beautiful part of creation, more luminous than the heavens, more resplendent than the sun, higher than the angels. You were not lifted up into heaven, and yet, remaining on earth, you have drawn down into yourself the heavenly Lord and King of all . . .

> What response, then, does holy Mary make to these words, the Virgin in body and spirit, pious, God-fearing, obedient, the honor of human nature, the gate of our life, the procurer of our salvation?

> Receiving the angel's words with a good disposition, she answers him: *Behold the handmaid of the Lord: let it be done to me according to your word* (Luke 1:38).[71]

To the Fathers of the Church, *full of grace* was not only a correct translation; it reflected the truth that Mary had received "the plenitude of grace." She was made "higher than the angels" and "the honor of human nature." St. Gregory of Nyssa, a contemporary of John and Basil, would put it this way in *On the Song of Songs,* 13:

---

71. Gambero, *Mary and the Fathers of the Church,* 272–281.

Just as she who introduced death into nature by her sin was condemned to bear children in suffering and travail, it was necessary that the Mother of life, after having conceived in joy, should give birth in joy as well. No wonder that the angel said to her, "Rejoice, O full of grace!" (Luke 1:28). With these words he took from her the burden of that sorrow which, from the beginning of creation, had been imposed on birth because of sin.[72]

It is important to note that John the monk and Gregory did not learn Koine Greek in a seminary as a dead language, but actually spoke it. And again, they understood the angel's name for Mary as a signal of her unique holiness. Soon we will see more of the relationship between Mary's new name and her sinlessness, and we will also see much more from the Fathers of the Church. But before we do, a word of caution would seem to be in order.

Two Objections

Many years ago, I was challenged with an objection to my understanding of Mary's new name from a very astute Protestant fellow citing Ephesians 2:8–9. He pointed out to me that this text uses the perfect tense and passive voice for the verb "to save" when it says of all Christians, "For by grace you *have been saved.*" Why wouldn't Catholics thus say that all Christians have received the fullness of salvation for all time in a manner similar to Mary's reception of grace?[73]

First, we have to understand the way in which the Catholic Church *does* teach that a newly baptized Christian is "full of grace."[74] This is Paul's context in Ephesians 2:8–9: about the initial

---

72. Ibid., 158–159.

73. I'm thankful to my former seminary Greek professor, Fr. Patrick T. Brannan, for helping me to formulate my response.

74. The exception here is the person baptized as an adult who has unrepented, ongoing sin in his life. If a person is about to be baptized, but is secretly (unknown to the priest) and knowingly (in his own conscience) living in a sinful relationship, for example, then that person would receive the sacramental seal of baptism, but the sanctifying grace normally communicated through baptism would not be communicated to him. The

grace of salvation received in baptism.[75] Thus, the use of the perfect tense would be expected. We could also say that all Christians who are truly walking with the Lord are "full of grace" at other times in their lives; for example, after making a good confession or receiving the Eucharist well-disposed. There are many ways in which God may work in our lives, "perfecting holiness in the fear of God" (2 Cor. 7:1). But because of the reality of original sin, we can pretty much guarantee that we are not going to stay that way.[76] We have not received the *name* "full of grace" as Mary did.[77]

We let God, of course, be the judge of our state of grace. St. Paul tells us in 1 Corinthians 4:3–4: "I do not even judge myself. I am not aware of anything against myself, but I am not thereby acquitted [Gr., *justified*]. It is the Lord who judges me. Therefore do not judge." Paul says we cannot judge our own state of grace in an absolute sense, much less another person's state of grace.[78]

sacrament would not be fruitful in his life because he would be holding up an obstacle to that grace. In the case of an infant, we can know he would be full of grace because he would be incapable of putting up an obstacle to grace.

75. The verses leading up to Ephesians 2:8–9 make this clear. "[W]e all lived in the passions of our flesh, following the desires of body and mind, and so we were by nature children of wrath ... even when we were dead in trespasses and sins ... (by grace you have been saved)" (3–5). However, in the very next verse (10), St. Paul emphasizes the necessity of the new adult Christian to begin working in faith and charity. Thus, there is the possibility that he will not stay in that initial state of grace. He says a Christian is "created in Christ Jesus unto good works." How does one get *in Christ Jesus* in the first place? Romans 6:3 tells us plainly: We are "baptized into Christ Jesus." Remaining in Christ is another question (see Rom. 11:22, Rev. 2:10, etc.). This state is not indicated to be permanent here in Ephesians as it is for Mary in Luke 1.

76. Cf. 1 John 1:8: "If we say we have no sin, we deceive ourselves and the truth is not in us."

77. Even the great apostle Paul, in Philippians 3:12, says he has "not been made perfect, but [he] press[es] on hoping." Paul claims no "fullness of grace" even for himself. Yet, as CCC 722 says, "The Holy Spirit prepared Mary by his grace. It was fitting that the mother of him in whom 'the whole fullness of deity dwells bodily' should herself be 'full of grace.' She was, by sheer grace, conceived without sin as the most humble of creatures, the most capable of welcoming the inexpressible gift of the almighty."

78. 1 John 5:13 teaches that we can "know that we have eternal life," but verse 14 clarifies that this is a "confident" assurance, rather than an absolute certainty. This is like you or me saying: "I know I am going to get an A on my Greek exam tomorrow." This use of the verb *to know* is proper but it is not being used as absolute. Paul uses "knowledge" similarly in Acts 20:25.

What we can say about Mary is that she was uniquely given the *name,* "full of grace," indicating that this state of grace was both completed and permanent. We can thus say with confidence, based on both Mary's new name and the context in which it was given, that the Mother of God was free from all sin.[79]

Another Protestant objection stems from a false presumption about divine revelation. Because there is so much evidence that the name *full of grace* reflects the sinlessness of Mary, some Protestants will demand that this one verse alone prove the Immaculate Conception. This is unreasonable. The historical reality of Mary's freedom from sin is reflected in this text (and others), to be sure. But this is just one text that gives us insight into the calling of Mary and her receiving the plenitude of grace; it is not a single and conclusive prooftext. One has to understand the scriptures as they have been communicated to us: in the context of the Tradition received in the life of the Church and aided by the power of the Holy Spirit as he speaks through the magisterial authority of the Church. The *Catechism* (95) states:

> Still, the Christian faith is not a "religion of the book." Christianity is the religion of the "Word" of God, a word which is "not a written and mute word, but the Word which is incarnate and living." If the Scriptures are not to remain a dead letter, Christ, the eternal Word of the living God, must, through the Holy Spirit, "open [our] minds to understand the Scriptures."

---

79. Some may argue here, "Is the sole difference between Mary and all Christians being 'full of grace' the fact that it is a name in Luke 1?" Well, no. The context is crucial as well. But the question betrays ignorance of the significance of names in Hebrew culture. That would be like saying, "You mean the only difference between the 'I am' of Exodus 3:14 and the way 'I am' is used elsewhere in Scripture is the fact that it is used as a name?" Well, name and context, to be sure, but, again, names given to us by God in Hebrew culture reveal something permanent about the one named. *Names* were a big deal in ancient Israel.

Dei Verbum (10, 3) adds:

> It is clear therefore that, in the supremely wise arrangements of God, sacred Tradition, Sacred Scripture, and the magisterium of the Church are so interconnected and associated that one of them cannot stand without the others. Working together, each in its own way, under the action of the one Holy Spirit, they all contribute effectively to the salvation of souls.

We must emphasize that not only the word *kecharitomene* but (even more important) the surrounding *context* gives us the needed clues to know Mary's sinlessness is being revealed. In coming chapters we will examine what John Paul II called the "revelations and ancient promises"[80] surrounding Luke 1:28, as well as levels of meaning in the verse itself revealing Mary to be the Ark of the Covenant, the Daughter of Zion, and the New Eve. We will also examine how Mary's uniquely "blessed" state is revealed not only through the message of the angel, but in the proclamation of Mary's cousin Elizabeth in verse 42. All of this and more will bring to light the full meaning of Mary's new name: "she who has been and is filled with grace."[81]

---

80. *Redemptoris Mater* 8.5.

81. St. Jerome, in the Vulgate, translated *kecharitomene* into Latin as *gratia plena* (*full of grace*) to get at that sense of Mary being having been filled with grace.

4

REVELATIONS AND
ANCIENT PROMISES
EVIDENCE FOR THE
IMMACULATE CONCEPTION

Perhaps now you're thinking, "Okay, I see what you are saying about Mary being free from sin, but how do you know she was free from sin *from the moment of her conception*? That seems more than a stretch!"

In other words, how do you demonstrate the dogma Immaculate Conception from Mary's having been named "full of grace?"

To answer this we must first recall that "full of grace" *by itself* does not prove the Immaculate Conception. For the full impact of Mary's renaming we need the full "Gospel context." Pope St. John Paul II wrote that this context,

> which mingles revelations and ancient promises, enables us to understand that among all the "spiritual blessings in Christ" this is a special "blessing" . . . the greeting and the name "full of grace" . . . in the context of the angel's announcement . . . refer first of all *to the election of Mary as Mother of the Son of God.* But at the same time the "fullness of grace" indicates all the supernatural munificence from which Mary benefits by being chosen and destined to be the Mother of God.[82]

---

82. *Redemptoris Mater* 8.5–9.1.

In biblical exegesis, context is everything. We argue that in the context of just twenty-eight verses of the first chapter of Luke's Gospel we find at least six key revelations and fulfillments of ancient promises painting a biblical portrait for us not only of Mary's sinlessness, but also her Immaculate Conception. In this chapter we'll examine five of them—reasons two through six.

REASON 2: Mary is revealed to be the prophetic "Daughter of Zion."[83]

In what is among the most simple and beautiful prayers in the Torah, Moses fervently prays for God to dwell in the midst of his people. It is a seemingly praiseworthy request, and yet God's answer is a firm "no." God's refusal was not because of any lack of desire on his part; God's will was always to dwell in the midst of his people. The problem was *Israel's sins.*

> The Lord said to Moses . . . Go up to a land flowing with milk and honey; but I will not go among you, lest I consume you in the way, for you are a stiff-necked people (Exod. 33:3).

> For the Lord had said to Moses, "Say to the people of Israel, You are a stiff-necked people; if for a moment I should go up among you, I would consume you" (Exod. 33:5).

God says he *could have* dwelt among them—but he would have destroyed them if he had! And yet in spite of the dire warnings, Moses entreats the Lord anyway, in Exodus 34:9, with this prayer:

> If now I have found favor in thy sight, O Lord, let the Lord, I pray thee, go in the midst of us, although it is a stiff-necked people; and pardon our iniquity and our sin, and take us for thy inheritance.

83. O'Carroll, *Theotokos*, 49–50, 116.

When we said Moses' petition would not be granted, that was true, but incomplete. It would be more correct to say it would not be granted in his lifetime, or even in the context of the Mosaic Covenant. Because of the sins of Israel, God would only dwell in the Ark of the Covenant made of wood and gold, in the tabernacle in the wilderness, or later on in the temple. However, the God-inspired longing of Moses' heart would one day be realized. Multiple prophets subsequent to the time of Moses prophesied God would indeed one day dwell in the midst of his people. But this ancient promise would only find its fulfillment in Jesus Christ . . . *and in his mother.*

The Prophecies of the Prophets

Let us first consider the prophet Isaiah. In the first eight chapters of the book that bears his name, in good prophetic tradition Isaiah brings a message of stern warning to Israel (and the surrounding nations) because of their abundant sins. But in later chapters we also see the promise of the coming Messiah. For our purpose we'll focus on chapters 11 and 12. You'll want to take note of how many times the inspired author prophesies of *that day*, which refers to the coming of the Messiah and the New Covenant.

> There shall come forth a shoot from the stump of Jesse, and a branch shall grow out of his roots. And the Spirit of the Lord shall rest upon him, the spirit of wisdom and understanding, the spirit of counsel and might, the spirit of knowledge and the fear of the Lord . . . In that day the root of Jesse shall stand as an ensign to the peoples . . . In that day the Lord will extend his hand yet a second time to recover the remnant which is left of his people . . . You will say in that day: "I will give thanks to thee, O Lord, for though you were angry with me, your anger turned away . . . Shout, and sing for joy, O inhabitant of Zion, for great in your midst is the Holy One of Israel."

The promise of the Lord dwelling *in the midst* of Israel was just that—a promise for the future.

And we should further note that in Isaiah and elsewhere, "the inhabitant of Zion" is also referred to as "the daughter of Zion," or even "the virgin daughter of Zion." For example, in Isaiah 37:22, Isaiah prophesies against Assyria, who had conquered Israel:

> [Assyria] despises you, she scorns you—the virgin daughter of Zion; she wags her head behind you—the daughter of Jerusalem.[84]

In Zephaniah, we find similar language. The Lord chastises Israel resoundingly for its sins, but then promises through the message of the prophet:

> (3:8) "Therefore wait for me," says the Lord, "for the day when I arise as a witness . . . (11) On that day you shall not be put to shame . . . (13) For they shall pasture and lie down, and none shall make them afraid. (14) Sing aloud, O daughter of Zion; shout, O Israel! Rejoice and exult with all your heart, O daughter of Jerusalem . . . (15) The King of Israel, the Lord, is in your midst . . .

And finally, after urging Israel to repent of their sins, Zechariah also prophesies: "Sing and rejoice, O daughter of Zion; for lo, I come and I will dwell in the midst of you, says the Lord" (Zech. 2:10).

We now fast-forward to Luke 1:28. When Luke records the greeting of the angel, "Hail, full of grace, the Lord is with you!" There are two keys to understanding this text in relation to Mary as the fulfillment of the ancient "daughter of Zion" prophecies.

1. The Greek word for *hail* is *kaire*, which can also be translated *rejoice*. In fact, the New King James Version of the Bible

---

84. Cf. Jer. 14:17; Lam. 2:13.

translates it as "Rejoice, highly favored one!" Because this "new name"—*kecharitomene*—is in the feminine, we could also translate it as "Rejoice, favored woman."

2. The angel does not say "the Lord *shall be with you*." He says, "The Lord *is* with you."

Could this hearken back to the prophetic "daughter of Zion" prophecies of old? There is really no biblical way around it. The ancient prayer of Moses was definitively answered in and through a teenage girl named Mary, and in a way beyond the wildest imaginings of the ancient prophets. Because of her "yes," after all of those centuries in waiting, God would finally dwell "in the midst of his virgin Daughter of Zion."

Indeed, this verse becomes an excellent example of what Scripture scholars refer to as the *polyvalent* or *multilayered* nature of Scripture. The angel's greeting not only signals that Mary is "full of grace," but that she is the true "Daughter of Zion."

So how does this relate to Mary being free from sin? We saw before that it was the sin of Israel that prevented God from dwelling "in the midst of" "the virgin daughter of Zion." How fitting indeed it is for the New Covenant Daughter of Zion—in the midst of whom the Lord would dwell bodily—to be free from all sin. The obstacle that kept God from dwelling in the midst of his people had been eliminated through Mary's Immaculate Conception, and Mary becomes the archetype of the Church—"holy and without blemish" (Eph. 5:27).

On one level, since she was "full of grace" Mary was the fulfillment of the prophecies concerning the Daughter of Zion even before the Incarnation. And yet, there was more to come. Mary's fullness of grace had prepared the New Covenant Daughter of Zion for something the Old Covenant people of God could never have fathomed. It was grace that made her fit to be a worthy vessel to bear the King of Glory *in her body*. The fulfillment of God's promise would not be *complete,* then, until Mary conceived Jesus in her womb.[85]

> "[Rejoice], full of grace, the Lord is with you! . . . the power of the Most High will overshadow you; therefore the child to be born will be called . . . the Son of God" (Luke 1:28–35).

I suppose an entire volume could be written on the significance of these prophecies. But I will conclude our thoughts here with a section from the *Catechism* and its succinct teaching on the significance of Mary as Daughter of Zion, in whom God promised he would dwell:

> The Holy Spirit *prepared* Mary by his grace. It was fitting that the mother of him in whom "the whole fullness of deity dwells bodily" should herself be "full of grace." She was, by sheer grace, conceived without sin as the most humble of creatures, the most capable of welcoming the inexpressible gift of the Almighty. It was quite correct for the angel Gabriel to greet her as the "Daughter of Zion": "Rejoice."[86]

REASON 3: Mary is the beginning of the new creation.

With her *fiat* in Luke 1:28—*Let it be done to me according to your word*—Mary becomes the first Christian. The unprecedented grace expressed in that verse is increased and perfected through her free cooperation with grace in Luke 1:38.[87] Mary becomes the first human person to receive the Son of God not just into her soul, but into her *body.* And she is the only person who would ever be called to bear God in her very womb. It is in this context John Paul II says of Mary:

---

85. O'Carroll, *Theotokos,* 49.
86. CCC 722.
87. Mary was already "full of grace," but now her capacity for grace is increased; thus, she receives even more of God's love and grace.

In the liturgy the Church salutes Mary of Nazareth as the Church's own beginning, for in the event of the Immaculate Conception the Church sees projected, and anticipated in her most noble member, the saving grace of Easter.[88]

His Holiness further says of the faith of Mary:

Mary's faith can also be compared to that of Abraham, whom Saint Paul calls "our father in faith" (cf. Rom. 4:12). In the salvific economy of God's revelation, Abraham's faith constitutes the beginning of the Old Covenant; Mary's faith at the Annunciation inaugurates the New Covenant.[89]

Mary inaugurates the New Covenant? Some might balk at this and point out that since Jesus Christ *is* the New Covenant, it must be he who inaugurated it. And they would be correct. Hebrews 10:9 tells us that Christ "abolishes the first [covenant sacrifices] in order to establish the second." Jesus said his blood "is the new covenant" (Luke 22:20). So how could John Paul II have said Mary inaugurates the New Covenant? The answer lies in Sacred Scripture and in the infallible decree of Pope Blessed Pius IX defining Mary's Immaculate Conception:

[I]n the first moment of her conception, by a unique gift of grace and privilege of Almighty God, in view of the merits of Jesus Christ, the Redeemer of mankind, [Mary was] preserved free from all stain of original sin.[90]

In the order of grace, Jesus is the inaugurator, the source—indeed, Jesus Christ *is* the New Covenant. But in the order of time, as the grace of Christ is actually communicated to the world—"the salvific economy of God's revelation"—Mary was the first human

---

88. *Redemptoris Mater* 1.3.
89. Ibid., 14.1.
90. Ott, *Fundamentals of Catholic Dogma*, 199; cf. Pope Pius IX, *Ineffabilis Deus*.

person to experience the redemption of Christ in her person. This grace, the grace of the New Covenant, was incarnate in Mary before the Incarnation—from the moment of her conception—and it was perfected in her through her declaration of faith and obedience.

The New Creation

Let us consider for a moment the nature of this New Covenant that begins in the life and person of Mary. The New Covenant represents a new law, a new priesthood, a new sacrifice, a new calendar, and more.[91] But even more fundamentally, the New Covenant represents *a new creation*.

Most Christians understand the concept of "a new creation" in the context of Revelation 21:1–2, which speaks of the coming of "a new heaven and a new earth." On a popular level, most think of this purely as a future reality; and there is a sense in which that is true. The "new heaven and new earth" will only be realized in full and on a cosmic level at the second coming of the Lord. Yet even now Christians are referred to as "a new creation" in Christ through baptism.[92] All Christians are revealed to "have a part in the first resurrection" and to experience the "powers of the world to come" now, in this life.[93] Mary, as the first Christian, was thus the beginning of the new creation.

In the first creation, the first man—Adam—was created from a pristine earth, untouched by the curse of original sin:

> And to Adam [God] said, "Because you have listened to the voice of your wife, and have eaten of the tree of which I commanded you, 'You shall not eat of it,' cursed is the ground because of you; in toil you shall eat of it all the days of your life; thorns and thistles it shall bring forth to you; and you shall eat

---

91. Cf. Heb. 7:11–12, 10:8–10; Col. 2:16.
92. Cf. 2 Cor. 5:17.
93. Cf. Rev. 20:5–6; Heb. 6:5.

the plants of the field. In the sweat of your face you shall eat bread till you return to the ground, for out of it you were taken; you are dust and to dust you shall return" (Gen. 3:17–19).

Notice that it was only *after* the fall that the earth was cursed. How fitting indeed that in the New Covenant, the new man or new Adam would come from a pristine source also untouched by sin. Hence Mary, as *the beginning of the new creation,* is preserved from all stain of original sin. Since New Testament fulfillments are always more glorious that their Old Testament antecedents, it would be unthinkable to have Mary conceived with the "curse" of original sin.[94]

What's Old Is New

This understanding of Mary as "the beginning of the new creation," the new earth from which the new man, Jesus Christ, would be formed, will be novel to some. Yet it is an ancient idea, dating to the Fathers of the Church and deeply grounded in Scripture, evidencing a highly developed understanding of Mary's role in salvation and her sinless nature very early in the Christian era. In the fourth century, St. Jerome wrote:

> "Can a bride forget her jewels, or a virgin her girdle?" (Jer. 2:32). Always in this very prophecy it is said that a great miracle occurred involving this woman: "The woman will surround the man and the virgin's womb will contain the parent of all."[95]

Jerome here references Jeremiah 31:22, which reads, "How long will you waver, O faithless daughter? For the Lord has created a new thing on the earth: a woman protects a man." The Douay-Rheims translates this last phrase closer to the Hebrew

---

94. Recall how Old Testament "types" are referred to as mere "shadows" in comparison to their New Testament fulfillment (cf. Heb. 10:1; Col. 2:16).
95. St. Jerome, *Against Iovinianum* I, 32.

original as "a woman shall compass a man." This text is given in the midst of a well-known chapter of Jeremiah that prophesies the coming of the New Covenant and is quoted to that end in Hebrews 8:7–12.

It is not difficult to see why the patron saint of Scripture scholars would have come to the conclusion that this "woman" would be Mary. According to the text, this "woman" would be a central part of this "new thing [created] on the earth," which is a reference to the New Covenant and *the new creation* in Jesus Christ. Specifically, it says she shall "compass a man." If we examine the Old Testament, we discover it was the first man—*Adam*—who "compassed" the woman—*Eve*, for she was created from him.[96] In the recapitulation of all things in the New Covenant, God deigned to reverse this order just as he was to reverse the curse of original sin: Jesus, the "second man" or "second Adam," comes from the new woman, Mary.[97] It was "the woman" who "compassed" the man.

Jerome developed this idea in his writings, in his commentary on the Psalms referring to Mary as the "new earth" out of which the "new Adam" would be created. He saw both Jesus and Mary in the "flower and the lily" of Song of Solomon 2:1 and more importantly the "fruit of the earth" from Psalm 67:6:

> Do you want to know what this fruit is? It is the virgin from the Virgin, the Lord from the handmaid, God from a human creature, the Son from a mother, the fruit from the earth.[98]

He says something similar in his commentary on Psalm 96. Here, he speaks of the Promised Land as a type of Mary:

> The land of David is holy Mary, Mother of the Lord, "who was born of David's seed according to the flesh" (Rom. 1:3). What

---

96. The term *woman* in Hebrew means *from man*.

97. Cf. 1 Cor. 15:47; Gal. 4:4.

98. Gambero, *Mary in the Fathers of the Church*, 211; cf. St. Jerome, *Tractus de Psalmo 66* and *96*.

was promised to David was fulfilled in Mary's virginity and birth, where a virgin is born from a Virgin.[99]

Jerome sees Mary as holy because she was to be the *new land* out of which would arise the new man or new Adam. We discover this idea of Mary being the *virgin soil* or *new earth* in many of the writings of the Fathers.

As early as the second century, St. Irenaeus defended the virginal conception of Christ in the womb of Mary by using as a type of the virgin birth, Adam formed from the "virgin earth" in Genesis.[100] According to Irenaeus, Mary is that "new earth" from which the Messiah would arise.

St. Ephrem of Syria:

Just as their bodies have sinned and die, and as the earth, their mother, is cursed (cf. Gen. 3:17–19), so because of this body which is the incorruptible Church, his earth is blessed from the beginning.

The earth is Mary's body, the temple in which a seed has been deposited. Observe the angel who comes and deposits this seed in Mary's ear. It is with this very clear word that he began to sow: "Salvation is with you; you are blessed among women" (Luke 1:42), showing that because of the first mother who was cursed, the second Mother bears the name of blessed.[101]

St. Epiphanius of Salamis:

---

99. Ibid.
100. O'Carroll, *Theotokos*, 190–191.
101. Ibid., 114, St. Ephrem, *Diatessaron* 4,15. Notice that here we have a connection between Mary's sinlessness as related to her "bear[ing] the name of blessed" (as St. Ephrem says) and Christ being called *blessed*. This is a reference to Luke 1:42, a text we will look at below, when Elizabeth, under the inspiration of the Holy Spirit, says to Mary, "Blessed are you among women and blessed is the fruit of your womb." This too has implications for the Immaculate Conception.

As Maker and Master of the thing [to be made] he formed himself from a virgin as though from earth—God come from heaven, the Word who had assumed flesh from a Holy Virgin.[102]

John the monk, disciple of St. Basil:

For by her virginal womb, I plan to renew the human race; by my condescension, I want to reestablish the image I molded; I want to restore the ancient image, reshaping it. I formed the first man from a virgin earth, but the devil, making himself master, plundered him as an enemy and threw him to the earth, thus mocking my fallen image. Now I want to remold a new Adam for myself from the virgin earth, so that nature might prepare a beautiful defense and receive the just crown against him who conquered her. [103]

St. John Chrysostom

Therefore he called it "Eden" or "virgin soil," because this virgin [the soil of paradise] was a type of that other Virgin. As the first soil produced for us the garden of paradise without any seed, so the Virgin gave birth to Christ for us without receiving any manly seed.

In case a Jew should ask you how the Virgin could give birth, answer him thus: How could a virgin soil make wondrous plants spring up? For, in the Hebrew language, "Eden" means "virgin soil."[104]

---

102. *Panarion* 79:7, 2.

103. This disciple of St. Basil goes on to conclude that Mary was "made worthy to provide a dwelling for such a Lord . . . the most pure workshop of the divine economy . . . worthy chariot for our Lord's entrance into life . . . the most beautiful part of creation, more luminous than the heavens, more resplendent than the sun, higher than the angels. "

104. Gambero, 178–179. Cf. St. John Chrysostom, *Commentary on the Psalms* 44, 7.

As Ephrem, Jerome, and Epiphanius point out, Mary as the new earth is an image that reveals her unique holiness. She is not only the "virgin soil" out of which would arise our Lord and Messiah, but she is also the pristine earth—*the beginning of the new creation*—untouched by original sin who would serve as a fitting source to provide a body for our Lord Jesus Christ.

REASON 4: Mary's *blessed* state.

As we move forward again in Luke 1, we find two verses indicating that Mary enjoys a uniquely "blessed" state. The first comes from the lips of Elizabeth in verse 42: "Blessed are you among women, and blessed is the fruit of your womb!" The second comes from the prophetic words of our Lady herself in verse 48: "For behold, henceforth all generations shall call me blessed."

In the context of the Annunciation, Elizabeth's words to Mary are no common blessing.[105] In fact, in them we discover a double blessing referring to Mary *and* Jesus: *eulogemene* and *eulogemenos* (Gr., *blessed* in the feminine for Mary and in the masculine for Jesus).[106] In drawing this parallel between Jesus and Mary, it is a blessing of a supreme sort.

Ludwig Ott points out:

---

105. Some may speculate about the degree to which Elizabeth understood the full depth of the words she was using. While we can't know for certain, Elizabeth *is* depicted as knowing of Mary's pregnancy via revelation from God. Further, she uses biblical language—*blessed are you among women* (cf. Judg. 5:24; Jth. 13:23) and *who am I that the mother of my Lord should come to me?* (cf. 2 Sam. 6:9)—and even knows of the *things promised* to Mary concerning her child being the Messiah, the Son of God. Did she know of the parallel blessing of Jesus and Mary here, indicating the blessed state of Mary? Perhaps—perhaps not. Prophecies are not always understood fully by the prophet (see Dan. 12:8–9).

106. These words are quite unsettling at first glance when we consider just who is being spoken of here. In the context of the oriental culture out of which Scripture arose, the person listed *first* in a series was very important. Recall the lists of the apostles in Matthew 10, Mark 3, and Luke 6. Peter is always first and Judas is always last. Are we attempting to say Mary is more important than Christ here? Of course not! However, there is no doubt that Mary is given a lofty status in this text.

Elizabeth, filled with the Holy Ghost, speaks to Mary: "Blessed art thou (*eulogeme'ne*) among women, and blessed is the fruit of thy womb" (*eulogeme'nos*). The blessing of God which rests upon Mary is made parallel to the blessing of God which rests upon Christ in his humanity. This parallelism suggests that Mary, just like Christ, was from the beginning of her existence, free from all sin.[107]

Some may object that we're making too much out of the word "blessed," as James White does when he asks, "[D]oes [this] mean that all Christians are sinlessly perfect because they are called blessed in Matthew 25:34?"[108]

The answer, of course, is no. In any human discourse, context is crucial to understanding what is being said. If we consider a simple command like: "Put the kitty on the table," only context would determine whether we're talking about a cat or a bet in a poker game. So it is with Scripture.

It is not simply the term *blessed* that gives us the significance of the passage; it is the parallel usage that indicates a fullness of blessing in the lives of both Jesus and Mary. All of this is seen in the context of Mary's being revealed to be full of grace, the beginning of the new creation, the Ark of the Covenant, and more. The Ark of the Covenant, as we will soon see, will become an especially important image because it too suggests a parallel relationship between Mary and Jesus.[109]

Again this is not to say Mary is *equal* to Jesus; but it is to see a similarity when it comes to the absence of sin. There is a true parallel. An example of this "parallelism" taught among the Fathers is Ephrem of Syria, ca. 350, in his Nisibene Hymns, 27:

---

107. Ott, *The Fundamentals of Catholic Dogma*, 200–201.
108. White, *Mary—Another Redeemer?*, 39.
109. Psalm 132:8 is an example in the Old Testament: "Arise, O Lord and go to thy resting place, thou and the ark of thy might." In the New Testament we have Revelation 11:19, which depicts both Jesus symbolized by *the temple* and Mary symbolized by *the ark* together in heaven. In Chapter 14 we will delve deeper into these texts when we consider the Assumption of Mary.

Thou alone and thy Mother are in all things fair: for there is no flaw in thee and no stain in thy Mother. Of these two fair ones, to whom are my children similar?[110]

Moreover, as we mentioned above, Ephrem also writes specifically concerning our text of Luke 1:42:

Just as their bodies have sinned and die, and as the earth, their mother, is cursed (cf. Gen. 3:17–19), so because of this body which is the incorruptible Church, his earth is blessed from the beginning.

The earth is Mary's body, the temple in which a seed has been deposited. Observe the angel who comes and deposits this seed in Mary's ear. It is with this very clear word that he began to sow: "Salvation is with you; you are blessed among women" (Luke 1:42), showing that because of the first mother who was cursed, the second Mother bears the name of blessed.[111]

Ephrem brings out quite beautifully the connection between Mary's sinless nature, or incorruptibility, and her "bear[ing] the name of blessed" in Luke 1:42 and 48. This fourth-century Father of the Church gives us a great example of the early belief among Christians of "the blessing of God which rests upon Mary [being] made parallel to the blessing of God which rests upon Christ in his humanity," as Ott suggested.[112] Indeed, so radical is this blessing in the life of Mary that it becomes another name for Mary: "*all generations shall call me blessed*" (Luke 1:48). Or, as Ephrem said it: "the first mother . . . was cursed, the second mother *bears the name of blessed.*"

---

110. Quoted in O'Carroll, *Theotokos*, 132. Here, St. Ephrem quotes the prophetic text of Song of Solomon 4:7, which many of the Fathers cite as a reference to Mary without sin and "spouse of the Holy Spirit": "You are all fair, my love; there is no flaw in you." This is another example of a parallel between Mary's holiness and the holiness of God.
111. *Diatesseron* 4, 15, quoted in Gambero, *Mary and the Fathers of the Church*, 114.
112. Ott, *Fundamentals of Catholic Dogma*, 200–201.

REASON 5: Mary is revealed to be "more blessed than all women."

Fr. Reginald Ginns brings out yet another profound but oft-missed truth found in Luke 1:42. Elizabeth's spontaneous ejaculation of praise for Mary, "Blessed are you among women, and blessed is the fruit of your womb," is a Hebraism that means Mary is *more blessed than all women.*[113] Because Hebrew has no special way of express-ing either the comparative (more/less) or superlative (most/least) for adjectives, idioms were used instead.[114] Among these, it was common to use "blessed among" a given category to get at the sense of being "the most blessed" in that category.

Thus, Mary is here declared to be not just blessed but rather *the most blessed* among the entire category of women, which would include Eve. Once again, she is revealed to be conceived without sin. For if she is *more blessed* than Eve, original sin is not something we could consider for her, biblically speaking.

It is interesting to note that we find types of Mary in the Old Testament about whom similar language is used, but with crucial qualification. Ja'el, for example, who delivers Israel from the wick-ed Canaanite King Jabin and his General Sisera, was lauded thusly:

> Most blessed of women be Jael, the wife of He'ber the Kenite, of tent-dwelling women most blessed (Judg. 5:24).[115]

Judith, who similarly delivers Israel from another wicked general, this time the Assyrian Holofernes, is also praised:

> O daughter, you are blessed by the Most High God above all women on earth; and blessed be the Lord God, who created the heavens and the earth, who has guided you to strike the head of the leader of our enemies (Jth. 13:18).

---

113. Ginns, *A Catholic Commentary on Holy Scripture,* 941.
114. Kautzsch, *Gesenius' Hebrew Grammar,* 429. Cf. ibid., 429–432.
115. Cf. 4:17–24.

Both of these women, who are types of Mary in that they are each used by God to deliver his people at different times, are referred to as "most blessed," but only above "tent-dwelling women" or "women on earth" well over 2,000 years ago. Mary's blessedness is above *all women* without qualification.

REASON 6: Mary, the Ark of the Covenant, is a fitting vessel for the Son.

We now want to focus our attention on four verses: Luke 1:35, 43, 44, and 56, with a special concentration on verse 43, as we examine how Luke's Gospel reveals another of the "revelations and ancient promises" fulfilled in Christ and Mary: Mary as *the New Covenant Ark of the Covenant*:

> And the angel said to [Mary], "The Holy Spirit will come upon you, and the power of the Most High will overshadow you; therefore the child to be born will be called holy, the Son of God . . . (43) [Elizabeth exclaimed,] "And why is this granted me, that the mother of my Lord should come to me? (44) For behold, when the voice of your greeting came to my ears, the child in my womb leaped for joy . . . (56) And Mary remained with [Elizabeth] about three months, and returned to her home.

First, consider these parallels between the ark of old, and the Mother of God revealed here:

1. The Ark of the Covenant contained three "types" of Jesus inside: Manna, Aaron's rod, and the Ten Command ments (cf. Heb. 9:4). In Hebrew, *commandment* (*dabar*) can be translated as *word*.	1. Mary carried the fulfillment of all these types in her body. Jesus is the "true [manna] from heaven" (John 6:32), the true "High Priest" (Heb. 3:1), and "the word made flesh" (John 1:14).

2. Exodus 40:34–35: "The cloud [overshadowed] the tent of meeting, and the glory of the Lord filled the tabernacle." The Greek word for "overshadow" found in the Septuagint is a form of *episkiasei*.	2. "The Holy Spirit will come upon you, and the power of the Most High will overshadow you; therefore the child to be born will be called holy, the Son of God" (Luke 1:35). The Greek word for "overshadow" is *episkiasei*.
3. David "leapt and danced" before the ark when it was being carried into Jeru- salem in procession in 2 Samuel 6:14–16.	3. As soon as Elizabeth heard the sound of Mary's sal- utation, John the Baptist "leaped for joy" in her womb (Luke 1:44).
4. After a manifestation of the power of God working through the ark, David ex- claims, "How can the *ark of the Lord* come unto me?"	4. After the revelation to Elizabeth concerning the true calling of Mary, and that she was carrying God in her womb, Elizabeth exclaims, "Why is this granted me, that the moth- er of my Lord should come to me" (Luke 1:43)?
5. The ark "remained in the house of Obededom . . . three months" in 2 Samuel 6:11.	5. "Mary remained with [Elizabeth] for about three months" (Luke 1:56).

No Christian denies that the Ark of the Covenant was holy. It was in fact uniquely holy, *because of the three types of Jesus Christ contained within it*. But is there really a biblical connection between the ark and Mary?

The parallels strongly suggest such a connection: The "glory of the Lord" *overshadowing the ark* in Exodus 40 and the Holy Spirit *overshadowing* Mary in Luke 1; David and John the Baptist each *leaping for joy*—David before the Old Testament Ark and St. John in the presence of Mary; as well as the fact that the Old Testament ark remained in the house of Obededom for "three months" and Mary "remained with [Elizabeth] for about three months." But the most important and perhaps the most obvious type/fulfillment relationship is found between 2 Samuel 6:9 and Luke 1:43. Elizabeth quotes 2 Samuel 6:9 upon her experiencing a powerful manifestation of the power of God at work in and through Mary.

A bit of background information is essential in order to help us better understand the connection. In Numbers 4:15–20, we discover God to have considered the Old Testament Ark of the Covenant so sacred that the high priest alone was given permission to touch it—*or even to look inside of it.* Moreover, among the Levites only the Kohathites were tasked by God to carry the ark, but even they had to use wooden staves overlain with gold that had been driven through golden rings on the outer edges of the ark so they would not come into contact with it while carrying it (see Exod. 25:13–15). Indeed, Scripture reveals that anyone, including Levites, presumptuous enough to touch or look inside the ark would be punished by death.

God meant what he said. In 1 Samuel 6, God slays seventy men of Bethshemes for merely looking inside the ark. Years later, in 2 Samuel 6, we find the ark in the care of the sons of Abinadab: Uzzah and Ahio. As the story goes, these two brothers were in charge of transporting the ark up to Jerusalem in obedience to King David's command. In the process, Uzzah made the grave error of touching the ark in order to steady it when it appeared it was going to fall to the ground. God struck him dead "for his rashness" (v. 8).

Protestant scholars generally agree with Catholics with regard to the ultimate cause of Uzzah's demise; it was a *sin problem.* R.C. Sproul, a well-known Calvinist theologian, has remarked:

It was an act of arrogance, a sin of presumption. Uzzah assumed his hand was less polluted than the earth. But it wasn't the ground or the mud that would desecrate the ark; it was the touch of man. The earth is an obedient creature . . . When the temperature falls to a certain point, the ground freezes. When water is added to the dust, it becomes mud, just as God designed it.

God did not want his holy throne touched by that which was contaminated by evil.[116]

Here is where the connection between the ark and Mary becomes crystal clear. Upon seeing Uzzah collapse in a heap, the inspired author declares David to have said, "How shall the ark of the Lord come to me?" (v. 9). There can be little doubt that this text is echoed in Luke 1:43. Verses 39–45 will give us the context:

In those days Mary arose and went with haste into the hill country to a city of Judah, and she entered the house of Zechariah and greeted Elizabeth. And when Elizabeth heard the greeting of Mary, the babe leaped in her womb; and Elizabeth was filled with the Holy Spirit and she exclaimed with a loud cry, "Blessed are you among women, and blessed is the fruit of your womb! *And why is this granted me, that the mother of my Lord should come to me?* For behold, when the voice of your greeting came to my ears, the babe in my womb leaped for joy. And blessed is she who believed that there would be a fulfillment of what was spoken to her from the Lord."

Both David and Elizabeth experienced dramatic manifestations of the power of the ark of the Lord—both its type and its fulfillment—with both passages of Scripture making clear it was not only what or who was dwelling *inside* the two arks that moved David and Elizabeth to the point of awe, but also *the arks themselves.* Elizabeth wondered that the *mother* of Jesus should come to her; similarly, David emphasized the *ark of the Lord* itself, or as

---

116. Sproul, *The Holiness of God*, 141.

Sproul calls it, the "holy throne" of God.

We emphasize again that it was *the contents* of both arks that made each holy. That is beyond dispute. But we would also do violence to both texts if we were to eliminate the importance placed on each of the arks. Evidently, the Ark of the Covenant was revered—*untouchable*—because of its instrumental role in bringing the presence of God to the people of God. Just ask Uzzah. Wouldn't it follow that the New Covenant fulfillment of the Ark of the Covenant is to be revered as well? That is precisely what we find revealed in Luke's Gospel. Mary is not just some insignificant conduit; she is revealed to be an instrumental cause of this divine encounter with Elizabeth. Indeed, it was not until Mary spoke—"the moment that the sound of [Mary's] greeting sounded in [Elizabeth's] ears"—in verse 44—that literally all heaven broke loose in Elizabeth's house.

The Inevitable Conclusion

How does all of this relate to the Immaculate Conception and Mary's sinlessness? The answer lies in considering just why the ark of old could not be touched by the hand of man. As Sproul pointed out so well, it could not be touched by a man because men are sinful. But imagine if the ark was more than acacia wood and gold. What if the ark or "holy throne" of God was *human*? Could such a person be just as sinful as a man who was struck dead by God for touching it . . . or better yet, *her*? Surely not! Well, the New Testament tells us that the new and true ark *is a human,* and her name is Mary.

The ark of the Old Testament was not only especially holy, but God himself designed it. It was made of the purest of materials, pristine from the time of its construction. Sound familiar? *It had to be holy from the moment of its construction,* if you will. Christians have, from the most ancient times, seen in this type the sinless Mother of God.

St. Hippolytus, writing ca. A.D. 190:

Now the Lord was without sin, being in his human nature from incorruptible wood, that is from the Virgin, and being sheathed, as it were, with the pure gold of the Word within and of the Spirit without.[117]

In this analogy the Ark of the Covenant is said to be the humanity of Christ, which bore divinity. But notice the intimate connection of the Ark to Mary. She is the *incorruptible wood* from which the ark is constructed. It is this wood that would carry the holy objects inside.

St. Athanasius, writing in 360:

O noble Virgin, truly you are greater than any other greatness, O dwelling place of God the Word. To whom among all creatures shall I compare you, O Virgin? You are greater than them all. O [ark of the New] Covenant, clothed with purity instead of gold! You are the ark in which is found the golden vessel containing the true manna, that is, the flesh in which divinity resides . . . If I say that the angels and archangels are great—but you are greater than them all, for the angels and archangels serve with trembling the One who dwells in your womb, and they dare not speak in his presence, while you speak to him freely.[118]

God himself personally designed the Ark of the Covenant in Exodus 25, but what he had in mind ultimately was not a wooden box overlain with gold. He had in mind the true Ark of the New Covenant who would contain within her womb the Lord God, creator of the universe incarnate. If God willed that the old ark should be pure and untouched by sinful man, as we have seen he did, how much more pure would the new ark be, considering that

---

117. O'Carroll, *Theotokos*, 50.
118. Gambero, *Mary and the Fathers of the* Church, 107, cf. *Homily of the Papyrus of Turin*. In referring to Mary as greater than the angels, in the context of referencing her "purity," St. Athanasius unmistakably implies her sinlessness. If she were a sinner, she would not be greater than the angels.

the type was only a shadow in comparison with its fulfillment?[119] It is only fitting, as Athanasius said over 1,600 years ago, that Mary would be "clothed with purity instead of gold" and even greater than the angels.[120]

Now we can see more clearly why John Paul II said Mary's *name* "full of grace" was surrounded by "revelations and ancient promises" that really bring into focus its true meaning. And now we can turn to the last and most profound of these revelations.

---

119. Cf. Hebrews 10:1.
120. We find among some great Christian writers and Doctors that they see the humanity of Christ as another valid fulfillment of the Ark of the Covenant. The *Catholic Encyclopedia* references St. Thomas Aquinas in this connection. The fact that some Fathers and Doctors of the Church saw Christ's humanity as a fulfillment of the ark indicates an agreement that it is, indeed, a symbol of sinless perfection. Some of them saw both Mary and Jesus as fulfillments of the ark, as we saw with St. Hippolytus. But in every case, the Ark of the Covenant is depicted as a symbol of purity. Its fulfillment would, it seems, also be most fittingly free from the taint of sin.

5

THE NEW EVE AND THE IMMACULATE CONCEPTION

Our seventh reason for the Immaculate Conception of Mary is the sixth and final of the "revelations and ancient promises" surrounding Luke 1:28 and the revelation of Mary's name as *full of grace*. It is arguably the most illuminating of all, carrying with it multiple dogmatic applications. In Luke 1:38 (and elsewhere in Scripture, as we will see), Mary is revealed as the *New Eve*. St. Irenaeus of Lyons, writing ca. A.D. 177, gives us a window into the early Church's understanding of this profound truth:

> Mary the Virgin is found obedient, saying, "Behold the handmaid of the Lord; be it unto me according to thy word." But Eve was disobedient; for she did not obey when as yet she was a virgin. And even as she, having indeed a husband, Adam, but being nevertheless yet a virgin . . . having become disobedient, was made the cause of death, both to herself and to the entire human race; so also did Mary, having a man betrothed [to her], and being nevertheless a virgin, by yielding obedience, became the cause of salvation, both to herself and the whole human race . . . And thus also it was that the knot of Eve's disobedience was loosed by the obedience of Mary. For what the virgin Eve had bound fast through unbelief, this did the Virgin Mary set free through faith.[121]

---

121. Irenaeus, *Against Heresies* III, 22, 4.

Irenaeus emphasizes the fundamental link between Mary as "the New Eve" and her central role in God's plan of salvation. If we consider again Old Testament types as necessarily inferior to their New Testament fulfillments, it would certainly be fitting to say— indeed, we argue it follows necessarily according to the revelation we have been given—that the *New Eve* would be conceived without sin. If she were conceived in sin, Mary would be inferior to the first Eve, who was created without sin.

Moreover, a true understanding of *the New Eve* renders null and void any thought of Mary ever having committed actual sins. Just as Eve's sinfulness led to the death of all of her children—as Irenaeus said—it would be Mary's obedience, or sinlessness, that would lead to life for all of her children.

Couldn't Mary have sinned *after* having obeyed God and conceived Jesus? It doesn't seem fitting that she would have. Just as the New Adam, Jesus, never fell into sin as the first Adam did, it is fitting that Mary would likewise repair the old Eve's sin with perfect obedience. Even a single sin from the Mother of God would represent a much greater fall than Eve's, because she was given so much more grace. That would be unthinkable.

Also, when we consider the manifold gifts in Mary's life we've already examined, from "Mother of God," "full of grace," and "Ark of the New Covenant" to the "beginning of the new creation" and more, and now "the New Eve," we see how each reveals the plenitude of grace in Mary's life in its own way. St. Augustine's famous words come to mind:

> With the exception of the holy Virgin Mary, in whose case, out of respect for the Lord, I do not wish there to be any further as far as sin is concerned, since how can we know what great abundance of grace was conferred on her to conquer sin in every way, seeing that she merited to conceive and bear him who certainly had no sin at all.[122]

---

122. St. Augustine, *On Nature and Grace*, 36, 42.

And finally, as we will see in more detail below, Mary's identity as the "New Eve," did not cease with her giving birth to Christ. She continues in that prophetic role from the wedding feast of Cana in John 2 to the foot of the cross in John 19, and indeed until the end of time in Revelation 12, bringing life to all of her spiritual children "who keep the commandments of God and bear testimony to Jesus" (Rev. 12:17). Because Scripture reveals her to be the New Eve throughout her life and into eternity, sin is out of the question, biblically speaking.

Back to the Beginning

In order to fully appreciate the biblical roots of the New Eve we must go back to the story of the first Eve in the very first book of the Bible. As the narrative goes, God placed our original parents, Adam and Eve, in the midst of paradise on earth, the garden of Eden, giving them a single prohibitive commandment:

> You may freely eat of every tree in the garden; but of the tree of the knowledge of good and evil you shall not eat, for in the day that you eat of it you shall die (Gen. 2:16–17).

The serpent enters into this scene as the tempter whose desire was to seduce our original parents into breaking God's law. And unfortunately, he was successful. He deceived and overcame "the woman," Eve, who in turn became an instrument in the devil's evil plot by leading Adam into what the Church calls "original sin."[123]

No doubt, the devil thought he had won when Adam and Eve fell into his trap, bringing death upon themselves and their posterity. After all, God had clearly declared to Adam that "in the day that you eat of [the tree of the knowledge of good and evil] you

---

123. CCC 389–390, 396–406.

shall die." All appeared to be lost: "through the envy of the Devil, [sin and] death entered into the world."[124]

All was not lost, however, because immediately after the fall, God spoke directly to the devil promising the coming of a new "woman" and her seed—a New Eve and a New Adam—who would together oppose and overcome both the devil and all of those who follow his ways—his spiritual "seed":

> I will put enmity between you and the woman, and between your seed and her seed: he shall bruise your head, and you shall bruise his heel (Gen. 3:15).

Scholars call this verse the *protoevangelium*, or "first gospel," because it is the first announcement in the Old Testament of the coming of the New. The *Catechism* comments:

> After his fall, man was not abandoned by God. On the contrary, God calls him and in a mysterious way heralds the coming victory over evil and his restoration from his fall. This passage in Genesis [Genesis 3:15] is called the *Protoevangelium* ("first gospel"): the first announcement of the Messiah and Redeemer, of a battle between the serpent and the Woman, and of the final victory of a descendant of hers.

> The Christian tradition sees in this passage an announcement of the "New Adam" who, because he "became obedient unto death, even death on a cross," makes amends superabundantly for the disobedience of Adam. Furthermore many Fathers and Doctors of the Church have seen the woman announced in the *Protoevangelium* as Mary, the mother of Christ, the "new Eve." Mary benefited first of all and uniquely from Christ's victory over sin: she was preserved from all stain of original sin and by

---

124. Cf. Wis. 2:24; cf. 1 Tim. 2:12, Rom. 5:12.

a special grace of God committed no sin of any kind during her whole earthly life.[125]

At first glance, the "woman" seems to have an unsettling prominence in the text. Considering that "the seed" of *the woman* represents the eternal Son of God, one does not expect him to take a back seat to her. Yet the emphasis is on her.

We also notice another "parallelism" similar to what we've examined earlier. Both *the woman* and *her seed* are placed in parallel and in opposition to—enmity with—the devil and his seed; they are placed in a separate category from the devil and his "seed," which represents all of fallen humanity. This has eye-opening implications for the Immaculate Conception. John tells us, "He who commits sin is of the devil" (1 John 3:8). Paul says that fallen human beings are "by nature children of wrath" (Eph. 2:3). In this sense, all of mankind is influenced by the devil and overcome by him at times and in varying degrees. We are all the serpent's seed.

Mary and *her* seed—Jesus Christ—are uniquely excluded from this category; thus, they are uniquely revealed to be free from all sin. Indeed, it bears repeating that the emphasis in the text seems to be on the absolute enmity between *the woman* and the serpent.[126]

New Testament Clarification

Many non-Catholic critics will be quick to object to this interpretation of Genesis 3. And, granted, taking these verses in isolation might make the "Catholic" interpretation seem a little obscure. However, the meaning and fulfillment of the *protoevangelium* is further illuminated and even to some extent interpreted for us in the New Testament, especially in Revelation 12:

---

125. CCC 410–411.

126. It may be that "the seed" of the devil applies in the first place to the anti-Christ, "the lawless one" (2 Thess. 2:8), and to all the rest of sinners via participation. The seed of the woman, similarly, would apply to Christ in the first place, but to the faithful via participation, or by allusion, as well. However, there is no doubt that in the fullest sense, this prophecy applies to Mary and Jesus—*the woman and her seed*—alone.

And a great sign appeared in heaven, a woman clothed with the sun, with the moon under her feet, and on her head a crown of twelve stars; she was with child . . . And the dragon stood before the woman who was about to bear a child, that he might devour her child when she brought it forth; she brought forth a male child, one who is to rule all the nations with a rod of iron . . . Now war arose in heaven, Michael and his angels fighting against the dragon . . . And the great dragon was thrown down, that ancient serpent, who is called the Devil and Satan . . . And when the dragon saw that he had been thrown down to the earth, he pursued the woman who had borne the male child . . . Then the dragon was angry with the woman, and went off to make war on the rest of her offspring, on those who keep the commandments of God and bear testimony to Jesus.

The mention of "the great dragon . . . that ancient serpent" is only our first clue that there is a connection between Revelation 12 and Genesis 3. Notice, too, that Eve is called "woman" repeatedly—nine times in sixteen verses in Genesis 3 alone—before she is named "Eve." In Revelation 12 John refers to Mary as "woman" eight times in seventeen verses. We also have the reference to the "offspring" of *the woman* in Revelation 12:17. The Greek word here is *spermatos*, or "seed," which hearkens back to *the seed of the woman* in Genesis 3:15.

We also find an allusion to the name of "Eve," which Genesis 3:20 tells us means "mother of all the living."[127] Mary is revealed to be the mother of all who live in Christ, or "those who keep the commandments of God and bear testimony to Jesus" (Rev. 12:17).

In the final analysis, there seems to be a rather obvious parallel between the three main characters of Genesis 3—Adam, Eve, and the devil—and the three main characters of Revelation 12—Jesus, Mary, and the archangel Michael. But perhaps most important of all for our purpose here is the clear and absolute enmity we see

---

127. This is actually a play on words here. The Hebrew word for "Eve" sounds similar to the word for "living." The inspired author fills in the holes.

between *the woman* and a fourth character, the *dragon*, in Revelation 12, also referred to as "that ancient serpent, who is called the devil and Satan" (v. 9)—an unambiguous fulfillment of the prophetic words from Genesis 3:15. "The serpent" of Revelation 12 hates *the woman* and pursues her, but he can never overcome her. In other words, he could never move Mary to sin as he had done with Eve. Thus, Scripture twice reveals the antipathy between the devil and Mary as *absolute*.

The Seven Days of the New Creation

If we had no more evidence of Mary as *the New Eve* in Scripture, we would have already proved our case, yet there is much more. In the Gospel that bears his name, John—who most likely penned the Book of Revelation—gives us more insight via allusions back to Genesis 1:

Genesis 1:1–26:	John 1:1–9:
In the beginning God created the heavens and the earth . . . (3) And God said, "Let there be light;" and there was light . . . (11) And God said, "Let the earth put forth vegetation . . . (20) Let the waters bring forth swarms of living creatures . . . (24) Let the earth bring forth living creatures according to their kinds . . . " (26) Then God said, "Let us make man in our image."	In the beginning was the Word, and the Word was with God, and the Word was God . . . (3) all things were made through him, and without him was not anything made that was made. (4) In him was life, and the life was the light of men. (5) The light shines in the darkness, and the darkness has not overcome it. (9) The true light that enlightens every man was coming to the world.

John's reference to the very first words of Genesis is instantly recognizable. Christ is revealed to be God and in multiple ways. First, John says, "In the beginning *was* the Word" using the imperfect form of the verb "to be." This verb form indicates a past ongoing reality. Thus, in the beginning, before there was any created thing, the Word was already in existence and *had been* from all eternity. Then, he simply says "the Word was God." Any questions? Next, he reinforces the point by declaring Christ to have been the creator of everything that was made, as well as the source of all "life" as well as the "light" we are so familiar with from Genesis.

St. John's point is not merely to say Jesus—*the Word*—is the God who created *in the past*, though he certainly affirms that to be true. His point is that Christ is the beginning of a new creation. The life he came to give is not mere biological life but the divine life that would be poured out in our hearts through the Holy Spirit.[128] He is not just the created "light" from Genesis; he is the source of light, "the true light that enlightens every man," bringing eternal light and life to all who would believe and abide in him. He not only creates man along with all of creation, but he re-creates man as the "true light that enlightens every man."

After John's theological introduction to his Gospel, drawing heavily on imagery from Genesis, he begins his historical narrative with the message of St. John the Baptist leading up to the beginning of Jesus' ministry at Cana—framed rather conspicuously by seven "days," no doubt echoing back to the creation story from Genesis.[129] Here are the seven days of the *re-creation* of the universe that is brought about by Christ.[130] Verses 18–28 represent the first day, 19–34 the second day, 35–42 the third day, and 43–51 the fourth day. Then, in 2:1, St. John skips to the seventh day when he says, "On the third day," meaning the third day after the fourth day mentioned in 1:43:

> And on the third day a marriage took place at Cana of Galilee, and the mother of Jesus was there. Now Jesus too was invited

---

128. The Greek word *zoe* ("life") is used in many places in the New Testament to represent the supernatural life of God gifted to men in Christ. Cf. Rom. 5:5; John 1:16–17, 15:26, 6:53, 10:10, etc.

129. *The Jerome Biblical Commentary*, p. 424.

130. Cf. Rev. 21:1; 2 Cor. 5:17, etc.

to the marriage, and also his disciples. And the wine having run short, the mother of Jesus said to him, "They have no wine." And Jesus said to her, "What is that to me and to you, woman, my hour has not yet come." His mother said to the attendants, "Do whatever he tells you" . . . This first of his signs Jesus worked at Cana of Galilee; and he manifested his glory, and his disciples believed in him.

That Mary's request was met by the language of rebuke from her divine son, yet he performed the miracle nonetheless, leaves no room to doubt Mary's essential intercessory role. But that intercession is not our focus right now, but rather the *nature* of the intercession—or more specifically, the nature of the *effects* of that intercession. As the first Eve moved Adam to sin, the New Eve now intercedes with the New Adam to perform a miracle that, according to the text, brought about (or shall we say, *gave birth to*) both the faith of the apostles and the manifestation of Christ's glory. Note, too, the reference to Mary as "woman" here in the context of the seven days of creation, or re-creation. Mary, the new "woman," has an even more prominent role in the new creation than did her antecedent in the old.

Bone of My Bones and Flesh of My Flesh

Adam and Eve were uniquely joined to each other in all of creation first of all by virtue of their lofty calling to be our original parents. But even more, when we examine the nature of their creation we find that Eve received her human nature from Adam *alone,* symbolized by God pulling a rib out of a sleeping Adam in order to create her (Gen. 3:21–22). No other two human beings could ever say that. This new person, named "woman," was truly flesh of Adam's flesh.

No two humans could ever say that *until the coming of the New Covenant.* The second Adam calls the New Eve "woman" as well, and in order to fulfill his lofty calling of re-creating the universe and saving fallen souls, the second Adam received his human nature entirely from the second Eve, Mary. This represents the reverse of Eve receiving her humanity from Adam in the context of *reversing the curse* of Genesis. The implications are staggering.[131]

The Crucifixion: John 19:25–27

But standing by the cross of Jesus were his mother, and his mother's sister, Mary the wife of Clopas, and Mary Magdalene. When Jesus saw his mother, and the disciple whom he loved standing near, he said to his mother, "Woman, behold, your son!" Then he said to the disciple, "Behold, your mother!" And from that hour the disciple took her to his own home.

Here we see perhaps the most profound revelation of Mary as the New Eve. The cross is referred to as a *tree* in Galatians 3:13, 1 Peter 2:24, and elsewhere in Scripture. Mary, in John's Gospel, is depicted at the foot of this tree upon which Jesus was crucified. Where Eve reached out in disobedience to the tree of the knowledge of good and evil and brought death to her children, Mary reaches out in faith to the tree of salvation, uniting herself with her son who brings eternal life. In so doing she becomes the mother to all those who live in Christ, which Jesus acknowledges in John 19:27 when he tells "the beloved disciple" (who represents all of us) to behold his mother. That John represents all Christians is confirmed in Revelation 12:17, when John himself tells us plainly that *the woman* who gave birth to Jesus Christ also gives birth to all "those who keep the commandments of God and bear testimony to Jesus."

A common objection to the above revolves around the identity of *the woman* of Revelation 12. Among those who deny it's Mary there's no consensus as to just who *the woman* is; they just know it's

---

131. There are more parallels to be found between John's Gospel and Genesis. Another possible example is the Holy Spirit descending upon Jesus in the context of John the Baptist's baptizing him; thus, God inaugurates his plan of salvation making man a new creation through faith and baptism (cf. Eph. 5:17; Luke 1:77). This seems to allude to the Holy Spirit "moving over the face of the waters" in the first creation (Gen. 1:2).

not her. And this only makes sense, for if she *is* Mary, much of the rest of Catholic Mariology falls into place. So we would almost expect an objection here.[132] However, *the nature* of the objections is not so expected.

When I was a Protestant, my rejection of Catholic Mariology was not so much based on scholarship as on a preconceived bias. I figured that *the woman* in Revelation 12 just *couldn't* be Mary, because Mary was just not that important in God's plan of salvation. Even well-known Protestant scholars exhibit a similar bias, struggling to find alternative explanations for the identity of the woman. One example is Alan F. Johnson:

> Who then is the woman? While it is not impossible that she is an actual woman, such as Mary, the evidence clearly shows that she, like the woman in chapter 17, has symbolic significance. At the center of chapter 12 is the persecution of the woman by the dragon, who is definitely Satan (v. 9). This central theme, as well as the reference to the persecution of the "rest of her offspring" (v. 17), renders it virtually certain that the woman could not refer to a single individual.[133]

William Barclay adds:

> This woman is in labor to bear a child who is undoubtedly the Messiah, Christ . . . where he is said to be destined to rule the nations with a rod of iron. That is a quotation from Psalm 2:9 and was an accepted description of the Messiah. The woman, then, is the mother of the Messiah.

> If the woman is the "mother" of the Messiah, an obvious suggestion is that she should be identified with Mary; but she is

---

132. A proper understanding of Revelation 12 is not essential to understanding Mary as the New Eve. Indeed, the earliest Christian writers we cited above use Luke 1 as their foundation. But Revelation 12 certainly helps clarify things.

133. Johnson, *The Expositor's Bible Commentary*, vol. 12, 513.

so clearly a superhuman figure that she can hardly be identified with any single human being.[134]

Both of these Protestant commentators suggest that *the woman* can be referred to as the Church or "God's people in every age,"[135] but when it comes to Mary there seems to be a mental block. Johnson says "it's not impossible" that *the woman* could be Mary, Barclay says it's even an "obvious suggestion" to say it represents Mary—yet in the very next sentence he says *the woman* is too glorious to be Mary, so it just can't be so! Johnson's reason for rejecting Mary as a possible interpretation is that the woman has "symbolic significance." As if an individual person can't have "symbolic significance"?

These Protestant authors seem compelled at least to acknowledge the obvious: It *appears* this text is speaking of Mary. But rather than allowing the words of Scripture to speak, they allow their own presuppositions—as I once did—to eliminate the obvious interpretation as a possibility. Catholics, without a preconceived bias against Mary, can simply go with what the text says.[136]

Theological Difficulties

In defense of our Protestant friends—Barclay and Johnson in particular—they do have their theological reasons for rejecting Mary as *the woman*. But we have to wonder if they are truly satisfied with them. We wonder whether these were serious attempts at exegesis

---

134. Barclay, *The Daily Study Bible Series*, 75–76.

135. Ibid., 76.

136. Another example of obvious bias can be found in: Geisler and MacKenzie, *Roman Catholics and Evangelicals—Agreements and Differences*, 313: "First, the 'woman' does not represent Mary, but the nation of Israel for whom there is 'a place prepared by God, that there she might be taken care of for twelve hundred and sixty days' (vs. 6) during the tribulation period before Christ returns to the earth" (cf. Rev. 11:2–3). This is perhaps an even more obvious case of *eisogesis*, or reading into a text, rather than *exegesis*, or *drawing out* of the text that which is presented by the inspired author. These authors read into the text a dispensationalist view that is minority even among Protestants. The dispensationalist view teaches *the woman* can only be Israel, so the authors state emphatically that *the woman does not represent Mary.*

or if they were more attempts to justify their presuppositions.

For example, both of these scholars emphasize that *the woman* is revealed to be too glorious—even "superhuman"—to be Mary or any single person. But isn't that the point of the text, no matter what or whom you interpret *the woman* to be? *She*, or *they*, or *it*, has been made "superhuman" by God's power. Even if you say *the woman* represents the Church, the Church is then depicted as "clothed with the sun, the moon under her feet, and on her head a crown of twelve stars" (v. 1). Barclay and Johnson's reasoning could logically be used to say this could not refer to the Church or any collection of humans either, rendering the text meaningless.

Johnson also eliminates Mary here because her "offspring" represents all of the people of God persecuted for the sake of Christ. This "renders it virtually certain that the woman could not refer to a single individual." Did he consider the fact that Abraham and Sarah are referred to as "father" and "mother" of the people of God hundreds of years after their respective deaths in Isaiah 51:1–2? Indeed, St. Paul says Abraham is the father of "all who believe" (Rom. 4:11) and that he (Paul) had "begotten" the Corinthians (1 Cor. 4:16). The fact that the "offspring" of these great saints includes too many souls to conclude a strictly "physical" interpretation does not mean they cannot refer to an individual in any sense.

The Woman and the Pangs of Labor

Perhaps the most pervasive theological reason we encounter as to why *the woman* of Revelation 12 cannot refer to Mary is found in "the suffering" of *the woman* in Revelation 12:1–3: "[T]he woman . . . was with child and she cried out in her pangs of birth, in anguish for delivery." Knowing that Catholic teaching has traditionally held that Mary did not suffer the pains of labor, the question is asked, how can Catholics believe this is Mary? Indeed, since Genesis 3:16 says labor pains are the result of original sin, wouldn't this prove too much? If it *was* Mary, wouldn't it disprove the Immaculate Conception? We will explain in more depth the teaching of the Church on this matter later, but there are two points to be made for now.

First, I know of no Protestant scholar who would interpret this text in any way other than to say that the "labor pangs" were spiritual in nature. If one held *the woman* to be Israel or the Church, "the labor pains" would obviously be spiritual. It should be no problem to interpret it that way if it were Mary.

Secondly, Mary did in fact suffer greatly throughout her life as a result of her calling to be the Mother of God. Right from the start, she had to suffer through being misunderstood—perhaps even by St. Joseph—with regard to her pregnancy.[137] She would have had some knowledge that her son was destined for great suffering from the time the angel revealed to her that he was to be the Messiah. This would be a source of suffering for any loving mother. Moreover, she was promised suffering by almighty God through the prophet Simeon in Luke 2:34–35: *A sword shall pierce your soul.* This would be dramatically fulfilled at the foot of the cross.

Ecclesiastes 1:18 says: "For in much wisdom is much vexation, and he who increases knowledge increases sorrow." Mary's unique and intimate knowledge of her son would have been a source of great consolation and great suffering. Any mother can readily see this even on a natural level; given the plenitude of grace in Mary's life, her intimate knowledge and therefore her suffering would have been multiplied exponentially. It is certainly no leap to see why she would be depicted as suffering "labor pangs" in Revelation 12:3—not physical pain from the head of her child passing through her birth canal, but just as real. In fact, spiritual suffering in the soul can be worse than any physical suffering. The body can go numb with intense pain, but there is no way to shut down the pain in a heart that loves.[138]

---

137. Scripture scholars tell us that in John 8:41, when the Jews were defending themselves against Jesus, who had been chastising them for their hypocrisy and challenging their claim to be "children of Abraham," they responded: "We were not born of fornication . . ." This is most likely a reference to the false rumor that had circulated for thirty years, that Christ was an illegitimate child. This would have been yet another source of pain for the Mother of God.

138. At least, not until it "obtain[s] the glorious liberty of the children of God" (Rom. 8:21).

In the final analysis, whether one is Catholic or Protestant, the text and context of Revelation 12 demonstrates Mary to be *the woman* at least in some sense for at least four reasons:

1. In Revelation 12:5, *the woman* of Revelation bears a male child "who is to rule all the nations with a rod of iron, but her child was caught up to God and to his throne." This child is obviously Jesus. If we begin on the literal level, there is no doubt that Mary is *literally* the one who bore Jesus.

2. Though there are multiple levels of meaning for the flight of *the woman* in verses 6 and 14, Mary and the Holy Family *literally* fled into Egypt in Matthew 2:13–15, with divine assistance.[139]

3. Mary can easily be seen to be the prophetic "woman" of Genesis 3:15 and Jeremiah 31:22. When you add to this Jesus' own reference to Mary as "woman" in John 2:4 and 19:26, it is no surprise that the same apostle John refers to Mary as *the woman* in Revelation 12. Scott Hahn provides:

> Tradition tells us that she is the same person whom Jesus calls "woman" in John's gospel, the reprise of the person Adam

---

139. An immediate objection to this will be to point out that "the woman fled into the wilderness" immediately after her child "was caught up to God and to his throne" in verse 5. This would then apply to the persecutions of the people of God through the centuries. And this certainly can represent one level of meaning for the text. However, we must also consider that Revelation is prophetic literature that cannot always and only be understood as simple chronological history. For example, in Revelation 12:3–4, the devil causes one third of the angels to be "cast down to the earth" out of heaven. This is placed after the revelation of the "woman clothed with the sun . . . [who] was with child . . . in her pangs of birth." When did this "casting down" of one third of the angels occur? It happened before man was created. Yet the devil was also "cast down" through the life, death, and ministry of Jesus and during the disciples' ministry, according to Luke 10:18, John 12:31, and Matthew 12:29/Revelation 20:2. And he will finally be cast into the lake of fire at the end of time (cf. Rev. 20:10). It is obvious this text is not intended to be understood in a strict, chronological sense; the *casting down* of Lucifer is depicted as occurring during the time of labor, but before the actual birth of Christ. A literal chronology does not work.

calls "woman" in the Garden of Eden. Like the beginning
of John's gospel, this episode of the Apocalypse repeatedly
evokes the *Protoevangelium* of Genesis.[140]

There are four main characters in the chapter: *the woman*, the
devil, Jesus, and the archangel Michael. No one denies that the
other three central characters mentioned are real persons on
the literal level. It fits the context exegetically to interpret the
woman, on that same level, also as a real person (Mary).[141]

Steeped in History

Even the earliest centuries of Christianity could not have been
any more certain in affirming Mary's ancient title of *New Eve*. The
Fathers who taught it were from both East and West, spanning the
centuries of Church history. From "Matheiteis," St. Justin Martyr
and St. Irenaeus, to Tertullian, St. Jerome and St. Augustine, to St.
Epiphanius, St. Gregory of Nyssa, St. John Chrysostom and more,
the Fathers are unanimous.

Here are a few examples:

The Epistle of Matheiteis to Diognetus, 12 (A.D. 140):

> Whereof if thou bear the tree and pluck the fruit, thou
> shalt ever gather the harvest which God looks for, which
> [the] serpent toucheth not, nor deceit infecteth, *neither is*
> *Eve corrupted, but is believed on as a virgin*, and salvation is set

---

140. Cf. Hahn, *Hail, Holy Queen*, 59. Hahn goes on to point out the parallels between
Genesis and our text: "The first clue is that John—here, as in the Gospel—never
reveals this person's name; he refers to her only by the name Adam gave to Eve in the
garden: she is 'woman.' Later in the same chapter of the Apocalypse, we learn also that,
like Eve—who is 'mother of all the living' (Gen. 3:20)—the woman of John's vision
is mother not only of the 'male child' but also to 'the rest of her offspring,' further
identified as 'those who keep the commandments of God and bear testimony to
Jesus' (Rev. 12:17) . . . The New Eve, then, fulfills the promise of the old to be, more
perfectly, the mother of all the living."

141. Ibid., 56–58.

forth, and the apostles are filled with understanding, and the Passover of the Lord goes forward, and the congregations are gathered together, and [all things] are arranged in order, and as He that teacheth the saints the Word is gladdened, through Whom the Father is glorified, to Whom be glory for ever and ever [emphasis added].[142]

This ancient text does not explicitly name the New Eve as Mary, but she is implied in the reference to her being "believed on as a virgin." She is depicted as being the opposite of Eve who had been corrupted.

St. Justin Martyr, a contemporary of "Matheiteis," in his *Dialogue with Trypho the Jew* (150):

For Eve, who was a virgin and undefiled, having conceived the word of the serpent, brought forth disobedience and death. But the Virgin Mary received faith and joy, when the angel Gabriel announced the good tidings to her that the Spirit of the Lord would come upon her, and the power of the Highest would overshadow her: wherefore also the Holy Thing begotten of her is the Son of God; and she replied, "Be it unto me according to thy word." And by her has he been born, to whom we have proved so many scriptures refer, and by whom God destroys both the serpent and those angels and men who are like him; but works deliverance from death to those who repent of their wickedness and believe upon him.[143]

Tertullian, in *On the Flesh of Christ,* 17, 5 (210):

Eve believed the Serpent; Mary believed Gabriel. The fault that Eve introduced by believing, Mary erased by believing.

142. We do not know who *Matheteis* actually was. There are different theories. The name means "disciple" in Greek and has been attributed to this unknown second-century Christian author.
143. *Dialogue with Trypho the Jew*, 100.

For perspective, if we add Irenaeus's reference we cited earlier to those of "Matheiteis," Justin, and Tertullian, we have references spanning three continents—Africa, Asia, and Europe, all concurring on this teaching of Mary as the New Eve. How did this understanding become this widespread so quickly? The source could only be apostolic Tradition going back to St. John himself. These four men were writing over 200 years before there was a uniform canon of Scripture, and three of the four were writing before we ever find the word "Trinity" mentioned in Christian writings.[144] At the very least, this should be a reason for any Christian to examine this teaching further.

St. Cyril of Jerusalem (ca. 350):

Through Eve yet virgin came death; through a virgin, or rather from a virgin, must the Life appear: that as the serpent beguiled the one, so to the other Gabriel might bring good tidings.[145]

St. Epiphanius of Salamis (360):

She it is, who is signified by Eve, enigmatically receiving the appellation of the Mother of the living. It was a wonder that after the fall she had this great epithet. And, according to what is material, from that Eve all the race of man on earth is generated. But thus in truth from Mary the Life itself was born in the world, that Mary might bear living things, and become the Mother of living things. Therefore, enigmatically, Mary is called the Mother of living things . . . Also, there is another thing to consider as to these women, and wonderful—as to Eve and Mary. Eve became a cause of death to men . . . and Mary a cause of life . . . that life might be instead of death, life excluding death which came from the woman.[146]

144. The first mention of the term is made by St. Theophilus of Antioch, in ca. A.D. 181.
145. *Catechetical Lectures*, 12, 15.
146. *Panarion* 78, 18.

St. Ephrem of Syria (ca. 360):

> Death entered by Eve's ear; that is why life entered by Mary's ear.[147] For as from the small womb of that ear death entered and spread about, so through the new ear of Mary life entered and spread about.[148]

> Because the serpent had struck Eve with his claw, the foot of Mary bruised him.[149]

> Mary and Eve, two people without guilt, two simple people, were identical. Later, however, one became the cause of our death, the other the cause of our life.[150]

St. John Chrysostom (390):

> A virgin drove us from paradise; through a Virgin we have found eternal life.[151]

> A virgin, the wood, and death were the symbols of our defeat. The virgin was Eve, for she had not yet known her husband; the wood was the tree . . . And behold, a second time, a virgin, the wood and death; the symbols of defeat have become the symbols of victory. For Mary is in the place of Eve.[152]

Space does not permit us to quote more, including St. Gregory of Nyssa, St. Athanasius, St. Ambrose, St. Jerome,[153] St. Cyril of

---

147. O'Carroll, *Theotokos*, 133.
148. Ibid.
149. *Diatesseron* 10, 13; quoted in Gambero, *Mary and the Fathers of the Church*, 117.
150. *Op. syr.* II, 37; quoted in Ott, *Fundamentals of Catholic Dogma*, 201.
151. Commentary on Psalm 44, 7, quoted in O'Carroll, *Theotokos*, 198.
152. Ibid., De Coemet. et de cruce, 2, quoted in O'Carroll, *Theotokos*, 198.
153. Jerome is famous for the phrase, "*Death through Eve, life through Mary*," which is quoted in the document of Vatican II, *Lumen Gentium* 56.

Alexandria, St. Peter Chrysologus, and St. Augustine.[154] Let these examples suffice to note that the Fathers and early Christian writers are virtually unanimous in connecting the *New Eve* to Mary's unique role in God's plan of salvation. They do not all make the connection to Mary's being without sin, though some—such as St. Ephrem—do. But neither do any of them object to it.

Although you won't find the words *Immaculate Conception* in these ancient works, from this truth of Mary as the New Eve, rooted in Scripture and Tradition, more ancient than the word *Trinity*, believed universally by Christians in both the East and West from the very beginning of the Christian era, the Immaculate Conception and the sinlessness of Mary necessarily follows.

---

154. Augustine saw Mary, "the New Eve," as the archetype of the Church who is "mother of the living."

6
ANSWERING OBJECTIONS

In this chapter, we will focus on the most common objections both to the Immaculate Conception and to the closely connected doctrine of Mary's sinlessness.[155]

The questions and objections surrounding these teachings are most often shrouded in misunderstandings ranging from the simple to the complex. For example, I was recently asked by a nine-year-old boy, "If Mary had to be without sin in order for her to carry Jesus in her womb, how could Jesus have come into a world where there is so much sin?" Quite a question coming from a child! Along these same lines many will ask, "If Mary had to be without sin in order to carry God in her womb, wouldn't Mary's *mother* have to be without sin in order to carry a sin-free Mary in her womb . . . and wouldn't the same be true for *her* mother . . . and *her* mother, etc.?"[156]

It is important for us to remember as we work our way through the Marian dogmas, that we are not talking about strict necessity with any of them. In other words, Mary did not *have* to be immaculately conceived in order to give birth to the Messiah. Jesus could have been born of a sinful woman if God had so willed

---

155. Whether Mary ever sinned personally has never been a matter of major dispute in the Church. As *Lumen Gentium* 56 says: "It is no surprise to find that the custom grew up among the Fathers by which they called the Mother of God all holy and free from all stain of sin, as though fashioned by the Holy Spirit and made a new creature." The document goes on to explain that Mary was not "held back by any sin, [and she] dedicated herself totally as the handmaid of the Lord to the person and work of her son."

156. This objection should not be scoffed at as it was held historically by none other than St. Bernard of Clairvaux in the twelfth century.

it. For that matter, God did not *have* to become incarnate in the world at all in order to save us. He could have saved us in any number of ways. He is all-powerful. But as the *Catechism* put it, it was *fitting* for God to have worked the way he did. The fathers of Vatican II put it this way: "For every saving influence that the blessed Virgin has on humanity arises not from any natural necessity but from the divine good pleasure; it flows forth from the superabundance of Christ's merits."[157]

What does the Church mean by *fitting*, or *from the divine good pleasure?* Think of it this way: If the president of the United States came to your hometown, it would not be a matter of strict necessity that there be television cameras, a parade, dignitaries, secret service agents, etc. The president could simply come to your town without any of the normal accompaniments. He is fully capable of it. However, it would not be fitting (and in his case, it might be dangerous). When the president comes to a town on an official visit, we expect to see a big to-do. Why? Because of the dignity of his office.

So it is with Mary. Her vocation is immeasurably greater than that of any king, president, or prime minister. She is the Mother of God. Hence, it was fitting that she be immaculately conceived in order to bring to the world "the King of kings and Lord of lords" (Rev. 19:16).

But what about the claim that Mary's mother—St. Anne—had to be sinless in order to bear a sinless Mary in her womb? Or what about the entire world needing to be untouched by sin in order for Jesus to live in it? There would obviously be no strict necessity in those cases, either. But there are two points to be made for clarity's sake. First, Jesus' relationship to the world—by virtue of being in it—is far removed from the intimacy of his relationship with Mary, his mother.[158] That intimacy increases the fittingness of

---

157. Tanner, *Decrees of the Ecumenical Councils*, vol. 2, 895.
158. Recall Mary as the *Ark of the Covenant*. The Old Covenant ark was certainly in our world of sin, but remember what happened when sinful men touched it or even dared gaze upon its inner contents? It is not just proximity that is involved here, but the *intimate nature of the contact* with the sacred thing or person that makes the difference

Mary's Immaculate Conception and sinlessness.

Moreover, there is an essential and infinite gap between Jesus and Mary that didn't exist between Mary and her mother.[159] Jesus was not just without sin; Jesus was God. St. Anne did not bear God in her womb, but Mary did; hence, Mary's preparation by God was radically different than St. Anne's, and fittingly so.

Bible-Based Objections

When speaking with Protestants, objections to Mary's sinlessness are certain as the sunrise, and they are equally as certain to come almost exclusively from the Bible. Here are some of my favorites I used to use when I was Protestant:

"How can you possibly believe Mary to be without sin when the Bible (Rom. 3:23) says *all have sinned and fallen short of the glory of God?*"

"Revelation 15:4 says God alone is holy. In claiming Mary to be without sin, you're making a goddess out of a mere woman!"

"Mary herself referred to God as *her savior* in Luke 1:47—and only sinners need saviors!"

When I was a Protestant, "go-to" arguments like these—and others we will examine—left no doubt in my mind that the Catholic Church was just dead wrong about Mary.

OBJECTION 1: The sin offering.

When the time came for their purification according to the law of Moses, they brought [Jesus] up to Jerusalem to present him

---

of whether something is acceptable or not.

159. James McCarthy is an example of Protestants who do not understand Catholic teaching in this matter. He says in *The Gospel According to Rome*, 223: "Indeed, Mary as defined by the Roman Catholic Church is virtually indistinguishable from the Son of God himself in excellency, power, and achievement. They differ only by degree." The Church teaches that Jesus is God; Mary is not. Therefore, there is an *infinite* difference between them. As a result, the Church teaches her faithful to adore Christ alone, while giving honor to the Mother of God. The difference between Jesus and Mary is a matter of essence and not merely degree.

to the Lord (as it is written in the law of the Lord, "Every male that opens the womb shall be called holy to the Lord") and to offer a sacrifice according to what is said in the law of the Lord, "a pair of turtledoves, or two young pigeons" (Luke 2:22–24).

"If Mary had to offer sacrifice for sin," the argument goes, "wouldn't that mean she was a sinner?"[160] On the surface, this very common Protestant objection seems tenable. That is, until we take a closer look. To begin, we have to examine the Old Testament passages referenced. Verse 23 alludes to Exodus 13:2, 12–13, which commanded every firstborn male child to be consecrated to the Lord and "redeemed."

Verse 24 contains a direct quotation from Leviticus 12:8, which is found in a context in which a woman having given birth to a child is said to be unclean; thus, a sacrifice had to be offered for her purification. This consisted of either a lamb for a burnt offering and a young pigeon or turtledove for a sin offering, or two turtledoves (one for a burnt offering, and one for a sin offering), or two young pigeons if one was poor. We'll quote verses 7 and 8 in order to capture a sense of the text:

> And [the priest] shall offer [the sacrifice] before the Lord, and make atonement for her; then she shall be clean from the flow of her blood. This is the law for her who bears a child, either male or female. [8] And if she cannot afford a lamb, then she shall take two turtledoves or two young pigeons, one for a burnt offering and the other for a sin offering; and the priest shall make atonement for her, and she shall be clean.

There can be no doubt that Mary offered a "sin offering" in Luke 2. Is she then being revealed to have been a sinner? Here are six

160. Found at www.dokimos.org. This is an Evangelical group of Christians who refer to themselves as "maverick Christians," claiming to be "unbranded," or nondenominational. They provide an excellent example of the commonly made assertion by Protestants in general: "Mary brings a sin offering to God, therefore, her own conception is not immaculate."

reasons why the answer is no:

1. The "uncleanness" being spoken of here in Leviticus 12 does not indicate a personal sin has been committed; rather, it speaks of ritual impurity. Leviticus 12:7 says the woman in labor becomes "unclean" because of "the flow of blood," not because of any personal sin she committed. One must recall that even a woman's menstrual period would render her "unclean" and in need of "purification" according to the Old Testament.[161] Thus, the fact that the Holy Family made this offering in accord with the law would not mean Mary sinned. She was "unclean" because of the "flow of blood" assumed by the law in the case of childbirth.

2. According to the teaching of Jesus Christ, the "sin offering" spoken of in Leviticus 12 cannot be understood to refer to a personal sin in the one offering the sacrifice. The *Catechism* (582) explains:

> Jesus perfects the dietary law, so important in Jewish daily life, by revealing its pedagogical meaning through a divine interpretation: "Whatever goes into a man from outside cannot defile him ... (Thus he declared all foods clean.)...What comes out of a man is what defiles a man. For from within, out of the heart of man, come evil thoughts ..." In presenting with divine authority the definitive interpretation of the Law, Jesus found himself confronted by certain teachers of the Law who did not accept his interpretation of the Law, guaranteed though it was by the divine signs that accompanied it.

Jesus declares that only what comes "out of the heart of man" defiles him, or "gives birth to sin," as St. James says it (James 1:15). Things that do not defile a man therefore include foods, blood, semen, spit, and other things that were said to "defile a man" in various Old Testament texts.[162] These things do not come forth "from the heart." For there to be personal sin involved, there must

---

161. Cf. Leviticus 15:19–30.
162. Cf. Leviticus 15, 17, etc.

be knowing and purposeful disobedience to God's law. Thus, it follows: Giving birth did not make Mary a sinner.

3. Although the sacrifice offered in Leviticus 12 is clearly for the purification of the woman who bears the child, there is a sense in which it is also said to be for the child who is "brought forth in sin" (Ps. 51:5). St. Thomas Aquinas explains:

> When the days of the mother's purification were expired, a sacrifice was to be offered either for a son or for a daughter, as laid down in Lev. 12:6. And this sacrifice was for the expiation of the sin in which the child was conceived and born; and also for a certain consecration of the child, because it was then presented in the Temple for the first time.[163]

Aquinas's reference to "for a son or for a daughter" refers to the different lengths of the period of purification determined by the sex of the child: forty days for a male child and eighty days for a female. Thus, the baby was seen as contributing to the necessity of the "purification," not just the mother. Whether this was because of the baby coming into contact with blood during the birthing process or because of that universal sense of sin to which St. Thomas refers and is attested to in Old Testament texts (such as Psalm 51:5) is not clear from the text, but the fact that both the mother and child were "purified" is abundantly clear.

This is most likely why Luke 2:22 specified, "When the time came for *their* purification." Both Mary *and* Jesus had to be presented for purification by sacrifices offered for both of them.[164] If one is going to argue that Mary had sin because she had to go through this "purification" rite of Leviticus 12, then Jesus had sin as well. The sacrifice being offered, according to the text, was for both of them.

Moreover, if someone is going to conclude that this "general

---

163. *Summa Theologica* III, Q. 37, Art. 3.
164. Both the King James and Douay-Rheims versions of Scripture—relying on inferior manuscripts—had it wrong when they rendered this text as "her purification." The Greek reads as "their purification."

sense of sin" that Aquinas spoke of would have to apply to Mary, he will also have to say it applies to Jesus as well. That simply cannot be.

4. Thomas Aquinas gives us multiple commonsense reasons why Mary would have offered sacrifice that involved a "sin offering" and "purification" in obedience to the law even though she had never sinned personally. Among them we find:

> Just as Christ, though not subject to the Law, wished, nevertheless, to submit to circumcision and the other burdens of the Law, in order to give an example of humility and obedience . . . for the same reasons He wished His Mother also to fulfill the prescriptions of the Law, to which, nevertheless, she was not subject.[165]

Circumcision consecrated or "made holy" the person being circumcised. In fact, anyone who was not circumcised was to be "cut off from his people" (Gen. 17:14). Christ did not *need* to be circumcised, but, as St. Thomas says:

> [Christ was circumcised] in order by His example to exhort us to be obedient. Wherefore He was circumcised on the eighth day according to the prescription of the Law (Lev. XII, 3) . . .

> Christ submitted to circumcision while it was yet of obligation.[166]

The same can be said for Mary's submission to the law's prescription of making a "sin offering," and for her being "purified" after childbirth.

5. Along these same lines, Luke 2:22 also references Exodus 13:2 and the Lord's command to "consecrate to me all the first-born" males. Exodus 13:13 then says, "Every first-born of man

---

165. *Summa Theologica* III, Q. 37, Art. 4.
166. Ibid., Art. 1.

among your sons you shall redeem." Christ did not *need* to be "redeemed," in any sense of the term, yet he was "redeemed" in obedience to the law.[167]

6. Perhaps the ultimate example of just why Mary would have offered sacrifice in obedience to the law is the example of her divine Son's baptism. Even though the very purpose of John the Baptist's baptism was to "give knowledge of salvation to his people in the forgiveness of their sins" (Luke 1:77), Jesus submitted to this baptism, as he himself said, "to fulfill all righteousness" (Matt. 3:15). Jesus did not need to be baptized because he had no sin. Mary, likewise, did not need to be purified by a temple sacrifice, but she was obliged to obey the law "to fulfill all righteousness."

Objection 2: Only God is good.

> Who shall not fear and glorify thy name, O Lord? For thou alone art holy. All nations shall come and worship thee, for thy judgments have been revealed (Rev. 15:4).

In his book, *The Gospel According to Rome*, James McCarthy claims this text indicates "God alone" can be said to be holy and good. So how can Catholics claim Mary to be without sin?

> Scripture leaves no room for any other exception [other than Christ]: "Indeed, there is not a righteous man on earth who continually does good and who never sins" (Eccl. 7:20). The angels above worship the Lord, proclaiming, "Thou alone art holy" (Rev. 15:4). The Lord Jesus said, "No one is good except God alone" (Luke 18:19) . . . Mary, like every other human being, was a sinner who needed to be redeemed.[168]

---

167. Christ was "redeemed" in a ceremonial sense only. He did not need to be redeemed in any sense.
168. McCarthy, *The Gospel According to Rome*, 196–197.

Each of the texts cited above is claimed to indicate a unique holiness in God that would exclude the possibility of a sinless man or woman. Of course, there is an obvious exception to all three of these texts in "the man Jesus Christ" (1 Tim. 2:5), as McCarthy admitted. But we should note here that a strict, literal interpretation of these passages would have to conclude that Jesus was a sinner, too. Protestants generally make an exception for Jesus, but as we will see, they should for Mary as well.

The fact that angels (and saints along with them, according to the text) in heaven are depicted as "singing the song of Moses" and saying "Thou alone art holy" in Revelation 15:4, or that Jesus can truly say that "God alone" is good, does not preclude the possibility that there are angels and saints in heaven who participate in the holiness of God *and are sinless*. In fact, the holy angels who did not fall, as Satan did, *never sinned at all,* and yet they could join with the saints in heaven proclaiming "God alone is holy."

This does not mean that *they* are not holy and good; it simply means that their holiness or goodness is dependent upon and is a participation in the holiness that alone belongs *by nature and absolutely* to God. Mary's holiness, like that of the angels and saints above, is a participation in the holiness of God that he alone possesses in an absolute sense.

Indeed, God who "alone is holy" is revealed to communicate his holiness so much so that Scripture refers to the people of God as "saints," or literally translated, "holy ones" (cf. Col. 1:2, 12).

OBJECTION 3: All have fallen short.

James McCarthy continues:

> Paul wrote, "all have sinned and fall short of the glory of God" (Rom. 3:23) . . . Mary, like every other human being, was a sinner who needed to be redeemed.[169]

---

169. Ibid., 197.

This verse deserves special treatment, along with 1 John 1:8 ("If we say we have no sin, we deceive ourselves, and the truth is not in us") and Romans 3:10 ("None is righteous, no not one") as the favorite prooftexts of the various non-Catholic sects attempting to disprove Mary's sinlessness. Where argument two says only God is perfectly good, so Mary couldn't be, this argument says that all have sinned, so that must include Mary.

When I'm asked about Romans 3:23, I like to respond with the same series of questions that a young Catholic Marine named Matt Dula asked me over twenty-seven years ago, when I was in the Marine Corps and just starting on my road to Rome. (I tried to convert him, but he ended up going a long way toward converting me!) I quoted Romans 3:23 and 1 John 1:8, and the resulting conversation went like this:

> MATT: "Do you mean to tell me that you believe Jesus Christ was a sinner? I've never heard of a Christian believing that before!"
>
> TIM: "Of course not!"
>
> MATT: "Well, if you believe literally that 'if any man says he has no sin, he is a liar' . . . I have to ask you: was Jesus Christ fully man?"
>
> TIM: "Well, yes, but he was also God!"
>
> MATT: "Yes, and Mary is the *Mother of God*, but that is not the question. Was Jesus *fully man*? If he was, and we are going to take I John 1:8 in a strict, literal sense, then Jesus was a sinner!"
>
> TIM: "Okay, I see your point, but Jesus was an *exception* to Romans 3:23 and I John 1:8. The Bible tells us so in Hebrews 4:15, which clearly says Christ was 'tempted as we are, yet without sinning.'"
>
> MATT: "Oh, so you admit there are exceptions, do you? What if I were to show you that there are *millions* of exceptions to 1 John 1:8 and Romans 3:23?"
>
> TIM: "Let's hear it!"

Matt then explained to me what I have explained to thousands since. First of all, we need to know that both 1 John 1:8 and Romans 3:23 are dealing with personal sin, not original sin. (Romans 5:12 will deal with original sin, and we can demonstrate two exceptions there as well.) 1 John 1:8 clearly refers to personal sin because in the very next verse John tells us, "If we confess our sins, he is faithful and just to forgive us our sins." We don't *confess* original sin because we didn't do it! Confession is only for personal sins. The context of Romans 3:23 is similar:

> None is righteous, no, not one; no one understands, no one seeks for God. All have turned aside, together they have gone wrong; no one does good, not even one. Their throat is an open grave. They use their tongues to deceive. The venom of asps is under their lips. Their mouth is full of curses and bitterness (Rom. 3:10–14).

Original sin is not something we *do*; it is something we've inherited. As a result of the sin of Adam, we have inherited a fallen nature. That is the essence of original sin.[170] Romans 3 also deals with personal sin because it speaks of sins committed by the sinner.

After explaining all of this, Matt asked, "Has a baby in the womb, or a child of two, ever committed a personal sin?"

"No, they have not," I had to concede. Romans 9:11 says of Jacob and Esau, "though they were not yet born *and had done nothing either good or bad.*"

"Or how about the severely mentally challenged who do not have the use of their intellects and wills; have they committed personal sins?"

I agreed the answer there is also no, they have not. In order to commit a sin, one must have knowledge of the sinful act and full use of the will in performing it.

"There!" declared Matt. "Millions of exceptions to Romans

---

170. Cf. CCC 404.

3:23 and 1 John 1:8!"[171]

My response at this point was similar to the response I often get today: "Well, that may be, but you can't show me why *Mary* is another exception." I had admitted there were exceptions, but how do we know that Mary is one, and further, that she is, among human persons, uniquely free of all sin, both personal and original?"[172] Here is where our positive reasons why Mary is free from all sin come in handy!

OBJECTION 4: Mary has a Savior.

And Mary said, "My soul magnifies the Lord, and my spirit rejoices in God my Savior (Luke 1:46–47).

James McCarthy says of this text, "[Mary] herself acknowledged [she was a sinner] when she prayed . . . 'my spirit has rejoiced in God my savior.'"[173] If Mary had to be "saved," does this not imply sin?

We should begin by making very clear that the Catholic Church agrees Mary was "saved." Yes, Mary *needed* a savior! But it does not necessarily follow from this that Mary sinned first. Catholics believe that Mary was given the singular privilege of grace to be saved completely from sin so that she never committed even

---

171. Some may argue that the multiplication of "exceptions" ends up eliminating the norm. This is not so. The general norm of "all have sinned" applies to every human person over the age of accountability (around age 7) except for those who do not have use of their intellect and will, and Jesus and Mary. This is hardly a danger to the norm.

172. For a full hearing of my conversion story, I recommend my CD set, *Jimmy Swaggart Made Me Catholic*, available from Catholic Answers.

173. McCarthy, *The Gospel According to Rome*, 197. McCarthy says: "[Mary] herself acknowledged [she was a sinner] when she prayed, 'My soul exalts the Lord, and my spirit has rejoiced in God my Savior' (Luke 1:46,47). The Church concedes that Mary was redeemed, but only from the *debt* of original sin. It claims that she was not redeemed from the *stain* of sin, for Mary 'was preserved free from all stain of original sin.' Scripture recognizes no such distinction." Here, McCarthy misrepresents Catholic teaching. The Church does not make the distinction he claims. Mary was "redeemed, in a more exalted fashion, by reason of the merits of her Son" (CCC 492, cf. LG 53, 56), but she was "redeemed from the moment of her conception . . . 'from all stain of original sin'" (CCC 491, cf. Pius IX, *Ineffabilis Deus*, 1854, DS 2803).

the slightest transgression. For salvation, according to Scripture, can refer to the forgiveness of sins *after* one commits personal sins, but it can also refer to being protected from sinning before the fact as well.

> Now to him who is able to keep you from falling and to present you without blemish before the presence of his glory with rejoicing, to the only God, our Savior through Jesus Christ our Lord, be glory, majesty, dominion, and authority, before all time and now and forever (Jude 24–25).

The great fourteenth-century Franciscan, Duns Scotus, gave us the now-famous analogy that has aided the understanding of millions in this regard: "Some have been raised up after they have fallen, but the Virgin Mary was sustained as it were in the very act of falling, and prevented from falling, like the two men who were about to tumble into a pit."[174]

Someone who falls into a pit would need someone to lower a rope and "save" him. Another who was warned or held back so that he did not fall into the pit at all would also have been "saved," but a step sooner. Analogously, Mary was saved from sin by receiving the grace to be preserved from sin. But she was still saved.

---

174. Quoted in Hardon, *The Catholic Catechism*, 153.

PART III

EVER-VIRGIN

7

VIRGIN AND MOTHER

SEVEN REASONS FOR FAITH
IN MARY'S PERPETUAL VIRGINITY

Catholics and non-Catholics alike tend to be surprised when they discover the large amount of biblical evidence in favor of the perpetual virginity of Mary—the dogma that Mary remained a virgin before, during, and forever after the birth of Jesus. Yet they should not be. This dogma, like all of the Marian dogmas, is revealed to us in Scripture as well as in Sacred Tradition.

This is not to say we find a detailed biblical *defense* or *definition* of Mary's perpetual virginity. We do not. This is most likely because no one objected to it in the first century, when the New Testament was written.[175] In fact, there would be no serious dissent from the dogma until the fourth century; hence, there was no need for the inspired authors of the New Testament to defend it.[176] However, what we do find in the New Testament is that

---

175. Similarly, the celibacy of Christ is never defended in Scripture because it was well-known, and therefore presupposed. One can infer that Christ was celibate by the fact that he enjoins celibacy as the most holy manner of living in Matthew 19:11–12. He also presented himself as the bridegroom of the people of God (cf. John 14:1–6), an image taught after him by the apostles (Eph. 5:21–32; Rev. 21:2,9). It is unlikely that Scripture would use this kind of language if Christ had a human bride. We will see with Mary that there are even more obvious inferences for her perpetual virginity. In fact, it would be just as unbiblical to hold that Mary had sexual relations with Joseph as it would be to hold the position that Christ was married.

176. The inspired authors of Scripture were writing in response to the raging controversies of the day. That is why you find more detail related to issues like the authority of the Church (against the Judaizers and antinomians), the full divinity and humanity of Christ (against the forerunners of the Gnostics), justification (against the Judaizers), etc. These were the "hot topics" of the first century.

Mary's perpetual virginity is often either implied or assumed. And perhaps most importantly, it *necessarily follows* from other truths that we find clearly revealed in Scripture.

In this chapter we will examine seven such examples of scriptural evidence for Mary's perpetual virginity.

REASON 1: "How shall this be?"

In Luke 1:34, when Mary is told by the angel Gabriel that she was chosen to be the mother of the Messiah, she asks the question, "How shall this be done, because I know not man?" (DRV).[177] This question makes no sense unless Mary was not only a virgin at that time, but was intent on remaining a virgin throughout her life.

St. Augustine famously comments on this text: "Had she intended to know man, she would not have been amazed. Her amazement is a sign of the vow."[178] Presumably Mary would have known how babies are brought into the world. If she had been expecting to have children in accordance with the normal course for marriage, Augustine reasons, she wouldn't have replied to the angel as she did.

Pope St. John Paul II adds:

> *Mary* is the first person in whom this *new awareness* [directed to the eschatological kingdom] is manifested, for she asks the Angel: "How can this be, since I have no husband?" *(Lk* 1:34). Even though she is "betrothed to a man whose name was

177. We cite the Douay-Rheims version of Scripture here because it translates the Greek verb *estai* properly as "shall." Though some Bibles will translate Luke 1:34 as, "How *can* this be . . . ?" and that certainly can be done, the first meaning of the verb *eimi* (*estai* is the third person singular for it) is simply "to be." See Newman, *A Concise Greek-English Dictionary of the New Testament*, 52; William D. Mounce, *The Analytical Lexicon to the Greek New Testament,*164. Thus, we chose to go with the DRV. Translating this as "how can this be" can mislead toward thinking Mary had doubts. She did not. She knew the word of the Lord through the angel was going to happen, she was asking a very good question in words to the effect of, "How are you going to do this, since I am not planning on having conjugal relations?"
178. *Sermon* 225, 2.

Joseph" (cf. *Lk* 1:27), she is firm in her resolve to remain a virgin. The motherhood which is accomplished in her comes exclusively from the "power of the Most High," and is the result of the Holy Spirit's coming down upon her (cf. *Lk* 1:35) . . . it is *a sign of eschatological hope.*[179]

Despite the historic Christian witness to Mary's perpetual virginity, exemplified in that passage from St. Augustine, millions of Protestants disbelieve in this dogma. James White explains the typical argument:

> Nothing about a vow is mentioned in Scripture. Mary's response to the angel was based upon the fact that it was obvious that the angel was speaking about an immediate conception, and since Mary was at that time only engaged to Joseph, but not married, *at that time* she could not possibly conceive in a natural manner, since she did not "know a man" . . . There is nothing in the words "I do not know a man" that suggests a vow. The verb is present tense, "I do not *know* a man." The passage does not say "I have pledged never *to know* a man" or "I *will never* know a man."[180]

But White makes three critical and common errors here.

1. White says that Mary was *engaged to Joseph*. In fact, there was no such thing as *engagement* (as it is understood in modern Western culture) in ancient Israel. The text says she was "betrothed" or "espoused" (Gr., *emnesteumene*). Betrothal or espousal would be akin to the ratification of a marriage with the exchange of wedding vows but before the consummation. So when Luke 1:27 says Mary was *betrothed*, it means they were *married*. In Hebrew culture, after the betrothal the husband would go off and prepare a home for his bride and then return and receive

179. *Mulieris Dignitatem* 20.
180. White, *Mary—Another Redeemer?*, 31–32.

her into his home where their already ratified union would be consummated.[181]

This is why Matthew 1:18–19 states that when Joseph found out that Mary was with child, he determined he would "send her away privately." The Greek verb translated *to send away* is *apolusai*, meaning *to divorce*.[182] Why would Joseph have to "divorce" Mary if they were only engaged? The answer is that they were not merely engaged, they were *betrothed* according to the custom of the time.

The angel then tells Joseph not to be afraid "to take Mary your wife," and when Joseph woke from his dream, "he took his wife" (20–24). Both the angel and the inspired author considered them husband and wife even though they were only said to be betrothed. Months later, when Joseph and Mary traveled to Bethlehem to be enrolled according to the decree of Caesar Augustus, they were still said to be "betrothed" (Luke 2:5).[183]

Joseph had already taken his espoused "wife" in to his home and was caring for her. He was her legal spouse and was becoming enrolled with her as a family; she was called his "wife" by an angel, yet they were still *betrothed*. To refer to them as "engaged" would be like calling a couple at their wedding reception merely "engaged" because they have not consummated their marriage yet.

Once we properly understand the context of Luke 1, and the fact that Mary and Joseph were already married, then the question Mary asks—"How [shall] this be, for I know not man?"—becomes all the more enlightening. Think about it: If you were a woman who had a ratified marriage and someone at your reception said—or "prophesied"—that you were

---

181. Jesus uses the language of the bridegroom in John 14:1–3: "I go to prepare a place for you . . . And when I go to prepare a place for you, I will come again and will take you to myself, that where I am there you may be also. "

182. This is the same word Matthew uses for *divorce* seven times when he recounts Jesus' teaching on marriage and divorce in Matthew 5:31–33, 19:3, 7–9.

183. Cf. Luke 2:5.

going to have a baby, that would not really be all that much of a surprise. That is the normal course of events. You marry, consummate the union, and babies come along. You certainly would *not* ask the question, "Gee, how is this going to happen?"

Mary never doubted; she simply asked a very valid question.[184] She believed the message of the angel—that she was going to have a baby—but she did not know how it was going to happen. If she had been *betrothed* in the normal course, she would know precisely how it would happen because St. Joseph would have had a right to the marriage bed. Her question indicates she was not planning on the normal course of events in her future with her husband.

2. White said, "It was obvious the angel was speaking about an immediate conception."

Obvious? Really?

The angel uses the future tense seven times before Mary's response. For example, "And behold, you *will* conceive in your womb and bear a son."[185] There is no indication in the text that Mary thought the conception was going to be either immediate or some time down the road, or that it would be non-sexual in nature. If we were to exclude the possibility that Mary had taken a vow, she would at least have thought that the angel was referring to her union with St. Joseph.

In fact, it was the only logical option. Remember, at this point the angel had not yet revealed that the conception would be by the Holy Spirit and non-sexual. That is precisely why Mary asked the angel, "How shall this be?" She would not have asked the question unless she had taken the vow. Otherwise, she would have simply rejoiced in the news that she and Joseph were going to be the biological parents of the Messiah.

184. There were even a few Fathers of the Church who thought Mary may have doubted. The Greek text does not bear this out. The text presents Mary as having a firm faith. She knew she was going to have a baby because God said so. Mary's question was, in effect, "How are you going to do this?"

185. Luke 1:31.

3. White continues:

> There is nothing in the words "I do not know a man" that
> suggests a vow. The verb is present tense, "I do not *know*
> a man." The passage does not say "I have pledged never *to*
> *know* a man" or "I *will never* know a man."[186]

The truth is: everything in the context indicates Mary was
thinking about the future.

Further, the text does not say "I do not know *a* man." It
literally reads, "I know not man."[187] Given the context, this
may well be a euphemistic response one would expect from
a celibate female. But even if we grant the translation, this
changes nothing. We still have a *future* conception revealed to
an espoused woman who, in normal circumstances, would have
known that she would soon be having marital intercourse. Add
to this that it would have been *impossible*, in Mary's mind, for
her to become pregnant *at that moment*, the context as well as
the text of Luke 1 contradicts White's claim.[188] Mary did not
ask, "How is this going to happen right at this moment?" but
"How could this ever happen at all?" As the Fathers of the
Church would say, the question betrays the vow.

Can There Really Be a Married Virgin?

White speaks for many Evangelicals when he claims:

---

186. White, *Mary—Another Redeemer?*, 32.
187. Koine Greek did not have the indefinite article *a*. Context determines whether one
would use *a*, or leave the translation without the article.
188. Svendsen, *Evangelical Answers*, 140. Svendsen also holds the position that Mary
was wondering "how she was going to become pregnant *right now* since she was
not currently having sexual relations with any man." Again, this interpretation is
unsupported by the context. Even if we were to discount the Perpetual Virginity of
Mary altogether, we would at least have to admit that Mary would think the angel
was referring to her marriage to Joseph. There is no way Mary could have known that
the pregnancy was only moments away until the angel told her of the nature of the
conception of the Son of God in verse 35 and in answer to her inquiry.

The idea of a "married virgin" . . . is an oxymoron . . . out of harmony with the Bible's teaching concerning the nature of marriage.

Eric Svendsen goes even further and says that the idea of the Perpetual Virginity of Mary

> introduce[s] an historical implausibility; namely, that there was such a thing as a *married virgin*. Such a notion cannot be supported either biblically or historically. Indeed, the very notion of a woman making a vow of lifelong chastity while at the same time planning a wedding is the stuff of which myths are made.[189]

This kind of reasoning is reminiscent of modern liberal scholars who make the similar claim that the very notion of a *virgin conceiving* is "the stuff of which myths are made." The fact that Mary gave birth to God has no historical precedent because it is a unique event. It should come as no surprise that the marriage of Joseph and Mary would be unique as well. Nobody else's spouse had ever been—or will ever be—called to give birth to God.

We could examine many other examples of unique situations in salvation history. The creation was a unique event. God does not "create" people anymore. He only did that once, in the case of Adam and Eve. He creates the soul of every human being, but every *person* is born, not created. However one interprets the story of Noah and the flood, it would certainly qualify as a unique event.[190] We can also rest assured that God will never again ask anyone to offer his teenaged son as a bloody sacrifice on an altar as he did with Abraham.

Given the example of other unique events in salvation history, it should not surprise us that at the greatest moment of salvation

189. Ibid.
190. A Catholic is free to hold a literal interpretation of the story of the flood, or to believe that the flood was a more local event in which "the whole world" known to Noah may have been flooded, rather than the belief that the entire globe was flooded. And there may be other possible interpretations as well.

history—*when the fullness of time had come*—some unique occurrences would accompany the life, death, burial, and Resurrection of Christ. And since there is no human person who had a more intimate role in Christ's life than his mother, it makes perfect sense for some of those occurrences to involve her.

The Jewish Connection

"Okay, Tim," you say. "I see your point about the Incarnation being a 'unique event.' But as a matter of history, in ancient Jewish thought, the man who does not marry 'sheddeth blood' and is 'no proper man.' And not being able to have children was considered a *curse*.[191] A 'married virgin' would represent something *contrary* to the Old Covenant as it was understood by the Jewish people."

Would the idea of Mary and Joseph living celibately in marriage be nonsense and even unbiblical to first-century Jews? Well, let us note first that this was not the response of the early Christian community. Part of the reason for this may well be the fact that celibacy had become more and more accepted in the ancient Jewish world in the centuries leading up to the advent of Christ. And this includes celibacy throughout one's life or even after marriage. Celibacy in marriage, whether permanent or temporary, was not completely alien to the first-century Jewish mind. There were exceptions to the norm that all should marry and reproduce—not only in the Old Testament but in the Talmud as well. Consider just these examples:

1. In Jeremiah 16:1–4, God commands Jeremiah *not* to take a wife. He was celibate for life.

---

191. Babylonian Talmud, *Yebamoth 63a*, "Any man who has no wife is no proper man; for it is said, *Male and female created He them and called their name Adam*." The idea here is, among many Jews, Genesis 5:2 (here quoted) means a man is only half a man without a wife because the text says God "named *them* man" (Heb., *Adam*). *Yebamoth 63b* declares the man who does not have children "sheds blood" because, "*Whoso sheddeth man's blood by man shall his blood be shed,*" and this is immediately followed by the text, "*And you, be ye fruitful and multiply.*"

2. Moses commanded the entire male Jewish community not to "go near a woman" for three days in anticipation of the giving of the Law by God on Sinai (see Exod. 19:15).

3. When David and his men were famished and asked in desperation for sustenance from the high priest, he told David he had nothing except the "bread of the presence" that was reserved for the priests alone. He would acquiesce to David's request but only if, according to 1 Samuel 21:4, "the young men have kept themselves from women."

4. David's concubines who had been taken by his son Absalom were received back by David as his concubines after Absalom's death, but he would never have conjugal relations with them again. "So they were shut up until the day of their death, living as if in widowhood" (2 Sam. 20:3).[192]

5. According to Jewish tradition, Moses remained celibate for the rest of his life after encountering the word of God on Mount Sinai.[193]

6. According to Jewish tradition, Elijah and Elisha were celibate all their lives while other prophets remained celibate, like Moses, after having encountered the word of God in prophecy.[194]

7. An extraordinary rabbi, Ben Azzai, who lived in the early second century A.D., refused to marry, claiming the Torah to be his wife.[195] This was condoned in this extraordinary case.

---

192. According to Deuteronomy 24:1–4 and Jeremiah 3:1–2, David could not have conjugal relations with them again, but he was still responsible to care for them. This may be considered to be an antecedent of St. Joseph, as we've seen, who cares for Mary, but can never have conjugal relations with her because she had been consecrated as spouse of the Holy Spirit.

193. Babylonian Talmud, *Shabbath 87a*; *Pesachim 87b*.

194. Opisso, *The Perpetual Virginity of Mary,* at www.ewtn.com/library/answers/talmud. htm.

195. Babylonian Talmud, *Yebamoth 63b*.

8. The first-century Jewish historian Josephus wrote of the now-famous Jewish sect called the Essenes having celibates among them contemporaneous with Jesus and the apostles.[196]

9. The first-century Jewish scholar Philo wrote of the Therapeutae, who also practiced celibacy, it appears, universally.[197] It's not difficult to figure out why this group did not endure!

It seems the pump had been primed for the coming of Christ and St. Paul, who both practiced and taught celibacy "for the sake of the kingdom of God" (Matt. 19:12).[198] St. Clement of Rome speaks of celibacy being commonly practiced by Christians in A.D. 90, St. Ignatius of Antioch speaks similarly in A.D. 107, and St. Justin Martyr tells us it was being practiced all over the Roman Empire by A.D. 150.[199] Joseph's entering into marriage with Mary as her celibate protector was not something with precedent, but given the fact that Mary was to "encounter" not only "the word of God," but "the *Word* of God" himself in a unique way, one can see the reasonableness of her being completely consecrated to God while needing Joseph as her protector.

With this as a context, we can see why the idea of Mary as perpetual virgin was far from being a problem in the early Church.

REASON 2: "Behold, your mother."

In John 19:26–27, Jesus gives his mother to the care of St. John, even though the responsibility to take care of her would have fallen to the next eldest brother of Jesus, if he had one, according to the law of the Old Testament. This is a strong indicator that Mary had no other children. It is highly unlikely Jesus would take his mother away from his family in disobedience to the law:

196. *The Antiquity of the Jews* 18, 1, 5.
197. Philo of Alexandria, *On the Contemplative Life* III–XI.
198. Cf. 1 Cor. 7:1, 7, 32–34, 38.
199. St. Clement of Rome, *Epistle to the Corinthians*, 38; St. Ignatius of Antioch, *Epistle to Polycarp*, 5; St. Justin Martyr, *First Apology*, 15, 29.

When Jesus saw his mother, and the disciple who he loved standing near, he said to his mother, "Woman, behold, your son!" Then he said to the disciple, "Behold, your mother!" And from that hour the disciple took her to his own home.

James White responds to the Catholic position:

His brothers were unbelievers. In fact, they had mocked Him in John 7, and would not come to faith in Him until after His resurrection. But more obviously, they were not at the cross. John was.

It is true that John 7:5 says, "For even his brethren did not believe in him," but this does not necessarily mean *all of them*. It certainly *could* do so, but the greater context of the Gospels excludes that as a possibility for several reasons.

1. James, the "brother of the Lord" from Galatians 1:19, was also *an apostle*. Scripture places "the apostles" and "brethren of the Lord" as groups in separate categories, for example, in John 2:12, Acts 1:12–14, and 1 Corinthians 9:5. For that reason alone it is very unlikely that "his brethren" would have included James in John 7:5.[200] He would most likely be set apart.

2. Jesus was Mary's "firstborn" according to Matthew 1:25. That would mean he was the oldest. In Near-Eastern culture 2,000 years ago, it was normally unacceptable for younger siblings to publicly rebuke an older brother.

3. If James were to be included in this unbelieving group—however unlikely that may be—it would only have been a temporary state of unbelief for him, among the others, because

---

200. James, as an individual, is referred to as "the brother of the Lord" in Galatians 1:19. The distinction between "apostles" and "brothers of the Lord" is made when it comes to considering them as groups.

biblical texts written before and after John 7:5 indicate that James (and we could add his brother, the apostle Jude) among the "brothers of the Lord," did believe.[201] John 2:11 tells us that as a result of the intercession of Mary that brought about Jesus' first miracle, "his disciples believed in him." That would include James and Jude. John 15:3 presents our Lord saying to the apostles—on the night before he was crucified—"You are already made clean by the word which I have spoken to you." Indeed, Jesus goes on to be very specific about the state of the apostles in John 17:12, when he says, "While I was with them, I kept them in your name (speaking to the Father), which you have given me; I have guarded them, and none of them is lost but the son of perdition."

And when we narrow our focus to the time represented by John 7:5, we discover that John claimed Jesus' "brethren" did not believe in him at the time of the *Feast of Tabernacles* (see John 7:2) in Jesus' third and final year of ministry on earth. The Feast of Tabernacles begins on the fifteenth of Tishrei and stretches for seven days (this is late October to late November on our calendar). It would be six months before the Passover and the Crucifixion. To attempt to drag out of that fact that *James* and *Jude,* "brothers of the Lord," did not believe in Jesus for the months leading up to the time of the Crucifixion? That is more than a stretch.

If the claim is that Jesus entrusted his mother to John because none of the "brothers of the Lord" were present *at the cross*—they fled and lost their faith for these few days of darkness—this reveals a rather "low" and unbiblical Christology that just doesn't fit with what we know about Jesus. Surely Christ would have known that James would one day become not only faithful, but a bishop, along with his brother Jude. And he would have known that their "return" to faith was only three days away!

In Matthew 26:13, Jesus knew the woman who anointed his

---

201. Cf. Jude 1:1.

head with oil would be remembered "wherever this gospel is preached in the whole world"; he knew beforehand of Peter's triple denial in Matthew 26:34; he knew of Peter's death in John 21:18–19; he knew Judas would betray him in Matthew 26:21; he knew all of the apostles would leave him in Matthew 26:31; he knew Peter would "strengthen" his brother apostles—including St. James—after the Resurrection in Luke 22:29–32; he knew he would be crucified and raised from the dead. In fact, Peter tells us in John 21:17 that Jesus "know[s] everything," and John tells us that Jesus "knew all men" (John 2:24–25). Surely Jesus would have had knowledge enough to give his mother into the care of one of his "brethren" who, though not present at Calvary, would soon be a believer again.

Simply speaking, there would have been no need to give his mother to John if he truly had multiple brothers and sisters. The fact is: Jesus had no brothers and sisters, so he had the responsibility, on a human level, to take care of his mother. And so he did.

Two final thoughts on the matter: First, there is no doubt that Jesus placed emphasis on the spiritual realm above the natural. There is no surprise here. In Matthew 12:50, Jesus said doing the will of God is more important than mere human bonds. However, to say this would be sufficient grounds for Jesus to ignore the fourth commandment (fifth according to Protestants' way of counting them), which commands honoring father and mother, is absurd.

In fact, Jesus had very strong words for those who shirked their responsibilities toward taking care of their parents for some "religious" reason. Even a cursory reading of Mark 7:9–12 should dispel any notion that Jesus would prevent his uterine siblings from fulfilling their duty to their mother. The only reasonable conclusion here is that Jesus did not *have* any uterine siblings; thus, he had the responsibility to entrust his mother to John.

In the same way, Mary would not have abandoned her other children. She gave birth to Jesus at a very young age—perhaps fifteen—so she would still have been relatively young when Jesus died on the cross. If the Protestant position were true, her other children would have been in their teens and twenties, and perhaps one or two of them even younger.[202] With these facts in mind, consider these words of St. Athanasius, the great fourth-century patriarch of Alexandria and defender of the Faith, as he presented his own defense of the Perpetual Virginity of Mary:

> For, if she had other children, the Savior would not have ignored them and entrusted his Mother to someone else; nor would she have become someone else's mother. She would not have [abandoned her own] to live with others, knowing well that it ill becomes [a woman] to abandon her husband or her children. But, since she was a virgin, and was his Mother, he gave her as a mother to his disciple, even though she was not really John's mother, because of his great purity of understanding and because of her untouched virginity.[203]

REASON 3: The power of the Most High overshadowed her.

Mary is depicted in Scripture as the spouse of the Holy Spirit. Joseph, knowing that she was consecrated to God, would never have considered having conjugal relations with her.

When Mary asked the angel how she was going to conceive a child, in Luke 1:34 the angel responded: "The Holy Spirit will come upon you, and the power of the Most High will overshadow you; therefore the child to be born will be called holy, the Son of God."

This language of *the power of the Most High* overshadowing Mary is pregnant with meaning. We have already seen how this text relates to Mary as the Ark of the Covenant. But the underlying Hebrew may well also hearken back to Old Testament texts where the husband "spreads his cloak" over his bride. That is, these words appear to represent *nuptial* language. Consider Ruth 3:9—

---

202. Scripture refers to four brothers of the Lord by name in Matthew 13:55 and to *at least* three sisters in verse 56 when the townspeople of Nazareth refer to "all his sisters" as still living among them when Jesus was preaching there. If Mary had one child about every two years, her youngest might have been as young as twelve.

203. Gambero, *Mary and the Fathers of the Church*, 104, cf. St. Athanasius, *On Virginity*.

"I am Ruth your handmaid, spread therefore your skirt (*kanaph,* "wing") *over your maidservant,* for you are next of kin."

God uses similar language with reference to his bride, Israel:

And you grew up and became tall and arrived at full maidenhood; your breasts were formed, and your hair had grown; yet you were naked and bare. When I passed by you again and looked upon you, behold, you were at the age for love; and *I spread my skirt over you . . .* and you became mine (Ezek. 16:7–8).

Considering the nuptial language used in Luke 1, conjugal relations between Joseph and Mary would have been out of the question. Simple enough. However, critics will claim this opens up more questions than it answers. Matthew 1:20 says Joseph "took Mary as his wife." How does this square with her being the "spouse of the Holy Spirit?" Is this bigamy? Did God cheat on St. Joseph?

This is definitely not bigamy and God did not cheat on Joseph. Bigamy, by definition, is entering into two marriages that are ordered to this life. Mary was not married to two men. In other words, Mary's earthly, temporal espousal to Joseph did not exclude the possibility of an eternal nuptial relationship with God. By analogy, our earthly, temporal marriages do not exclude the possibility of *our* having a nuptial relationship with God.[204] The two unions are of entirely different orders.

The unique case of Mary and Joseph reminds us that the order of grace must always have primacy over the order of nature. In the end, there is no real contradiction because grace never destroys or contradicts nature; rather, grace always builds on and perfects nature. However, fallen humanity must recall: It is the order of grace that brings clarity to nature where nature is limited or even impaired.

St. Peter Chrysologus, writing in the early fifth century, speaks

204. According to Revelation 21:2, Christ is our bridegroom to whom, Paul says in 1 Corinthians 11:2, we have been "espoused."

to this very subject with a clarity we would do well to take to heart:

> The messenger flies to the spouse, in order to remove every attachment to a human marriage from God's spouse. He does not take the Virgin away from Joseph but simply restores her to Christ, to whom she had been promised when she was being formed in her mother's womb. Christ, then, takes his own bride; he does not steal someone else's. Nor does he cause separation when he unites his own creature to himself, in a single body.[205]

Fr. Luigi Gambero, a professor of Patristics at the Marianum (Rome) and the International Marian Research Institute (University of Dayton), comments on this text:

> The text excludes an incompatibility between the two types of marriage, because they take place on two different levels; however, Peter [Chrysologus] does not hesitate to affirm the clear superiority of the divine marriage over the human marriage. The divine marriage belongs to the eternal plan of divine election, according to which the creature is bound to its Creator before anything else; the marriage with Joseph, upon which our author does not place much emphasis, is part of the order of human possibilities. The only condition imposed by the realization of the divine plan is the attitude of total detachment from the human situation that would result.[206]

Let's Get Practical

We have explained this third reason for Mary's perpetual virginity mostly by demonstrating how her simultaneous unions with Joseph and the Holy Spirit were possible. But we must also consider the practical necessities involved. The Holy Spirit entered into a

---

205. Sermon 140, 2.
206. Gambero, *Mary and the Fathers of the Church*, 297.

nuptial relationship with Mary for one obvious reason: God was about to become incarnate in the womb of Mary. But Joseph became Mary's spouse and protector on this earth for at least two pragmatic reasons:

First, St. Matthew points out in his genealogy (1:1–17) that Joseph was of the line of David for a reason: Jesus had to be of the royal line in order to fulfill prophecy. He was to be the true "son of David" and king of Israel.[207] As the only son, even though adopted, he would have been in line for the throne. Remember, the Herods were usurpers, not true kings of Israel by right. They were not even Jews.[208] The sons of David were the rightful heirs to the throne. According to Matthew, Joseph and Jesus were in line for the throne.

Secondly, Jesus needed an earthly father and Mary needed a spouse, especially in a culture that did not take too kindly to adultery. Even though the Romans had taken from Israel the authority to execute malefactors, there was still what we would today call "street justice" there. We often encounter this situation with Jesus—when people began to pick up stones to stone him after he declared that he was God, for example.[209] Without Joseph as her protector, Mary would have been in mortal danger if she was believed to have become pregnant by someone other than her earthly spouse.

REASON 4: Mary was consecrated to the Holy Spirit.

As we said above, the marriage between Mary and the Holy Spirit, and Mary and Joseph are not incompatible because they are of entirely different orders. However, unlike, say, all Christians' "nuptial" relationship with the Lord, in the case of Mary and the Holy Spirit, *a child was conceived*. "The Word was made flesh and dwelt

207. See 2 Sam. 7:14, Heb. 1:5, Rev. 19:16, 22:16.
208. Scott Hahn writes in *Hail, Holy Queen*, 57: "Herod . . . was a non-Jew, appointed by the Romans to rule Judaea."
209. Cf. John 5:17–18, 8:58–59, etc.

among us" (John 1:14). In a unique and unrepeatable fashion, the two orders *intersect*.

Thus, Mary's consecration to God for the purpose of the Incarnation brings with it biblical challenges. We've already seen how Joseph and Mary's betrothal to each other was equal to a legal spousal contract, according to Scripture. The word for *betrothed* in Hebrew is *kiddush*, which is derived from the Hebrew word *kadash*, meaning *holy* or *consecrated*. This betrothal was considered a sacred event binding spouses to each other. It was because of this understanding of the sacredness of the bond of matrimony that adultery was considered such a serious sin. Marriage was a *consecrated* state. Desecrating this state by adultery left a woman defiled and was punishable by death, or in some circumstances, left her unfit to return to conjugal relations with her husband.[210] (This seems odd to us today, but things were very different among the ancient, tribal people with whom our Lord was dealing.)

The latter cases, where a desecration of a marriage left women unfit to return to relations with their husbands, are of particular interest to us now. We see an example of this in 2 Samuel. Absalom, one of David's sons, tried to usurp the throne of his father by, among other things, sleeping with ten of David's concubines:

> Ahithophel said to Absalom, "Go in to your father's concubines, whom he has left to keep the house; and all Israel will hear that you have made yourself odious to your father, and the hands of all who are with you will be strengthened." . . . [A]nd Absalom went in to his father's concubines in the sight of all Israel (16:21–22).

Later, when Absalom's attempted coup d'état failed and he was killed, King David did not forget his concubines. Scripture tells us David "took the ten concubines, whom he had left to care for

---

210. Cf. Deut. 22:22–29. In verse 23–24, in particular, a "betrothed virgin" who sleeps with a man who is not her husband commits adultery. Both were subject to stoning because "the man . . . violated his neighbor's wife."

the house, and put them in a house under guard, and provided for them, but did not go in to them. So they were shut up until the day of their death, living as if in widowhood" (20:3).

David would not have conjugal relations with these ten concubines again because they were "defiled" by Absalom. But he did have the responsibility to care for them and protect them after Absalom's death, because he (Absalom) could no longer care for them. And they were David's concubines, so he had a real responsibility for their well-being.

It is hard for us to fathom this in the twenty-first century. How could King David and Joseph have the responsibility to care for their wives, but then not be able to have conjugal relations with them? We have to understand this through the revelation given to us in the Old Testament. Deuteronomy 24:1–4 and Jeremiah 3:1 reveal to us that a woman who was divorced by her husband and then wedded to another could never return to her former husband even if her new husband were to die. Deuteronomy 24:4 declares:

> Then her former husband, who sent her away, may not take her again to be his wife, after she has been defiled; for that is an abomination before the Lord, and you shall not bring guilt upon the land which the Lord your God gives you for an inheritance.

It was the sexual bond that was evidently the cause of the "defilement" in the relationship. Hence, King David could receive his concubines into his home after they were "defiled" by Absalom, but he could never have conjugal relations with them again.

In Jeremiah 3:1, God himself refers to this law, when he speaks metaphorically of his relationship with Israel:

> "If a man divorces his wife and she goes from him and becomes another's wife, will he return to her? Would not that land be greatly polluted? You have played the harlot with many lovers; and would you return to me?" says the Lord.

Very much rooted in this Old Testament understanding, the Talmud taught divorce to be mandatory in the case of an espoused woman who became pregnant by another. The espoused woman who conceived by another would then belong to that other and could never return to her former husband. The ancient rabbis said:

A woman made pregnant by a former husband and a woman who was giving suck to a child by another husband . . . do not receive the marriage contract . . . A man should not marry a woman made pregnant by an earlier husband or giving suck to a child born to an earlier husband, and if she married under such conditions, he must put her away and never remarry her.[211]

When we take into account the Old Testament background and ancient Hebrew culture, we understand Matthew 1 and the situation with the Holy Family. In Joseph's mind, once she was pregnant, Mary would have belonged to the father of the child within her. His choices were either to expose her publicly and endanger her to mob violence or to do what we see he actually resolved to do in Matthew 1:19: divorce her quietly. But notice what Scripture then tells us in verses 20 and 21:

But as [Joseph] considered this, behold, an angel of the Lord appeared to him in a dream, saying, "Joseph, son of David, do not fear to take Mary your wife, for that which is conceived in her is of the Holy Spirit."

When the angel told Joseph that Mary's child was conceived of the Holy Spirit, he knew what was required of him. Just as we saw with King David in 2 Samuel 20:3, Joseph knew that he was to take his wife into his home and care for her, though he could never have conjugal relations with her. According to Scripture and ancient Jewish tradition, Mary belonged to the father of her child—the Holy Spirit. However, the Holy Spirit could not be

211. Neusner, *The Babylonian Talmud*, vol. 11, 123.

the protector that Mary needed. The Holy Spirit could not sign legal documents and be Mary's legal spouse. But Joseph was ready and willing—just man that he was—to care for Mary as his lawfully wedded spouse.[212]

REASON 5: Mary is the temple gate.

In Ezekiel 44:1–2, the prophet was given a vision of the holiness of "the gate" of the temple, which would be fulfilled in the Perpetual Virginity of Mary:

> Then he brought me back to the outer gate of the sanctuary, which faces east; and it was shut. And he said to me, "This gate shall remain shut; it shall not be opened, and no one shall enter by it; for the Lord, the God of Israel has entered by it; therefore it shall remain shut."

No Christian would deny that in the New Testament *Jesus* is revealed to be the temple. In John 2:19, when Jesus said, "Destroy

---

212. When the angel said, "Fear not to take Mary your wife," Matthew does not record him as using the Greek word commonly used for "coming together" in conjugal relations, *sunelthein* (Gr., *come together* or *go in unto*. In the New Testament this term is sometimes translated as "to conceive," as in conceiving a child, as we see in Luke 1:36.). This is significant because just two verses earlier, Matthew had used a form of *sunelthein* in order to express the notion of conjugal relations (see 1:18). Yet, when the angel told Joseph to "take Mary" as his wife (v. 20), Matthew used a different word—*paralambano*. See the different meanings in Barclay M. Newman's *A Concise Greek-English Dictionary of the New Testament*, 173, 133:

> *Sunelthein*, inf. *sunerkomai*: Come together, gather; assemble, meet; come or go with, accompany, be with; be married, have marital relationships (Matt. 1:18).
> *Paralambano*: Take; receive, accept (often a tradition); learn (1 Thess. 4:1); take charge of (John 19:16b).

The wording here seems to indicate that Joseph was to "take charge of" Mary and be her protector. Understanding ancient Jewish culture as well as the Old Testament helps us to understand why Joseph's first thought would have been of divorce. It also confirms for us that Joseph would never have thought for a moment about taking conjugally one who belongs to someone else, especially if that someone else is God! The only other option available to Joseph would have been to take Mary in and be her guardian while refraining from ever having conjugal relations with her. This scenario as well as the change in words seems to confirm our Catholic understanding.

this temple and in three days I will raise it up," the Jews thought he was speaking of the enormous stone edifice that stood in Jerusalem, but, as John tells us two verses later, he was actually speaking of his own body. So if Christ is the prophetic temple of Ezekiel 44, into which God himself has entered for our salvation, who or what is this prophetic gate that is the conduit for God to enter into his temple? *Mary* is the natural fulfillment. She is *the gate* through which not just a spiritual presence of God has passed, but God in the flesh. How much more would the New Testament gate remain forever closed? As we've seen, St. Jerome commented on this very text in the fourth century:

> Only Christ opened the closed doors of the virginal womb, which continued to remain closed, however. This is the closed eastern gate, through which only the high priest may enter and exit and which nevertheless is always closed.[213]

REASON 6: Mary is the untouchable ark.

According to multiple parallel texts in Scripture, as we have already seen, Mary is depicted as the New Testament Ark of the Covenant.

The encounter of Mary and Elizabeth in Luke 1:39–45, shortly after Mary conceived Jesus at the Annunciation, is clear evidence of this. Let's review briefly. We noted especially Elizabeth's exclamation when Mary entered her home and greeted her: "And why is this granted to me, that the mother of my Lord should come to me?" This refers back to 2 Samuel 6:9, in which the Old Testament type of Mary—the old Ark of the Covenant—was carried into the presence of King David. He said, "How can the ark of the Lord come to me?" The ark remained there three months. In a New Testament fulfillment of the type, Luke 1 records that Elizabeth gave Mary an identical greeting, and that Mary remained with Elizabeth for the same three months.

---

213. *Against the Pelagians*, 2, 4.

According to Hebrews 9:4, the Ark of the Covenant bore the Ten Commandments, a small amount of manna, and the staff of Aaron, the high priest. All of these were types of our Lord. According to John 6:31–33, Jesus is the true manna. According to Hebrews 3:1, Jesus is our true high priest. In Hebrew, the Ten Commandments can be referred to as the ten *words* (*dabar* in Hebrew). Jesus is the *Word* made flesh according to John 1:14.

According to the Old Testament, no one except the high priest could touch the ark or even look inside of it.[214] If anyone else touched or looked inside the ark, the punishment was death.[215]

If this was the case for the Old Testament type, which according to Hebrews 10:1 is no more than a shadow of the true New Testament fulfillment, then it would seem fitting that Mary would remain "untouched" by Joseph as well. When we understand this, we understand why great saints such as Jerome and Epiphanius would have been so indignant when they encountered the first heretics to posit even the possibility that Joseph could have had conjugal relations with Mary. This was absolutely foreign to the Christian consciousness of the first four centuries.

REASON 7: Mary is "the virgin."

According to St. Epiphanius (d. 403), Christians gave Mary the *title* of "virgin," which indicates permanence:

> For I hear that someone has a new notion about the holy, ever-virgin Mary, and dares to cast a blasphemous suspicion on her ... Why all this ill will? Why so much impudence? Isn't Mary's very name ["Virgin"] a testimony, you troublemaker? Doesn't it convince you? Who, and in which generation, has ever dared to say St. Mary's name and not add "Virgin" at once when

---

214. Cf. Exod. 28–29.
215. We saw two dramatic examples of this in 1 Samuel 6:19 and 2 Samuel 6:7.

asked? The marks of excellence show from the titles of honor themselves.[216]

Epiphanius, a brilliant linguist and scholar,[217] teaches two crucial points here:

1. Isaiah 7:14, "Behold, a virgin shall conceive and bear a son," is not just a description of the Virgin Mary, but gives to her what would become a *title*, just as Abram was given the *name* or *title* of father of a multitude—*Abraham*. As we have seen before, in Hebrew culture a name reveals something permanent about the one named. Such is the case with the Virgin Mary.

2. This title was recognized among Christians from the very beginning. She has always been referred to as "*the Virgin* Mary." On that basis, he identified the heresy of denying Mary's perpetual virginity as a novelty that contradicted universal Christian belief.[218]

We have not exhausted the reasons we have as Catholics for faith in the Perpetual Virginity of Mary, but we believe the reasons we have examined should give even the most skeptical among skeptics reasons to rethink their position. And yet, another question comes to mind immediately: *Why is this teaching so important to begin with?*

In our next chapter, we will answer that very question.

---

216. *Panarion* 78:5, 5; 6,1.
217. Cf. Jurgens, *The Faith of the Early Fathers*, vol. 2, 67. Jurgens tells us of Epiphanius's reputation for learning: "It is Jerome who calls [Epiphanius] a Pentaglot, for his knowledge of Greek, Syriac, Hebrew, Coptic, and Latin."
218. Cf. CCC 92. Some might argue here that some Protestants also refer to Mary as "the Virgin Mary," but that doesn't mean they believe in her *perpetual* virginity. Granted. But it is worth noting that the early Fathers, such as Epiphanius, believed the title implied *perpetual* virginity. That is how Christians understood it from the very beginning.

8

THE BIG DEAL

WHY MARY'S
PERPETUAL VIRGINITY MATTERS

Protestants who don't initially understand the importance of the *Theotokos* usually don't take long to grasp it once they understand that it's the nature of Jesus Christ himself that is ultimately on the line. If you miss it on Mary as Mother of God, then you have to answer the question: "To whom did she give birth?"

Even more people fail to get the full import of the Immaculate Conception, but generally speaking, when they're shown how unthinkable—and unbiblical—it would be for the living God to dwell bodily in anything or anyone other than the most pure of vessels, most come to understand and accept the truth of it.

But when it comes to the Perpetual Virginity of Mary there seems to be an even greater disconnect, and a greater task to explain the truth. For too often their objections aren't based on Scripture—though we certainly encounter a lot of those, too—but on a dismissive attitude. "What does it really matter anyway? Mary gave birth to Jesus and that is what she was called to do. So what if she had more children?"

In fact, when it comes to this dogma both non-Catholics and Catholics—who ought to know better—think this dogma has no impact on their spiritual lives one way or the other. Both those who deny it and those who nominally accept it think it's just *not a big deal.*

Truth Matters

We must first be clear that *all doctrine* taught in Scripture as faithfully interpreted by the magisterium of the Church is a big deal!

> Take heed to yourself and to your teaching; hold to that, for by so doing you will save both yourself and your hearers (1 Tim. 4:16).

When it comes to the teaching of the Church, the Bible says souls are on the line. The *Catechism* likewise connects the dogmas and our spiritual lives:

> There is an organic connection between our spiritual life and the dogmas. Dogmas are lights along the path of faith; they illuminate it and make it secure. Conversely, if our life is upright, our intellect and heart will be open to welcome the light shed by the dogmas of faith (89).

There is no clause here excluding the Perpetual Virginity of Mary. Indeed, *Lumen Gentium* 65, which we have referenced before, is a reminder for us of just how those words apply to *all* of Mariology:

> For Mary, who has entered deeply into the history of salvation, in a certain way unites within herself the greatest truths of the faith and echoes them; and when she is preached about and honored she calls believers to her son, to his sacrifice and to the love of the Father.

As we've said, Mary is nothing apart from Christ. Everything that is good in her and every reason why she is important comes entirely from him. She is like the moon that reflects the sun: She has no light of her own apart from her Son. The same can be said of Mariology. Its subject, Mary, indeed, "unites in her person and re-echoes the most important doctrines of the faith," bringing the teachings of Christ into focus for us and challenging us to consider these essential truths. They cease being abstractions and become real for us in the life of a real disciple of Jesus Christ.

So how does the Perpetual Virginity of Mary do this? First, it helps us see that God is always the initiator in the spiritual life of the Church as well as of individuals. Secondly, it aids us in understanding as a category the importance of the *sacred*. In this category, we could include the consecrated life, the sacraments—in particular the sacredness of the sacrament of marriage—and more.

God, the First Cause of All Things

The first and most important teaching the Perpetual Virginity of Mary safeguards is God's "absolute initiative" in the Incarnation and in the lives of every Christian.

> Mary's virginity manifests God's absolute initiative in the Incarnation. Jesus has only God as Father. "He was never estranged from the Father because of the human nature which he assumed . . . He is naturally Son of the Father as to his divinity and naturally son of his mother as to his humanity, but properly Son of the Father in both natures" (CCC 503).

The only thing any human person has to offer God is his free cooperation with God's initiative. God's gracious invitation stretches back into eternity while man's temporal response—still aided by grace—is all that man has to give to God. As such Mary is the most perfect image of the Church, as the *Catechism* goes on to say:

> At once virgin and mother, Mary is the symbol and the most perfect realization of the Church: "the Church indeed . . . by receiving the word of God in faith becomes herself a mother. By preaching and Baptism she brings forth sons, who are conceived by the Holy Spirit and born of God, to a new and immortal life. She herself is a virgin, who keeps in its entirety and purity the faith she pledged to her spouse" (507).

Mary's Perpetual Virginity protects both the initiative of God in all things and the essential nature of human cooperation in order for God's plan to be fruitful in our lives. Even more, as both virgin and mother, she is the unique and most perfect realization of what the Church is called to be and to accomplish. The Church is a virginal bride "without spot or wrinkle . . . without blemish" (Eph. 5:27), "prepared as a bride adorned for her husband" (Rev. 21:2), yet, like Mary, she also gives birth to all "those who keep the commandments of God and bear testimony to Jesus" (Rev. 12:17).

Protectress of the Sacred

Our Blessed Mother was *consecrated to God* in the context of a nuptial union with God for the specific and sacred purpose of bringing Christ into the world for the salvation of all. This truth is central to understanding Mary's vow of perpetual virginity. But in order to appreciate it, we have to first consider what it means to say Mary was consecrated to God.

In Scripture, once something or someone is consecrated or *set apart for God's use*, often accompanied by sacred vows, the thing or person so consecrated is generally not to be used for anything else. This has obvious implications for Mary's perpetual virginity. If Mary was consecrated to God in a nuptial union in order to bring forth Christ, there would be no question of Joseph's ever having conjugal relations with her.

This is clear to the informed Catholic, but among the thousands of Protestant sects there is an alarming loss of even a basic understanding of the profoundly biblical notions of consecration and sacred vows that quickly renders the obvious not so obvious. And this loss of understanding plays itself out in Christian communities in manifold ways. We argue that true devotion to Mary is a gift to the Church that can restore to the Christian world a true understanding of what consecration, sacraments, vowed celibacy, and especially the sacrament of holy matrimony mean. But before we go there, perhaps we need to take a brief walk through the Bible and consider—or reconsider—the biblical notion of consecration, and what it means biblically to take a vow before God.

In the Bible, whether we are speaking of a priest, the offerings, the temple, the Ark of the Covenant, and more in the Old Testament, or of consecrated celibacy, the Eucharist, marriage, and more in the New Covenant, the same truth holds: Once something or someone is consecrated for God's purpose, to use it for another purpose would be a sin of the worst order—*a sacrilege*. In Scripture, vows that consecrate are binding upon those who make them, under the pain of often-grave consequences.

The Priest
Exodus 29:1–9

> Now this is what you shall do to them to consecrate them, that they may serve me as priests . . . Then you shall bring his sons, and put coats on them, and you shall gird them with girdles and bind caps on them; and *the priesthood shall be theirs by a perpetual statute.* Thus you shall ordain Aaron and his sons.

The Priestly Garments
Exodus 28:40–43

> And for Aaron's sons you shall make coats and girdles and caps; you shall make them for glory and beauty. And you shall put them upon Aaron your brother, and upon his sons with him, and shall anoint them and ordain them and consecrate them that they may serve me as priests. And you shall make for them linen breeches to cover their naked flesh; from the loins to the thighs they shall reach; and they shall be upon Aaron, and upon his sons, when they go into the tent of meeting, or when they come near the altar to minister in the holy place; *lest they bring guilt upon themselves and die.* This shall be *a perpetual statute* for him and for his descendants after him.

The consecration of the priest was seen as sacred and permanent. Desecration of this sacred office was often punishable by death.

The Offerings
Exodus 29:31–34

> You shall take the ram of ordination, and boil its flesh in a holy
> place; and Aaron and his sons shall eat the flesh of the ram
> and the bread that is in the basket, at the door of the tent of
> meeting. They shall eat those things with which atonement was
> made, to ordain and consecrate them, *but an outsider shall not
> eat of them, because they are holy.* And if any of the flesh for the
> ordination, or of the bread, remain until the morning, then you
> shall burn the remainder with fire; *it shall not be eaten, because
> it is holy.*

The offerings were consecrated to be the food for the priest. No
one else was permitted to consume them.

The Sanctuary
2 Chronicles 30:8

> Do not now be stiff-necked as your fathers were, but yield
> yourselves to the Lord, and come to his sanctuary, which *he
> has sanctified forever,* and serve the Lord your God that his fierce
> anger may turn away from you.

The consecration of the sanctuary was both sacred and permanent. To use the temple or abuse it in any way brought about the
fierce anger of the Lord.

The Ark of the Covenant
Numbers 4:17–20

> The Lord said to Moses and Aaron, "Let not the tribe of
> the families of the Kohathites be destroyed from among the
> Levites; but deal thus with them, that they may live and not die
> when they come near to the most holy things: Aaron and his
> sons shall go in and appoint them each to his task and to his

burden, but *they shall not go in to look upon the holy things even for a moment, lest they die.*"

As we've seen, both the "men of Bethshemesh" in 1 Samuel 6:19–7:2 and Uzzah, the Kohathite, in 2 Samuel 6:1–9, found out in dramatic fashion that God is very serious about the things he has consecrated for his purpose. They were killed by the Lord himself for misusing and therefore desecrating what was consecrated to God! Remember: they were punished by death for merely *looking upon* or *touching* that which was consecrated for God's sacred purpose.

The Nazirite Vow
Judges 13:3–5

> And the angel of the Lord appeared to [the mother of Samson] and said to her, "You are barren and have no children; but you shall conceive and bear a son. Therefore beware, and drink no wine or strong drink, and eat nothing unclean, for behold, you shall conceive and bear a son. No razor shall come upon his head, for the boy shall be a Nazirite from birth; and he shall begin to deliver Israel from the hand of the Philistines.

We've all heard the story of Samson and his strength that was rooted in his Nazirite vow—which vow is described in detail in Numbers 6.

There are many other examples of vows and consecrations in the Old Testament that were binding upon the faithful with varying degrees of punishment if the vows were broken or if that which was consecrated was desecrated, but these should suffice as we move to the New Testament.

New Covenant Consecration

Did the ideas of vows and consecration disappear with the advent of Christ, or were they at least diminished dramatically? You might think so if your sphere of Christian experience were con-

fined to Protestant circles or to quasi-Christian sects. When is the
last time you heard of Protestants making vows to the Lord, still
less of shaving their heads as a sign of their vows? Yet we see Paul
doing that twice in Acts (18:18 and 21:23–24). Here we have an
apostolic foundation of the tonsure, in which religious brothers
shave their heads as a sign of their consecration to God.

Consecrated celibates span the globe in the Catholic Church.
But we do not find them in the Protestant world, even though
Paul teaches on consecrated celibacy in 1 Timothy 5:9–12. (More
on that below.)

Where in the Protestant world do we find an understanding of
the Eucharist that includes Paul's declaration that if you desecrate
this sacrament, you condemn yourself? In the Old Testament, as
we saw above, the punishment for desecrating that which had
been consecrated to God could include death. In the New Covenant, the punishment is far worse—damnation:

> For I received from the Lord what I also delivered to you . . .
> Whoever, therefore, eats the bread or drinks the cup of the
> Lord in an unworthy manner will be guilty of profaning the
> body and blood of the Lord. Let a man examine himself, and so
> eat of the bread and drink of the cup. For anyone who eats and
> drinks without discerning the body eats and drinks judgment
> upon himself. That is why many of you are weak and ill, and
> some have died (1 Cor. 11:23–30).

Whether or not one believes in the Real Presence, it's obvious that
the bread and cup of the Lord are consecrated and must be treated
with the utmost respect; otherwise, the punishment is decisive—
and can be *eternal*. The grape juice and crackers I casually received
when I was Protestant did not match what I read here from Paul.

Outside the Catholic and Orthodox churches there is very little to be found on these topics of vows and the consecrated life.
Even where you do find talk of vows—of marriage for example—
the understanding of those vows is superficial, or even errant. Indeed, in the modern Protestant "me and Jesus" theology—fruit of

Luther's notion of justification as the central Christian doctrine— sacred things like vows, sacraments, and consecration are mere trivialities. Yet this is not the lesson of Scripture.

The good news is that Protestants—and all of us—can guard against loss of the sacred by recognizing and meditating upon Mary's Perpetual Virginity.

We begin with one sentence from the patron saint of Scripture scholars, Jerome, defending the Perpetual Virginity of Mary some 1,600 years ago:

Would he [Joseph], who knew such great wonders, have dared touch the temple of God, the dwelling place of the Holy Spirit, the Mother of his Lord?[219]

To Jerome (and we could add a litany of Fathers of the Church), this is a no-brainer. And did you notice the sense of near-outrage in his words? Joseph wouldn't have *dared* to touch Mary. She was the chosen "temple of God," mother of the Redeemer, and spouse of the Holy Spirit, consecrated as such to God. To even consider that Mary—chosen to bear God in her womb—could ignore this great calling as if nothing had happened to her and then have conjugal relations with Joseph was inconceivable to Jerome, and it is inconceivable from the perspective of biblical teaching on holy matrimony.

Until Death Do Us Part

The New Testament makes very clear that marriage has been elevated to a new level—a supernatural level—with the advent of Christ. When Jesus was tested by the Pharisees and asked whether it was "lawful to divorce one's wife for any cause" in Matthew 19, he answered:

"Have you not read that he who made them from the beginning made them male and female, and said, 'For this reason a man

219. *On the Perpetual Virginity of Blessed Mary Against Helvidius*, 7.

shall leave his father and mother and be joined to his wife, and the two shall become one?' So they are no longer two but one. What therefore God has joined together, let no man put asunder" (4–6).

As was the case more than once during his ministry, Christ found himself in the middle of a Pharisee-Sadducee argument. The Pharisees asked this question because the Sadducees were teaching that it was lawful for a man to divorce for "any cause." The Pharisees were stricter, saying the reasons had to be serious. Whose side Jesus would support? Neither. Both sides needed correction. The Pharisees then responded:

"Why then did Moses command one to give a certificate of divorce, and to put her away?" [Jesus] said to them, "For your hardness of heart Moses allowed you to divorce your wives, but from the beginning it was not so" (v. 8).

In one fell swoop Jesus declared that there are *never* grounds for remarriage after divorce, and this was God's plan from the very beginning. God had only temporarily allowed for divorce through Moses because of the "hardness of hearts" of the Old Covenant people of God.

Jesus did more than simply restore marriage to its original state; he *elevated* marriage to the level of sacrament. This means that there could never again even be an accommodation like Moses'. Paul would confirm this radical new understanding in multiple places in his teaching.

Thus a married woman is bound by law to her husband as long as he lives; but if her husband dies she is discharged from the law concerning the husband. Accordingly, she will be called an adulteress if she lives with another man while her husband is alive. But if her husband dies she is free from that law, and if she marries another man she is not an adulteress (Rom. 7:2–3).

A wife is bound to her husband as long as he lives. If the husband dies, she is free to be married to whom she wishes, only in the Lord (1 Cor. 7:39).

Now concerning the matters about which you wrote . . . To the married I give charge, not I but the Lord, that the wife should not separate from her husband (but if she does, let her remain single or else be reconciled to her husband)—and that the husband should not divorce his wife (1 Cor. 7:1, 10–11).

Mary, Protectress of the Dignity of Marriage

Since Mary's marriage to the Holy Spirit is archetypical of the espousal and future marriage of the Bride of Christ, the Church, to Jesus Christ, losing sight of her Perpetual Virginity is devastating. For if Mary could ignore her nuptial consecration to the Holy Spirit, what does that say about the consecration of spouses in marriage? What does that say about consecration in general?

In an age where divorce and remarriage are rampant, it is tragic that the Catholic Church stands virtually alone in defense of marriage's indissolubility. It is difficult today to find individual Protestants, much less whole churches, standing with us. Even the Orthodox allow for second and third "marriages," even as divorce is wreaking havoc across the world, such as we have not seen in Christian history. Has there ever been a time when the fullness of truth—*the Catholic truth*—about marriage was more important to proclaim?

We would do well to remember these words from CCC 2384: "Divorce does injury to the covenant of salvation, of which sacramental marriage is the sign." We all know all too well that divorce tears the lives of the spouses apart and traumatizes children who are so often caught in the middle while it "introduces disorder into both the family and society" at large.[220] But even more devastating is the fact that divorce is a "grave offense against the moral

220. CCC 2385.

law. It claims to break the contract, to which the spouses freely consented, to live with each other till death."[221] And it has a "contagious effect that makes it truly a plague on society."[222] This is not to mention that if a new union is attempted by either spouse, "the remarried spouse is then in a situation of public and permanent adultery."[223]

The Perpetual Virginity of Mary serves as a stark reminder—a visible sign for all the world that has become a "sign of contradiction" in our day—of the permanent nature of the gift of marriage. To deny it is to betray the union of God and the Virgin Mary, archetype of all consecrations and a fulfillment of that which the sacrament of marriage is an earthly sign. It is the prototype of the marriage of Christ and his Church, and as such is exclusive, faithful, and permanent.[224] It is no coincidence that a loss of faith in the Perpetual Virginity of Mary goes hand-in-hand with the loss of an understanding of the sacredness of marriage and of the nature of a consecrated life before almighty God.

Contradictory Consecrations?

If what we are saying about consecration in Scripture is true, there appears to be a contradiction. Were not Joseph and Mary also consecrated to each other at their espousal? How, then, could Mary also be consecrated to God as his spouse?

There are three points to consider here:

1. Mary was already consecrated to God long before her espousal to Joseph. As we will demonstrate in Appendix II below, we know this as a matter of history not only from the *Protoevangelium of James*, written in A.D. 140, the testimony of

---

221. Ibid., 2384.
222. Ibid., 2385.
223. Ibid., 2384.
224. Revelation 12:17, for example, depicts the Blessed Virgin Mary, "the woman," as continuing in her nuptial relationship with God and bringing forth "offspring . . . who keep the commandments of God and bear testimony to Jesus."

the Fathers, and the teaching of the Church, but from Luke 1:34, where Mary responded to the angel's message of her future delivery of a child: "How [shall] this be for I know not man?" As we've seen, the question reveals the vow.

2. The espousal to Joseph was necessary in order to fulfill the prophecies declaring the Messiah to be the true king of Israel. According to Matthew's Gospel, Joseph was in the genealogical line of royalty that stretched back to David. It was also necessary to provide a protector for Mary in a culture that did not take kindly to women pregnant by someone other than their spouse.

3. In order to fulfill her calling to be the Ark of the Covenant and God's spouse, Mary could not be touched by man. This was a *higher calling* than Mary's espousal to Joseph. Indeed, Mary and Joseph's earthly union is an unambiguous reminder for all married couples that everything is *not* permitted in marriage. We must listen to God's word. Our nuptial union with God takes precedence over our nuptial unions on earth. Earthly marriage is "until death do us part," but the marriage supper of the Lamb at the end of time is everlasting. Joseph was truly Mary's spouse, but her union with God was of a higher order.

At this point, some may argue: "If both Mary's nuptial union with Joseph and her union with God were valid, why could she not go back to Joseph and have normal conjugal relations after giving birth to Jesus? Why would a physical relationship with Joseph impede a spiritual union with God?"

Consecrated Virginity

I fear all of this talk of consecrated lives and "perpetual virginity" may be leaving my non-Catholic readers cold. "Consecrated Virginity? Where is *that* in the Bible?" Add the idea that vows of consecrated virginity are gravely binding, and to people from the various sects that have formed since the Reformation you will sound like you are from another planet.

Yet these concepts are both reasonable and clearly taught in Scripture. For example, in 1 Timothy 5:9–12:

> Let a widow be enrolled if she is not less than sixty years of age, having been the wife of one husband; and she must be well attested for her good deeds, as one who has brought up children, shown hospitality, washed the feet of the saints, relieved the afflicted, and devoted herself to doing good in every way. But refuse to enroll younger widows; for when they grow wanton against Christ they desire to marry, and so they incur condemnation for having violated their first pledge.

It is certainly within the legitimate prerogative of someone who has lost a spouse to remarry. So why would Paul say these widows incur condemnation for remarrying? The reason is found in the concept of *enrollment*, which he elaborates. This was the first-century equivalent of taking a vow of celibacy. To break that vow, according to Paul, was to bring condemnation upon oneself.

In my own odyssey to the Catholic Church, I will never forget my interlocutor, Matt Dula, with whom I was engaged in what seemed to be a perpetual argument about the Faith, sharing this text with me. When he told me there was such a thing as "consecrated celibacy" in Scripture, I denied it. And when he told me about 1 Timothy 5:9–12 without actually citing it chapter and verse, I said, "That's not in the Bible!"

Well, There It Was!

As a Protestant I had never heard a sermon that even touched on this passage, or on Matthew 19:12, where Jesus recommends celibacy specifically in the context of the calling of the twelve apostles: "He who is able to receive this [celibacy], let him receive it." When Peter says shortly thereafter, "Behold, we have left everything and followed you," Jesus responds:

Truly, I say to you, in the new world, when the Son of man shall sit on his glorious throne, you who have followed me will also sit on twelve thrones, judging the twelve tribes of Israel. And every one who has left houses or brothers or sisters or father or mother or children or lands, for my name's sake, will receive a hundredfold, and inherit eternal life (Matt. 19:27–29).

Luke's version of this same saying adds "wife" to the equation:

And Peter said, "Lo, we have left our homes and followed you." And [Jesus] said to them, "Truly, I say to you, there is no man who has left house or wife, or brothers or parents or children, for the sake of the kingdom of God, who will not receive manifold more in this time, and in the age to come eternal life (18:28–30).

I had to ask myself, "Where are all of the Protestants forsaking wife and children for the sake of the kingdom and receiving a hundredfold in this life and eternal life as their reward?"

Some Final Thoughts

Whether the loss of a truly biblical understanding of sacraments, the consecrated life, vowed celibacy, and the sacrament of matrimony among Protestants preceded and perhaps contributed to loss of belief in the Perpetual Virginity of Mary (as it did for followers of Luther, Zwingli, Calvin, and Wesley, all of whom adhered to the dogma[225]) or followed from it (as it did for the later sons and daughters of the "reformers" who rejected it), reflecting on the nature of the sacred as it is profoundly echoed in Mary's Perpetual Virginity can serve as an antidote to the error.

But even for Catholics, this teaching is a unique aid to under-

---

225. For examples see Pelikan and Lehman, *Luther's Works,* vol. 22, 23; Pipkin, *Selected Writings of Huldrych Zwingli,* vol. 11, 275; Benson, *The Works of the Reverend John Wesley,* 110; John Calvin, Commentary on a Harmony of the Evangelists, Matthew, Mark, and Luke (see his commentaries on Matt. 1:25, and Matt. 13:55).

standing God's primacy in the order of grace in our own lives
and marriages. It compels us to rethink what we believe about
marriage and of consecrated virginity, because Mary and Joseph
lived both. It teaches us that consecration to God is permanent
and holy. Mary was consecrated to God from the time of her
childhood, and she observed that consecration to the end of her
life. What about us?

Moreover, the Perpetual Virginity of Mary teaches us that God
must come first in *our* marriages. Mary was committed to her
earthly spouse as far as she could be, but she reminds us in a
powerful way that it is God who joins man and woman together, and our consecration to God takes precedence even over our
consecration to husband or wife. Obedience to God's word must
be absolute.

If we Catholics pursued a greater devotion to Mary's Perpetual
Virginity, we would be renewed in our sense of the sacred, and of
what consecration to God truly means. We would have stronger
marriages and holier priests and religious. We would approach the
altar with more reverence. We would be a changed people. That's
a big deal!

9
ANSWERING OBJECTIONS

The Perpetual Virginity of Mary is perhaps the easiest of all of the Marian dogmas to understand conceptually. Nonetheless, when the topic is brought up with those who reject it, there is no lack of objections, misinformation, and misunderstandings. As we will see shortly, some objections are examples of "straw man" arguments, relatively easy to correct, while some are more complicated biblical and historical contentions, requiring a more detailed and precise response.

OBJECTION 1: Brothers of the Lord.

It's hard to say which objection to the Perpetual Virginity is the most common, but in my experience, the verses dealing with Jesus' brothers and sisters top the list.

Matthew 12:46–50:

> While he was still speaking to the people, behold, his mother and his brethren stood outside, asking to speak to him.

Matthew 13:55–56a:

> "Is not this the carpenter's son? Is not his mother called Mary? And are not his brethren James and Joseph and Simon and Judas? And are not all his sisters with us?"

On the surface, these texts do seem troubling for the Catholic position. After all, our Protestant friends insist, would not Jesus' having "brothers" indicate that Mary had other children? Eric Svendsen plainly states: "The New Testament mentions several times that Jesus had biological brothers and sisters."[226]

The first point of reply is a simple one: The Bible never claims Jesus had *biological* brothers and sisters. This is a classic example of *eisogesis*, or reading into a text something that is not there, due to a preconceived notion. As we will see below, "brothers of the Lord" actually refers to cousins or relatives other than uterine brothers. This will come to light when we understand Scripture properly given both the language and culture of ancient Israel.

But before we get to the texts in question, we would argue that if Svendsen and those who agree with him were consistent, they would also have to conclude that Joseph was Jesus' "biological" father. This is something no Christian would ever or could ever hold to be true. Yet John 6:42 records "the Jews" saying of Jesus: "Is not this Jesus, the son of Joseph whose father and mother we know? How does he now say, 'I have come down from heaven'?" Luke refers to Joseph as Jesus' "father" in Luke 2:33, and even Mary does, in Luke 2:48, without any clarification.

As our Protestant friends would agree, any Jews who believed Joseph was Jesus' biological father were simply wrong. He was not Jesus' father *by nature*. He was his father by adoption.[227] And though Luke as well as our Lady herself refer to Joseph as the "father" of Jesus, this could not mean that they believed he was the biological father of Jesus. In the same way, any scriptural reference to Jesus' relatives as his "brothers" does not necessarily equate to a scriptural proof they were indeed his *uterine* brothers.

---

226. Svendsen, *Evangelical Answers*, 137.

227. We know St. Joseph was Jesus' father by adoption through other scriptures, such as Luke 1:35, which reveal to us that Jesus was born of the Holy Spirit. Analogously, the inspired authors refer to some of Jesus' relations as "brothers," but other texts, as we will see below, reveal to us that these were not *uterine* brothers.

Oh, Brother!

The term *brother* had a wide semantic range in the Hebrew of the Old Testament, the Aramaic spoken by Christ, and in the Greek of the New Testament. The *Catechism* (500) explains:

> Against this doctrine the objection is sometimes raised that the Bible mentions brothers and sisters of Jesus.[228] The Church has always understood these passages as not referring to other children of the Virgin Mary. In fact James and Joseph, "brothers of Jesus," are the sons of another Mary, a disciple of Christ, whom St. Matthew significantly calls "the other Mary."[229] They are close relations of Jesus, according to an Old Testament expression.[230]

It was common in Hebrew and in Hebrew culture at the time of Christ for cousins, uncles, or nephews to call one another *brother* even though they were actually more extended relatives. This probably stemmed, at least in part, from the fact that both Hebrew and Aramaic did not have a specific word for *cousin*. It became common to use *brother* or *sister* when speaking of cousins, which led to using the term for other family relations as well.[231] The *Catechism* cites Abraham and Lot as classic examples of this in Genesis 13:8 and 14:16. Though they were uncle and nephew by relation, they called one another *brother*.

We also find a wide semantic range for *brother* in the New Testament. For example, in Matthew 23:8 Jesus told us to call one another *brothers*.[232] No sane person would conclude from this that all mankind comes from the same physical uterus. Jerome explained:

---

228. Cf. Mark 3:31–35, 6:3; 1 Cor. 9:5; Gal. 1:19.
229. Cf. Matt. 13:55, 27:56, 28:1.
230. Cf. Gen. 13:8, 14:16, 29:15, etc.
231. Shearer, *A Catholic Commentary on Sacred Scripture*, 844.
232. See also Acts 7:2, 9:17, and 1 Cor. 2:1.

In Holy Scripture there are four kinds of brethren—by nature, race, kindred, and love. Instances of brethren by nature are Jacob and Esau, the twelve patriarchs, Andrew and Peter, James and John. As to race, all Jews are called brethren of one another . . . Moreover they are called brethren by kindred who are of one family, that is *patria*, which corresponds to the Latin *paternitas*, because from a single root a numerous progeny proceeds. In Genesis we read, "And Abram said unto Lot, Let there be no strife, I pray thee, between me and thee, and between my herdmen and thy herdman; for we are brethren . . . " But to be brief, I will return to the last of the four classes of brethren, those, namely, who are brethren by affection, and these again fall into two divisions, those of the spiritual and those of the general relationship. I say *spiritual* because all of us Christians are called brethren . . . I say *general*, because we are all children of one Father, there is a like bond of brotherhood between us all.[233]

Jerome goes on to explain how Scripture never says the *brothers* of the Lord are brothers by nature:

I now ask to which class you consider the Lord's brethren in the Gospel must be assigned. They are brethren by nature, you say. But Scripture does not say so; it calls them neither sons of Mary, nor of Joseph.[234]

It is clear that our Lord's brethren bore the name in the same way that Joseph was called his father: "I and thy father sought thee sorrowing" (Luke 2:48). It was his mother that said this, not the Jews![235]

Eric Svendsen and many others definitely go beyond what is written when they claim the Bible teaches Christ had biolog-

---

233. *Against Helvidius* 16–17.
234. Ibid., 17.
235. Ibid., 18.

ical brothers, born of a sexual relationship between Joseph and Mary.[236]

It's All Greek to Me

When we get to the Greek of the New Testament, our Protestant friends will turn up the heat in the discussion. Svendsen provides an example:

> There are two other words that were in use by the New Testament writers when they wanted to convey the meaning "cousin" or "relative." One of these words, *anepsios,* occurs in Col. 4:10 to refer to Mark, the "cousin" of Barnabas. The other, *sungenis,* occurs in Luke 1:36 and is used to refer to Elizabeth, the "cousin" of Mary . . . That they knew of the distinction between these words and *adelphos* is evident from Luke 21:16 which uses both *adelphos* and *sungenis,* but in reference to different groups ("You will be betrayed even by parents, *brothers, relatives* and friends").[237]

What do we make of these arguments? First of all, Luke 21:16 only proves that *adelphos* can be used in the context of uterine brothers—an undisputed point. It also proves that *sungenis* can be used for extended relatives—another undisputed point. But what it doesn't prove is that *adelphos* cannot be used with a wider semantic range in other contexts.

But what about the fact that Greek did have a specific word for *cousin*—*anepsios*—as we see it used in Colossians 4:10? And what about *sungenis*? If these relations of Jesus were cousins, why did the inspired author use the word for brother—*adelphos*—instead of these other two words that clearly can be used for cousins or other relations?

Well, to translate Luke 1:36 as *cousin* with reference to Mary and Elizabeth is a stretch, but may well be correct. *Sungenis* means *relative,* and so could be used as *cousin.* But because Mary was a

236. Cf. 1 Cor. 4:6.
237. Svendsen, *Evangelical Answers,* 138–139.

young espoused bride and Elizabeth was beyond child-bearing years, they would most likely have been related as niece to aunt or in some other way.[238] But whether they were cousins, aunt/niece, or some other extended relation, we must again recall that in Hebrew and Aramaic—the first language of Christ and the apostles—it was common to refer to such relatives as *sisters*, or as here, *relatives*. This was a common cultural phenomenon rooted in the Hebrew and Aramaic languages of the Jewish people,

The apostles were Jews, and so they spoke (and wrote) Greek with a "Jewish accent." Since in Hebrew and Aramaic it was common to refer to all sorts of male relations as *brothers*, it is not surprising that when they spoke or wrote in Greek they tended to refer to all extended male relations as *brothers*. And so the real question is not whether Greek has a word for *cousin* or not. The question should be: Did first-century Jews—and the authors of Sacred Scripture here in question, who were Jewish converts—use the Greek word for *brother* the same way they used its Hebrew and Aramaic equivalents?

The "Septuagint-Conditioned" New Testament

The answer to the above is a definitive *yes*. In the Septuagint (the Greek translation of the Hebrew scriptures, often abbreviated as LXX), we have multiple examples. Leviticus 10:4 uses a form of *adelphos* to refer to the cousins of Moses and Aaron. In 1 Chronicles 23:22, the cousins of the daughters of Eleazar are called *adelphoi*. And in Tobit 7:2–4 we have forms of both *anepsios* and *adelphos* used as synonyms within two verses of each other: "Then Raguel said to his wife Edna, 'How much the young man resembles my *cousin* Tobit!' . . . So he said to them, 'Do you know our *brother* Tobit?'"

The Septuagint was translated over a considerable period of

---

238. Cf. Luke 1:27, 1:18. If *sungenis* means *cousin* here, as Svendsen suggests, this only proves that the inspired authors of Scripture did not only use *anepsios* for *cousin*.

time, from ca. 250 B.C. until ca. 100 B.C.[239] The first books translated were the Torah and then the writings of the prophets. Because Tobit was not even written first in Hebrew or Aramaic until ca. 200 B.C.,[240] we know it would have been one of the later translated books to be added to the Septuagint, in ca. 140–100 B.C. The translators of the LXX *could* have used *anepsios* or *sungenis* for *cousin*; and, in fact, at times they did. However, they obviously did not *have* to do so. They chose to use *adelphos* as well—for *cousin* or *relative* as well as for *brother*.

To his credit, Eric Svendsen responded with what appears on the surface to be a compelling rejoinder to a similar point made by Karl Keating in *Catholicism and Fundamentalism*:[241]

> But to transfer the Septuagint meaning of this word into the New Testament without any clear first-century examples betrays a misinformed, if not irresponsible approach. The fact is, *adelphos never* means "cousin" in the New Testament. Keating is guilty of the exegetical fallacy of semantic obsolescence; that is to say, he is guilty of foisting a meaning on the New Testament usage of *adelphos* that it had 200-odd years prior to the penning of the New Testament, but that it did not have at the time of that penning.[242]

There are three main problems with Svendsen's reasoning. First, he begs the question by asserting that *adelphos* could not be used for *cousin* in the first century because . . . *adelphos* could not be used for *cousin* in the first century. Secondly, he fails to recognize the influence of the Septuagint upon the New Testament. Fr. Mateo writes:

239. *The Oxford Dictionary of the Christian Church*, 1483. See also pages 1016–1017, where the final books of the Old Testament included in the Septuagint, *the Books of Maccabees,* are said to have been *written* in Greek ca. 100 B.C.

240. Ibid., 1628.

241. Keating, *Catholicism and Fundamentalism*, 283.

242. Svendsen, *Evangelical Answers,* 138.

From the middle of the second century B.C., many Jews in Egypt . . . and throughout the Diaspora had lost touch with Hebrew . . . By the time of Christ, for most Jews, the Septuagint *was* the Bible. This became true also for several generations of early Christians. Thus the influence of the Septuagint on the Greek language, as spoken and written by early Christians and by the Jews of the Diaspora and even in Palestine, was enormous. Almost 80 percent of the Old Testament citations and allusions in the New Testament come from the Septuagint . . . Stylistically, much of the New Testament, especially the four Gospels and Acts, is heavily dependent upon the Septuagint.[243]

Fr. Mateo also quotes David Hill of the University of Sheffield, who says:

The *vocabularies* [emphasis Fr. Mateo's] of the Greek Old Testament and the Greek New Testament have a great measure of similarity; and research into the syntax of the Greek of the Septuagint has revealed its remarkable likeness to that of the New Testament . . . The language of the New Testament . . . reveals in its syntax and . . . in its *vocabulary* [emphasis Hill's] a strong Semitic case, due in large measure to its indebtedness to the Jewish biblical Greek of the Septuagint.[244]

Fr. Mateo rightly points out that the Jewish writers of the New Testament (which would exclude only St. Luke) would have been "Septuagint-conditioned." And it could be argued that even Luke, being a Greek-speaking Gentile, would most likely also have been influenced by the Greek Septuagint.[245]

---

243. Fr. Mateo, *Refuting the Attack on Mary,* 13.
244. Ibid., 13–14. Fr. Mateo quotes David Hill, *Greek Words and Hebrew Meanings,* 16–18.
245. There is a theory that St. Luke may have been a Gentile convert to Judaism before his conversion to Christ; if so so this would only add to the importance of the LXX in his life. See www.newadvent.org/cathen/09420a.htm.

Brothers from Another Mother?

This leads to the third problem with Svendsen's reasoning: He overlooks the fact that the New Testament clearly uses *adelphos* to refer generally to *relatives*, just as the Septuagint does. For example, John 19:25 refers to "[Jesus'] mother's sister (*adelphe*), Mary the wife of Clopas," being present at the foot of the cross along with Mary and Mary Magdalene. It is highly unlikely that there would be two *uterine* sisters with the same name of *Mary*. This is surely an example of some other kind of relation being called *sister*.[246]

Further, after Matthew 13:55 mentions the brothers of the Lord, "James and Joseph and Simon and Judas," verse 27:56 tells us who their mother was: "Mary, the mother of James and Joseph." Protestant and Catholic scholars generally agree that this Mary is *not* the Blessed Mother. (In Scripture Mary is always called *the mother of Jesus*, or *mother of the Lord*, and would have been especially so-called in the context of her following her divine Son at the time of the Passion.) Yet the children of this other Mary are called *brothers of the Lord*. Thus we have another example of *brother* being used as *relative* or *cousin* in Scripture.

In addition, the fact that this "Mary" of Matthew 27:56 has children called *brothers of the Lord* would most likely connect her to the Mary mentioned in John 19:25 as the *sister* of Mary, the mother of Jesus. Thus, even more weight is added to the argument that these *brothers of the Lord* were actually cousins or some sort of extended relations, depending upon how closely related to our Lady her *sister* Mary was.

---

246. Some will claim that Mary is *Miriam* in Greek while her sister is *Maria*. However, in Scripture, the two spellings are actually used interchangeably, as we see in the case of Mary Magdalene in Mark 15:40 (she is called "Maria"); and Matthew 27:56 ("Maria"), 27:61 ("Mariam"), and 28:1 ("Mariam"). They are essentially the same name.

More About the "Brothers" of Jesus

Galatians 1:18–19 is another biblical text often used to "prove" Jesus had at least one uterine brother:[247]

> Then after three years I [Paul] went up to Jerusalem to visit Cephas, and remained with him fifteen days. But I saw none of the other apostles except James the Lord's brother.

Notice two very important points. First, the James whom Paul mentions was a *brother of the Lord*. Sound familiar? And secondly, he appears to be an apostle—not just in an extended sense, but one of the Twelve. In verses 17–19, Paul says:

> Nor did I go up to Jerusalem to those who *were apostles before me*, but I went away into Arabia; and again I returned to Damascus. Then after three years I went up to Jerusalem to visit Cephas, and remained with him fifteen days. But I saw *none of the other apostles* except James the Lord's brother.

There were some apostles, such as Barnabas, who were not of the Twelve. These were sent by Christ through the ministry of the Church to go to various areas of the world with a mission to preach the gospel.[248] But here Paul is writing about an experience he had shortly after his conversion when he speaks of *not* going to Jerusalem to those who "were apostles before [him]." This would have been, at most, only one to three years after the Resurrection

---

247. Svendsen, *Evangelical Answers*, 137. Galatians 1:19 is one among a list of seven texts that Svendsen uses to "prove" Mary gave birth to other children through conjugal relations with Joseph.

248. The Greek word *apostolos* means *sent one* or *emissary* (CCC 858). Some will include, for example, Andronicus and Junias as apostles in this sense in Romans 16:7. The text is unclear. It says they were "of note among the apostles," not necessarily that they were apostles. But Barnabas is clearly referred to as an apostle, along with Paul, in Acts 14:14. Moreover, 1 Corinthians 15:5–7 lists *the twelve* and *the apostles* as two distinct categories, indicating there were apostles beyond the Twelve. See also 1 Thessalonians 1:1, 2:6.

of Christ.[249] The apostles were still in Jerusalem at that time.[250] It is unlikely, then, that Paul is referring here to those who are apostles in an extended sense.[251] We will speak more about this later when we look at Eusebius and some historical data. But for now, let's just say that we can reasonably conclude that the text is referring to James, the *Lord's brother*, as being one of the twelve apostles.[252]

There were two apostles named James among the twelve. The first was the "son of Zebedee." He would not be the James that Paul spoke about in Galatians 1, because according to Acts 12:1–2 he was martyred very early. That leaves the other apostle James. According to Luke 6:15–16, his father's name was Alphaeus—not Joseph. That means that the apostle James whom Paul calls *the Lord's brother* could not have been Jesus' uterine brother.[253]

We also know that "Judas" (Jude) was the brother of James, according to Jude 1:1. So here we have two of the four *brothers of the Lord* mentioned in Scripture, but they were definitely not Jesus' uterine brothers. Add Joseph, whom Matthew 27:56 establishes could not be Jesus' uterine brother, and you've got three out of the four "brothers of the Lord" from Matthew 13:55–56 as some sort of relation of Jesus, but not brothers *by nature*.

---

249. Cf., *The Navarre Bible*, "The Acts of the Apostles," 107.

250. Acts 8:1.

251. There is no record in Scripture of an *apostle* in an extended sense—beyond the Twelve—called such *before* Paul was called to be an apostle. Barnabas was the closest to this. He was called, sent, and referred to as an apostle at about the same time Paul was called (see Acts 14:14). Again, it would be unlikely that Paul would be referring to anyone other than the Twelve when he refers to apostles who were "before him."

252. Orchard, *A Catholic Commentary on Sacred Scripture*, 1115. This well-respected biblical scholar agrees that this visit was a visit to "the twelve" and that among them he saw only Peter and James. St. Jerome, in *The Perpetual Virginity of Mary—Against Helvidius*, 15, concurs.

253. In *The Perpetual Virginity of Mary*, 14, Jerome adds: "James is called 'the less' (cf. Mark 15:40) in order to distinguish him from James the Greater, who was the son of Zebedee" among the Twelve. This is more evidence that the James who is called "the brother of the Lord," was one of the twelve apostles.

Alphaeus or Clopas?

At this point, a question invariably arises. Luke 6:15–16 tells us the father of James is Alphaeus, whereas the father of the James of Matthew 27:56 is called Clopas. How do we reconcile these statements?

First, neither one of these is Joseph, so we still know that we are not talking about the uterine brothers of Christ. But we should also consider that in the first century it was common to have more than one name, as is demonstrated in the cases of Jude/Thaddeus and Matthew/Levi.[254] Karl Keating suggests:

> More probably Alphaeus and Cleophas (Clopas in Greek) are the same person, since the Aramaic name for Alphaeus could be rendered in Greek in different ways, either as Alphaeus or Clopas. Another possibility is that Alphaeus took a Greek name similar to his Jewish name, the way that Saul took the name Paul.[255]

The second-century historian Hegesippus reported that Clopas was actually the brother of Joseph and that his son was Simon, the *brother of the Lord*, adding enormous weight to the contention that the brothers of the Lord were relatives or cousins.[256] Thus we have strong historical and biblical evidence that all four brothers of the Lord mentioned in Matthew 13:55 were related to Jesus, but not as uterine brothers. Any way you slice it, the "brothers of the Lord" can only be "cousins" or "relatives."

254. In the lists of apostles, Luke 6:16 and Acts 1:13 refer to "Jude/Thaddeus" as Jude, while Matthew 10:3 and Mark 3:18 refer to him as Thaddaeus. As far as "Matthew/Levi" is concerned, in comparing the synoptic Gospels where each present the calling of the apostle, Matthew 9:9 has him named "Matthew," while Mark 2:14 and Luke 5:27 have him named "Levi." Most likely, Matthew was his Greek name, while Levi was his Hebrew name.

255. Keating, *Catholicism and Fundamentalism*, 288.

256. Hegesippus is referenced in Eusebius of Caesarea, *Ecclesiastical History*, 4:22:4, and 3:11:1.

A Final Objection

At this point, some may object: "The James and Joseph of Matthew 27:56 are different from the James and Joseph of Matthew 13:55, because Matthew does not tell us that the James and Joseph of chapter 27 are specifically *brothers of the Lord* like he did in chapter 13.'"

Even a cursory examination of this objection reveals its weakness. Matthew had already mentioned James, Joseph, Simon, and Judas as *brothers of the Lord* in chapter 13. It is quite common for writers to abbreviate references when they are repeated. For example, an author may describe a man as, "Bill Smith, the plumber from Arlington, Virginia." But after a first introduction, the author may just say "Bill Smith," "Smith," or "the plumber." Further, if our hypothetical author was subsequently going to refer to a *different* person named "Bill Smith" he would specify who he was so that we wouldn't confuse him with the previously mentioned plumber from Arlington, Virginia. Thus, if the James and Joseph of chapter 27 had been different from the James and Joseph of chapter 13, Matthew would have identified them differently. He did not do so.

OBJECTION 2: The straw men.

Protestant author Dave Hunt is an excellent example of one who objects to the dogma of the Perpetual Virginity of Mary, at least in part, using a classic straw man argument. He claims:

> The Catholic argument goes on to insist that for Christ to be born of a womb that would later conceive and give birth to other children would somehow contaminate him.[257]

Anti-Catholic literature is peppered with misconceptions like this one. Eric Svendsen adds a different twist in creating his straw man:

257. Hunt, *A Woman Rides the Beast*, 436.

He claims it is not Jesus who would have been contaminated, but Mary:

> The Catholic emphasis on preserving Mary from any impurity seems to be the engine that drives this idea.[258]

Both of these are distortions. First of all, the Perpetual Virginity of Mary has nothing to do with making sure Mary doesn't "contaminate" Jesus by having other children as Dave Hunt claims the Catholic Church teaches. As we have seen, God could have chosen to come into the world through the instrumentality of a sinful woman if he so willed. If that's the case, he certainly could have come into the world through a woman who would later have normal conjugal relations with her lawfully wedded husband. The Catholic Church teaches that marriage is a holy state willed for man and woman from the beginning of creation.

The reason why Mary would have sinned if she'd had sexual relations with Joseph was because she was already consecrated to God as the spouse of the Holy Spirit—not because it would have "contaminated" Jesus.

But if it were the case that God willed to come into the world through a woman who would have other children, we would find a very different revelation of God's will in this matter and a very different historical account than what we find in Sacred Scripture and Sacred Tradition. In teaching the Perpetual Virginity of Mary, the Church is "driven" by nothing other than the revelation God committed to its care 2,000 years ago.

Svendsen is much closer to the truth here. We have already stated how it was both fitting and biblical that Mary would not have experienced even the slightest sin. But Svendsen's charge seems to suggest that the Catholic Church is somehow saying marital relations are "impure." This is false. As we have seen, the reason why Mary would have committed sin if she'd had conjugal relations with Joseph was that she belonged nuptially to God. She was the

---

258. Svendsen, *Evangelical Answers,* 137.

spouse of the Holy Spirit and Joseph was her earthly protector. There would be nothing inherently impure about Mary and Joseph having conjugal relations were it not for the fact that she had a previous nuptial commitment.

OBJECTION 3: "Before" and "until."

If the claim that the "brothers of the Lord" in Matthew 13:55 were his uterine brothers represents the most common objection to the Perpetual Virginity of Mary, in the top three is a wrong-headed application of Matthew 1:18: "Before they came together [Mary] was found to be with child of the Holy Spirit." If the text says "before they came together," doesn't that imply that they did eventually come together in conjugal relations? Eric Svendsen claims:

> The phrase "before they came together" makes sense here only if Mary *did not* make a vow of lifelong virginity. Matthew is making a point of letting his readers know that the child was conceived before any sexual union took place.[259]

Actually, this text makes perfect sense if we consider that the word *before* (Gr., *prin*) can be used—both in Greek and English—to emphasize a present or past event or state of being rather than a future event. It does not necessitate any event *after* the time of emphasis.

For example, consider this statement: "Tom died before he graduated high school." This statement uses the word *before* to emphasize a particular time, that is, to emphasize that Tom died young. Would anyone claim that the phrase "before he graduated high school" implies that Tom went on to graduate high school sometime after death?

Svendsen is half right: Matthew 1:18 emphasizes that Mary conceived of the Holy Spirit before any conjugal relations occurred. Matthew's purpose is to emphasize the virginal concep-

259. Svendsen, *Evangelical Answers*, 144.

tion of Jesus. But there is no evidence that the text is concerned with whether or not Joseph and Mary had a sexual union at a later time. There would need to be more information to demonstrate whether or not that took place.

John 4:49 is an example of a similar usage of *prin* in the New Testament. A man with an ill child approached Jesus and said: "Sir, come down before my child dies." Jesus then healed his child. There is no evidence in the text that this father was upset with Jesus for healing the child. "I told you I wanted my child to die! Why did you heal him?" This desperate father was not concerned with anything other than the immediate healing of his child. He is not concerned with the future beyond that.

A similar and equally common argument is found in Matthew 1:24–25:

> When Joseph woke from sleep, he did as the angel of the Lord commanded him; he took his wife, but knew her not until she had borne a son; and he called his name Jesus.

Dave Hunt makes hay from these verses:

> The Bible [Matt. 1:25] teaches that Mary was a virgin until the time that Jesus was born. Subsequently, she had a number of other children by Joseph, her husband.[260]

Does Matthew's use of the word *until* mean that Joseph eventually did come to know Mary conjugally? No; as with *before,* this implication is unfounded. The word *until* can be used to mean "leading up to the time of" without implying a change afterward. For example, I may say to a friend, "God bless you, until we meet again." Does that mean that if we meet again, I want God to stop blessing him?

Jerome responded to this very question:

---

260. Hunt, *A Woman Rides the Beast,* 436.

And the savior in the Gospel tells the apostles, "Lo, I am with you always, even unto the end of the world." Will the Lord then after the end of the world has come forsake his disciples, and at the very time when seated on twelve thrones they are to judge the twelve tribes of Israel will they be bereft of the company of their Lord?

I could give countless instances of this usage, and cover the verbosity of our assailant (Helvidius) with a cloud of proofs; I shall, however, add only a few, and leave the reader to discover others for himself.[261]

Here are some of the plain biblical examples confirming Jerome's words:

2 Samuel 6:23: "And Michal the daughter of Saul had no child to the day of her death." Does this mean she had children after she died?

1 Timothy 4:13: "Till I come, attend to the public reading of scripture, to preaching, to teaching." Does this mean Timothy should stop teaching after Paul arrives?

1 Corinthians 15:25: "For he (Christ) must reign until he has put all his enemies under his feet." Does this mean Christ's reign will end? (On the contrary, Luke 1:33 says, "He will reign over the house of Jacob *forever* and of his kingdom there shall be no end.")

Matthew 28:20: "And lo, I am with you always, to the end of the age." As Jerome asked, does this verse mean Christ will not be with us after the end of the age?

---

261. *On the Perpetual Virginity of Blessed Mary,* 6.

1 Timothy 6:14: "I charge you to keep the commandments unstained and free from reproach until the appearing of our Lord Jesus Christ." Does this mean they can break the commandments after Jesus comes?

Much Ado About a Preposition

Eric Svendsen fires back by claiming a nuance in meaning in Matthew 1:25: that this text uses the Greek words *heos hou* for *until,* whereas the New Testament texts I cited above use *heos* alone.[262] Responding to Karl Keating, he writes:

> This Greek construction (*heos hou* or *heos hotou*) has only two major connotations in the New Testament. In a few instances it has the temporal meaning "while" (a meaning that can hardly be applied to the passage in question). The other meaning is "until" and, without exception, implies a discontinuation of the action of the main clause . . . There are a handful of instances in the Septuagint where this construction has the meaning Keating wants to assign to Matt. 1:25. Between the completion of the Septuagint and the writing of Matthew there is not even one unambiguous instance of *heos hou* in the available literature of the centuries immediately surrounding the birth of Christ, where the construction has the meaning Keating assigns to Matt. 1:25. Keating's argument is thereby rendered groundless.[263]

Svendsen's claim is that *heos hou,* translated as "until" in Matthew 1:25, implies "a discontinuation of the action of the main clause"—in this case, that Mary's virginity was "discontinued."

One very large problem with Svendsen's theory is that not a single work of Greek scholarship agrees with it.[264] Moreover, the

---

262. Svendsen, *Evangelical Answers,* 143. I should note that 1 Corinthians 15:25 uses *arki hou,* another synonym for *until.*

263. Ibid., 143–144.

264. An example of what is found generally in Greek grammar books is found in Wenham,

evidence from Scripture and history further refutes Svendsen's claim. In the Bible, *heos hou* and *heos* are used interchangeably and have essentially the same meaning—amazingly, Svendsen himself admits that we see this in the Septuagint, and that alone is devastating to his claim. But we also see it in contemporary works in the period in which he claims there is "not even one unambiguous instance," and in the New Testament itself. Acts 25:21 alone should suffice to clear up the matter. In this text Paul is brought before the Roman governor of Caesarea, Festus, who says:

> But when Paul had appealed to be kept in custody for the decision of the emperor, I commanded him to be held *until* (Gr., *heos hou*) I could send him to Caesar.

Does this text mean that Paul's custody would be "discontinued" after he was sent to Caesar? Not according to the biblical record. Paul was kept in custody *before* the time he was sent, *while* he was in transit (Acts 27:1), and *after* he arrived in Rome (Acts 29:16). The action of the main clause did not cease with *heos hou*.

One might argue that Festus simply meant that Paul was to be held *in Caesarea* until Festus sent him to the emperor, meaning that the action of the main clause *did* cease when Paul was sent to Rome because he was no longer being held *in Caesarea*. But this simply does not fly, for three reasons.

1. The "main action" of the clause was not that Paul be "kept in Caesarea." It was simply that he was to be "kept in custody." That action did not cease with *heos hou*.

The Elements of New Testament Greek, 161: "An indefinite *heos* is frequently followed by *an* or *hou* (genitive of the relative pronouns) and sometimes by *hotou* (the irregular of *hostis*) . . . The addition of *han, hou* or *hotou* makes no difference to the sense. In the case of *hou* and *hotou* the word *kronou* (time) is understood. Such clauses are usually indefinite because they refer to something future and unfulfilled. If the clause refers to something which has actually happened in the past, it will be in the Indicative." According to Wenham, there is no essential difference in sense between *heos* alone and when *heos* is followed by *hou*.

2. Paul clearly appealed to the emperor that he be "kept in
   custody" *eis tein tou Sabastou diagnosin*, which means literally,
   "up unto the diagnosis (or investigation) of the emperor." Here
   Paul was exercising his rights as a Roman citizen. Festus was
   bound by Roman law to meet Paul's request or else it would
   be Festus who would be in grave danger from his superiors.
   The context indicates he was granting Paul's request to be
   kept in custody until Caesar could investigate his case.

3. It is in that context that Festus says, "I ordered him to be
   held until I could send him to Caesar." If the emperor had
   actually ordered him only to be kept in custody *in Caesarea*,
   then the centurion and soldiers who held him in custody until
   he arrived in Rome and beyond would have been disobeying
   orders. This is highly unlikely, given the high price Roman
   guards paid for disobedience (see Acts 16:27).

For a more thorough dismantling of Svendsen's claim, we recommend the writings of John Pacheco.[265] At his site, he and his
guest writers accumulate numerous examples of authors from the
time period between ca. 100 B.C. and A.D. 100 who use *heos hou*
where the action of the verb continues beyond the "until" of the
main clause. Among these works are *Joseph and Aseneth, 4 Maccabees, Josephus's Antiquities,* and the *Apocalypse of Moses.*

For brevity's sake, here is just one unambiguous example, 4
Maccabees 7:1–3:

> For like a most skillful pilot, the reason of our father Eleazar
> steered the ship of religion over the sea of the emotions, and
> though buffeted by the storms of the tyrant and overwhelmed
> by the mighty waves of tortures, in no way did he turn the
> rudder of religion until [*heos hou*] he sailed into the haven of
> immortal victory.

265. catholic-legate.com/Apologetics/MaryAndTheSaints/HeosHouPolemic.aspx.

The context here is one in which Eleazar is said to have held firm to his religion and never to have steered awry. It can be clearly seen that the use of *heos hou* continues the action of the main clause.

We will conclude our thoughts by revisiting the Septuagint, which Svendsen dismisses because it was written before his arbitrary 200-year period. Yet it should not be shelved so readily. As we said before, it was deeply influential to the New Testament's inspired authors. And in it we see *heos hou* continuing the action of the main clause in many instances. For example:

Genesis 8:5: "And the waters continued to abate until [*heos hou*] the tenth month; in the tenth month, on the first day of the month, the tops of the mountains were seen."

2 Samuel 6:23: And Michal the daughter of Saul had no child to [*heos hou*] the day of her death.

Psalm 94:13 (LXX 93:13): To give him respite from days of trouble, until [*heos hou*] a pit is dug for the wicked.

Song of Solomon 2:17: Until [*heos hou*] the day breathes and the shadows flee, turn, my beloved, be like a gazelle, or a young stag upon rugged mountains.

Song of Solomon 3:4: Scarcely had I passed them, when I found him whom my soul loves. I held him, and would not let him go until [*heos hou*] I had brought him into my mother's house, and into the chamber of her that conceived me.

In each of these texts, *until* is used and the action of the main clause continues beyond the action of the main clause. There is simply no reason to give credence to Svendsen's claim.

OBJECTION 4: The first-born.

A final common objection, made by Hunt and countless others, charges that Scripture (for example, Luke 2:7) confirms Mary had other children by referring to Jesus as her "first-born son." According to many Protestants, if Jesus was the first-born, wouldn't this imply at least a second-born?

Not necessarily. Exodus 13:1–2 tells us something very important about the "first-born" in Israel: "The Lord said to Moses, 'Consecrate to me all the first-born; whatever is the first to open the womb among the people of Israel, both of man and beast, is mine.'" Notice that they are not called *first-born* because there is a second-born. They are called first-born *at birth*. Jerome explains pointedly:

> The word of God defines *first-born* as everything that openeth the womb. Otherwise, if the title belongs to such only as have younger brothers, the priests cannot claim the firstlings until their successors have been begotten . . . The word of God compels me to dedicate to God everything that openeth the womb if it be the firstling of clean beasts: if of unclean beasts, I must redeem it and give the value to the priest. I might reply and say, "Why do you tie me down to the short space of a month? Why do you speak of the first-born, when I cannot tell whether there are brothers to follow? Wait until the second is born. I owe nothing to the priest unless the birth of a second should make the one I previously had the first-born."

PART IV

ASSUMED INTO HEAVEN

IO

RAISED BY LOVE

PROOFS FOR THE
FOURTH MARIAN DOGMA

On November 1, 1950, in his apostolic constitution *Munificentis-simus Deus*, Pope Pius XII infallibly proclaimed the truth of the Assumption of the Blessed Virgin Mary: "the Immaculate Mother of God, Mary ever Virgin, when the course of her earthly life was ended, was taken up body and soul into the glory of heaven."[266] This dogma is deeply rooted in Scripture and has profound implications for all Christians.

We've already seen how Mary's Immaculate Conception reveals the dignity of man and God's original (sinless) plan for him. Mary's Assumption is the complement to the Immaculate Conception in that it reveals mankind's ultimate destiny: a sharing, in both body and soul, in the very life and glory of God. The Assumption of Mary gives us a glimpse of the glory that is yet to be fully revealed; it is a source of hope for Christians. In the Mother of God all can see actualized in a real human person what awaits all of God's children who are "faithful unto death" and thus promised to receive the "crown of life."[267]

The Assumption in Scripture

The truth of the Assumption of Mary is profoundly beautiful; yet, at the same time, for many the doctrine presents seemingly

266. *Munificentissimus Deus* 44.
267. Cf. Rev. 2:10.

impenetrable obstacles to full communion with the Catholic
Church. When I was Protestant I used to say that "the assumption
of the Assumption is no more than an assumption, because there
is nothing of it to be found in Scripture or in the early Church!"

Today we frequently hear a similar refrain from non-Catholic
inquirers: "Mary is hardly ever seen in Scripture at all, and there
is *nothing* about her being bodily assumed into heaven." And yet
Pope Pius XII, when he promulgated the dogma of the Assumption of Mary, said:

> [T]his truth is based on Sacred Scripture and deeply embedded
> in the minds of the faithful; it has received the approval of
> liturgical worship from the earliest times; it is perfectly in
> keeping with the rest of revealed truth, and has been lucidly
> developed and explained by the studies, the knowledge and
> wisdom of theologians.[268]

"Based on Sacred Scripture" does not normally mean reliant on
one prooftext. And indeed, there are *many* biblical texts revealing
this ancient truth in manifold ways. Let's look at seven examples
of biblical texts or categories of texts among many more we could
consider.

1. The woman of Revelation 12 is Mary.

We have already examined at some length how Mary is the woman of Revelation 12. The chapter presents a remarkably clear depiction of the Mother of God in heaven. Pope St. Pius X elaborates on the Catholic perspective:

> "A great sign," thus the apostle St. John describes a vision
> divinely sent him, appears in the heavens: "A woman clothed
> with the sun, and with the moon under her feet and a crown of
> twelve stars upon her head." Everyone knows that this woman

---

268. *Munificentissimus Deus* 41.

signified the Virgin Mary, the stainless one who brought forth our Head. The Apostle continues: "And, being with child, she cried travailing in birth, and was in pain to be delivered." John therefore saw the Most Holy Mother of God already in eternal happiness, yet travailing in a mysterious childbirth.[269]

Pope Benedict XVI adds:

Also at the heart of the visions that the Book of Revelation unfolds, is the deeply significant vision of the Woman bringing forth a male child and the complementary one of the dragon, already thrown down from heaven but still very powerful.

This woman represents Mary the Mother of the Redeemer, but at the same time she also represents the whole Church, the people of God of all times, the Church which in all ages, with great suffering, brings forth Christ ever anew. And she is always threatened by the dragon's power.[270]

Some might say at this point: "Even if we acknowledge that Revelation 12 depicts Mary in heaven, how would that prove Mary is *bodily* in heaven? There are lots of people in heaven, but they do not have bodies. Why wouldn't we say Mary is just another Christian in heaven?"

Body and Soul

The woman of Revelation 12 is anything but "just another Christian in heaven"! She is revealed in verse 1 as having "the moon under her *feet*, and on her *head* a crown of twelve stars," in verse 5 as giving birth to the Messiah, and in verse 17 as giving birth to all "those who keep the commandments of God and bear testimony

---

269. *Ad Diem Illum Laetissimum* 24.
270. Pope Benedict XVI, General Audience, "John, the Seer of Patmos," Castel Gandolfo, Italy, August 23, 2006.

to Jesus." This depiction of her is in marked contrast to other texts of Scripture, in which saints in heaven are referred to as the "*souls* of those who had been slain*" (Rev. 6:9) or "the *spirits* of just men made perfect" (Heb. 12:23). Those who have gone before us and are in heaven (or purgatory) await the resurrection of their bodies, so it is no wonder that they appear as "souls" and "spirits." Compare this to Mary's depiction in Revelation 12 and it becomes evident that she is an exception to the norm; she is depicted as not just present in heaven, but *bodily* so.

Some might object that the bodily language is figurative. They might cite Luke 16:24, the story of Lazarus and the rich man, in which Jesus depicts the rich man in the torments of hell, saying, "Father Abraham . . . send Lazarus to dip the end of his finger in water and cool my tongue; for I am in anguish in this flame." Just because Jesus uses the terms *finger* and *tongue,* they might say, does not mean that souls in hell have literal body parts.

Most Christians would indeed concur that Luke 16 speaks figuratively of Lazarus having a finger and the rich man having a tongue in the next life, before the resurrection of the body at the end of time. Why wouldn't the same be true for Mary in Revelation 12? Why wouldn't her head and feet also be figurative?

The answer is found, first of all, in the context of the Book of Revelation, which offers a clear contrast between the disembodied "souls of the martyrs" in 6:9 and the embodied Mary in Chapter 12. But the further context of Revelation 12 brings out even more definitive evidence that "the woman" is in heaven, *body* and soul.

2. The ark in heaven is Mary.

Just one verse before Revelation 12 (11:19) and the unveiling of the woman, we find *the Ark of the Covenant* revealed to be in heaven:

> Then God's temple in heaven was opened, and the ark of his covenant was seen within his temple; and there were flashes

of lightning, loud noises, peals of thunder, an earthquake, and heavy hail.

Because of the division between Chapters 11 and 12, some miss the association between these two verses, but Scott Hahn explains why it is critical to understand their connection:

> There were no chapters in John's original Apocalypse; it was one continuous narrative . . .
>
> John has shown us the Ark of the Covenant—and it is a woman.
>
> The Apocalypse might indeed seem strange. Earlier we saw a bride that appeared as a city [Rev. 21:2]; now we see an ark that appears as a woman.[271]

Notice the connection between *the ark* and *the woman*, both referring to Mary, paralleling the connection in Revelation 21:2 between *the bride* and *the city*, both referring to the Church. How does John use these terms elsewhere in his writing? Can we get at what he had in mind when he used them? We believe we can.

We will make the argument that we don't actually need Revelation 12:1 to be able to see that Revelation 11:19 is referring to Mary's Assumption. It certainly illuminates the truth of the matter, but we argue 11:19 can stand on its own given a truly biblical understanding of both *the temple* and *the ark*.

The Temple Revealed

Protestants and Catholics generally concur that *the ark* and *the temple* of Revelation 11:19 do not refer to the ark of Exodus 25 and temple of 1 Kings 6. Protestant scholars generally agree these images are symbolic of a greater fulfillment in the New Covenant;

271. Hahn, *Hail, Holy Queen*, 54–55.

but that is as far as they go.[272] The deeper question that they tend not to address is: *how* do the ark and temple represent the New Covenant? We will contend John 2:19–21 and Revelation 21:22 give us the answer, and in fairly plain terms—at least regarding the temple.

According to John 2:19–21, just after Jesus performed his first miracle through the intercession of his mother (transforming water into wine), he proceeded to the temple, where he made a whip out of cords and cleared out those who were selling oxen, sheep, and pigeons for sacrifices, along with the infamous "money changers." The Lord of the temple had come to clean house, as they say. We can only imagine the drama and the power of the moment. In a word, God got mad that day! But notice the response of the Jews there present. They immediately and, no doubt, nervously, asked Jesus for a sign to demonstrate his authority to do these things. Both Jesus' response and John's commentary are revealing:

> Jesus answered them, "Destroy this temple, and in three days I will raise it up . . ." But he spoke of the temple of his body.

Here Jesus reveals that the true temple of God was not that massive house of worship made with stone and mortar it took the Jews forty-six years to build. To a Jewish people who considered the temple of the Lord to be the center of their universe, that would have been quite disturbing, to say the least. But John's commentary on Jesus' words makes it unmistakable: The temple was Christ's body—the same body that would die and be buried for three days before being resurrected from the dead.

In the light of these plain words from John 2, Revelation 21:22—not insignificantly penned by the same apostle—leaves

272. Johnson, *The Expositor's Bible Commentary*, vol. 12, 510. Johnson says in passing, "[the temple and ark of Revelation 11:19 are] symbolic of the new covenant established by the death of Christ." It is hard to imagine he could be satisfied with this. St. John sees an abstraction in heaven? This does not fit the context of St. John's vision, where he sees angels and men, St. Michael, Jesus, etc.

little room for doubt as to the nature of *the temple* John sees in heaven:

I saw no temple [in heaven], for its temple is the Lord God the Almighty and the lamb.

Obviously, John is not saying there is no temple in heaven *in any sense;* rather, there is no temple in the New Covenant resembling Solomon's rebuilt temple of old. Both represent the dwelling place of God, but one is a building and the other is a lamb—whom John identifies as the God-man Jesus Christ—the "lamb of God who takes away the sins of the world" (John 1:29).

Jesus did not suffer and die as a disembodied spirit. His body "was wounded for our transgressions . . . bruised for our iniquities . . . and with his stripes we are healed" (Isa. 53:5). So what could constitute "the lamb" of Revelation 21:22 that John identifies as *the temple* of the New Covenant along with "the Lord God the almighty?" The conclusion seems inescapable: *the temple* of Revelation 11:19 and 21:22 is Christ, and more specifically Christ's *physical body*, just as Jesus identified it in John 2:18–21.

The Ark Revealed

Now we need to take the next logical step. If John viewed the new and true temple, which is Christ's glorified physical body in heaven, would he not also have viewed the new and true Ark of the Covenant, which is Mary? This seems to fit the context of Revelation 11–12 while harmonizing perfectly with what we saw earlier about Mary's being revealed as the Ark of the Covenant in the wider scope of the New Testament. Moreover, just as the new temple is Christ's physical body, the new ark is *the glorified physical body of Mary*. It was Jesus' physical body that suffered and was raised, and it was Mary's physical body that bore the Lord of heaven and earth. If that body is revealed to be in heaven, it had to have been assumed by God in order to get there.

3. The Ark of the Covenant is prophesied.

> Arise, O Lord, and go to thy resting place, thou and the ark of your might.

Christians generally agree that Psalm 132 is a messianic psalm. It has multiple references to the messiah and the kingdom of Christ that will endure forever within it. For example:

> For the Lord has chosen Zion; he has desired it for his habitation: "This is my resting place for ever; here I will dwell, for I have desired it . . . There I will make a horn to sprout for David; I have prepared a lamp for my anointed" (vs. 13–14, 17).

Moreover, Acts 2:30 specifically cites Psalm 132:11 as referring to Christ:

> The Lord swore to David a sure oath from which he will not turn back: "One of the sons of your body I will set on your throne."

On the literal level, Psalm 132 refers to the then-future building of the ancient temple in Jerusalem that would house the Ark of the Covenant and the presence of God, from which the king of Israel would rule. Christians and Jews could generally agree here. But for Christians the prophetic character of this psalm is most important. Thus, the references to *the temple* and *the ark* have enormous significance. In verses 1–5, the inspired author wrote:

> Remember, O Lord, how . . . [David] swore to the Lord and vowed to the Mighty One of Jacob, "I will not enter my house or get into my bed; I will not give sleep to my eyelids, until I find a place for the Lord, a dwelling place for the Mighty one of Jacob."

While speaking of the future dwelling place of God and the future messianic kingdom the inspired psalmist makes this prophetic statement in verses 7–8, part of which we cited above:

> Let us go to his dwelling place; let us worship at his footstool! Arise, O Lord, and go to thy resting place, thou and the ark of thy might.

From a Christian and prophetic vantage point, the ultimate place of rest and the dwelling place of God is *in Christ* and *in heaven*, not in a temple made with human hands.[273] It is thus no wonder, as Ludwig Ott points out, that

> The Fathers . . . refer passages such as Psalm 131 (132):8 in a typical sense to the mystery of the bodily assumption.[274]

When the Lord was prophesied to "arise . . . and go to [his] resting place," the reference was to the Resurrection. In Psalm 132:7–8, the ark prophesied to go to this same place of rest would be fulfilled in Revelation 11:19 in the true Ark of the Covenant, *Mary*.

4. The ark is holy and powerful.

In this section we will not just cite one text but a series of revealing texts concerning the Ark of the Covenant. First, Exodus 40:34–35:

> Then the cloud covered the tent of meeting, and the glory of the Lord filled the tabernacle. And Moses was not able to enter the tent of meeting, because the cloud abode upon it, and the glory of the Lord filled the tabernacle.

273. Cf. Heb. 4:4–16.
274. Cf. Ott, *Fundamentals of Catholic Dogma*, 209.

As we examine Revelation 11:19 we notice a very definite manifestation of the power and glory of God surrounding the Ark of the Covenant (Mary) and the temple (Jesus) in heaven: "[T]here were flashes of lightning, loud noises, peals of thunder, an earthquake, and heavy hail." It's hard to imagine that the early Jewish Christians presented with these images would not hear the echoes of Old Testament texts such as 2 Samuel 6:1–9—which we examined earlier—where David experienced an extraordinary manifestation of the power of the Old Covenant ark. Or, perhaps 1 Samuel 5–6, where both the Philistines and the Israelites experienced dramatic displays of the glory of God emanating out through the ark. Joshua 3–4, where the "waters of the Jordan were cut off before the ark of the covenant" (4:7) is another powerful example.

But perhaps more immediately, it may well have brought to mind Exodus 40:34–35, in which the glory of God descends upon the newly erected tabernacle (which housed the ark) so powerfully that "Moses [himself] was not able to enter the tent of meeting." It seems that in the Old Testament, the *glory of God* and the *Ark of the Covenant* were resplendently wedded. Where the ark was, there you would find the glory of God.

The intimate relationship between *the tabernacle* and *the ark* is also important to note. When John teaches us about the Incarnation of Christ in his Gospel (1:14) he writes: "And the Word became flesh and dwelt among us . . . we have beheld his glory, glory as of the only-begotten Son from the Father." The Greek word for "dwelt" is *eskenosen*, which means literally "tabernacled"—Christ *tabernacled* among us—connecting Jesus not only to the temple of old, but also to the glorious tabernacle of old.[275] If Jesus Christ, the new and true temple/tabernacle, has ascended into heaven and is now experiencing "the glory which [he] had with [his Father] before the world was made" (John 17:5), it follows that the new and true ark—Mary—would be there as well. Where the glory of God is, there you will find the Ark of the Covenant.

---

275. Robertson, *Word Pictures in the New Testament*, 187.

5. The king calls for the ark.

> So David went and brought up the ark of God from the house
> of Obededom to the city of David with rejoicing (2 Sam. 6:12).

Examining the truth of Mary as the Ark of the Covenant confirms the ancient axiom of St. Augustine: "The New Testament is hidden in the Old, and the Old Testament is manifested in the New." Mary's Assumption is again brought into focus when we consider the relationship between the king of Israel, the Kingdom of Israel, and the Ark of the Covenant.

In 2 Samuel 6, we discover King David's first order of business after having conquered Jerusalem: With the intention of making it the capital of Israel and the "dwelling place" of God, he called for the Ark of the Covenant to be brought forth. Scripture tells us it was brought into "the city of David" in glorious procession and with a huge feast—enough to feed "the whole multitude of Israel, both men and women" (2 Sam. 6:19).

How fitting indeed that the first order of business of the true "King of kings and Lord of lords" of Revelation 19:16, after being established in his kingdom through his Resurrection and Ascension into heaven, would be to call for the true Ark of the Covenant to be brought into *the heavenly city* and *the heavenly banquet* containing every blessing—enough to feed the entire Church, "the Israel of God." Mary's Assumption is the fulfillment of the events of 2 Samuel that, however wondrous, are but a mere shadow. King Jesus has come fully into his kingdom and brought the ark with him.

6. Mary is incorruptible.

> This Jesus . . . you crucified and killed . . . But God raised him
> up . . . because it was not possible for him to be held by [death].
> For David said concerning him . . . "For you will not abandon
> my soul to Hades, nor let your Holy One see corruption (Acts
> 2:23–27)."

Though Peter will go on to make clear in verses 29–32 that he is speaking about a prophecy from Psalm 16:10, in which David "foresaw and spoke of the Resurrection of the Christ" (Acts 2:31), this text could also be applied to Mary. It was because of Christ's unique holiness that God would not allow his body to see corruption. By this principle, all of the arguments for Mary's sinlessness could also be applied to her Assumption. According to the prophecy of Psalm 16:10, corruption is not possible where there is sinlessness.

In *Munificentissimus Deus* 26, Pope Pius XII speaks of another way the scriptures get at Mary being "incorruptible":

> Often there are theologians and preachers who, following in the footsteps of the holy Fathers, have been rather free in their use of events and expressions taken from Sacred Scripture to explain their belief in the Assumption. Thus, to mention only a few of the texts rather frequently cited in this fashion, some have employed the words of the psalmist: "Arise, O Lord, into your resting place: you and the ark, which you have sanctified" [references Psalm 132:8]; and have looked upon the Ark of the Covenant, built of incorruptible wood and placed in the Lord's temple, as a type of the most pure body of the Virgin Mary, preserved and exempt from all the corruption of the tomb and raised up to such glory in heaven. Treating of this subject, they also describe her as the Queen entering triumphantly into the royal halls of heaven and sitting at the right hand of the divine Redeemer [references Psalm 45:10–14ff].

In a moment we will see the significance of our Holy Father's use of Psalm 45 and reference to Mary as "Queen . . . sitting at the right hand of the divine Redeemer." But the idea of the "incorruptible" ark is where we want to focus now. This idea comes from a pre-Christian Jewish tradition that claimed the acacia wood of the Ark of the Covenant mandated by divine commandment was "incorruptible." According to the ancient Jewish historian Josephus, who was a contemporary of the apostles,

There was also an ark made, sacred to God, of wood that was naturally strong, and could not be corrupted.[276]

That this tradition was well understood among the Jews at the time of Christ and slightly before can be seen in the Septuagint—translated a little more than a hundred years before Christ—and its translation of the description of the Ark of the Covenant in Exodus 25:10–11:

> And thou shalt make the ark of testimony of incorruptible wood; the length of two cubits and a half, and the breadth of a cubit and a half, and the height of a cubit and a half. And thou shalt gild it with pure gold, thou shalt gild it within and without.

The ark became a perfect symbol of Mary's sinlessness and therefore incorruptibility. Not only was its wood "incorruptible," but it was gilded with "pure gold," a further symbol of Mary's unique purity. If the type—acacia wood overlain with gold—was so pure and incorruptible, how much more would its fulfillment be? To say Mary could have sinned and her body corrupted in the grave would be incongruent with what we know of the Ark of the Covenant.

7. Where there's a king there's a queen.

> Your divine throne endures forever and ever. Your royal scepter is a scepter of equity; you love righteousness and hate wickedness. Therefore, God, your God, has anointed you with the oil of gladness above your fellows . . . at your right hand stands the queen in gold of Ophir (Ps. 45:6–9) .

Catholic readers will recognize this text not only because of Pius XII's reference above, but as part of the readings proclaimed at Mass on the Feast of the Assumption, celebrated on August 15.

276. *The Antiquities of the Jews* III, 6, 5.

All should recognize the first part of this reading, as it is quoted in Hebrews 1:8–9, confirming its prophetic and messianic nature.

As for its relationship to Mary's Assumption, we first point out the setting of Psalm 45: the wedding of the king, most likely Solomon. The princess is being brought before the king with "daughters of kings" as "ladies of honor" in the procession.[277] The "queen" in gold of Ophir represents the queen mother who stands at the king's "right hand," which is a symbol of power and authority.

We will revisit this text in more detail in Chapter 14, when we examine Mary's role as "Queen of queens" in the kingdom of God, but for now we note that Hebrews 1 sets the context of our Lord being established in his eternal kingdom and having "sat down at the right hand of the Majesty on high" in verse 3. With the king on his throne in the kingdom, we would expect nothing less than his queen mother to be standing at his right hand in her glorified body and gloriously clothed in royal apparel.

---

277. Cf. Psalm 45:9.

II
ANSWERING OBJECTIONS

After presenting positive proofs for the Assumption of Mary, one always has to be ready for the biblical and historical arguments often used against it. These objections can be broken down into four sections: The first two contain arguments from biblical passages, the third section is an argument from history, and the fourth, reminiscent of what we saw when we considered the Perpetual Virginity, questions whether the Assumption really matters.

OBJECTION 1: No one has ascended to heaven.

> No one has ascended into heaven but he who descended from heaven, the Son of man (John 3:13).

This text is usually cited by the Christian or quasi-Christian sects that deny the natural immortality of the soul, e.g., Seventh-day Adventists, Christadelphians, Jehovah's Witnesses, and the Iglesia Ni Cristo; however, some Fundamentalists use it, too. Here St. John was writing at a time likely long after Mary had ended her earthly life. So if he said that "no one has ascended into heaven," the argument goes, that would include Mary.[278]

There are at least four reasons why this text does not contradict the Assumption of Mary:

1. John was quoting words our Lord had spoken around A.D. 30. At that time Mary was still alive on earth.

---

278. One example from the Christadelphians can be found here at www.christadelphia.org/pamphlet/p_mary.htm.

2. Jesus could not have been saying that no one will *ever* be taken to heaven except him. If that's the case, then what is all this Christianity stuff about? You know, heaven and all?[279]

3. One could also interpret John 3:13 as referring to Christ's unique Ascension to heaven. The key here would be the word *ascended*. Mary did not ascend; she was *assumed*. Jesus ascended by his own divine power as he prophesied he would in John 2:19–21: "Destroy this temple, and in three days I will raise it up . . . he spoke of the temple of his body." Mary was powerless to raise herself; she had to be assumed into heaven. In a similar way, all of the elect will be assumed into heaven, so to speak, at the time of the resurrection of the body, as opposed to Christ, who alone ascended into heaven.

4. There are a couple of nuances in this text that many miss. According to St. Irenaeus in the second century, John wrote his Gospel with an emphasis on demonstrating the errors of the fathers of Gnosticism and the heresiarch Cerinthus in particular, who—among his many errors—denied the divinity of Christ.[280] Thus, in quoting these words from Jesus he intended to demonstrate that "the Son of man descended" from heaven as the "only begotten Son," a divine person, sharing his Father's nature.[281] In other words, "the Son of man" is the same *person* who was eternally with the Father in heaven and who descended to the earth in the Incarnation.[282]

---

279. Even Jehovah's Witnesses believe that the 144,000 chosen ones will rule and reign with Christ in the "heavenly realm." Most would agree that Jesus is not making a statement that no one will ever ascend into heaven. Christadelphians and a few similar sects would be excepted. They believe no one will ever go to heaven except Jesus; the rest will be on earth forever. But most importantly, the text never says never as far as the future is concerned.

280. *Against Heresies* III, 11, 1.

281. Cf. John 3:16.

282. St. Thomas Aquinas, *Commentary on the Gospel of St. John*, Part 1, 467–469. Thomas warns against the error of Valentinus, who said "the Son of man" descending from heaven meant he received his body from heaven and not from the Virgin Mary;

Moreover, his point was that even while Christ walked the earth with his disciples in Galilee he was in possession of heaven, experiencing the beatific vision, as true God and true man.

His human body would not be glorified until after the Resurrection, but, according to John, Christ could already "see" the Father while on earth.[283] Thus, while we human beings must "walk by faith, not by sight" (2 Cor. 5:7), Christ did not have "faith;" he had the "sight" of God that brings about "knowledge."[284] Thus, Pope Pius XII would declare:

> For hardly was [Christ] conceived in the womb of the Mother of God, when he began to enjoy the Beatific Vision. [285]

Consequently, Jesus, in his human nature, had already "ascended into" or possessed heaven—the beatific vision being the essence of what heaven is—even from his mother's womb.[286] Because he was and is both God and man, he could say that he had already "ascended" to heaven precisely because as God "he" had brought about this great mystery by his own power. Our Lord's words and

therefore, it was purely spiritual, not material. "And therefore to indicate that he is said to have come down in this way, because he assumed a [human] nature, he said, the Son of man came down, i.e., insofar as he become Son of man" in the Incarnation.

283 Cf. John 5:19. Jesus says he "can do nothing on his own . . . but only what he sees the Father doing."

284. Cf. John 11:41–42. When Jesus prays for Lazarus, he says, "I knew that you always hear me, but I have said this on account of the people . . . that they may believe." Jesus has knowledge; "the people" have faith.

285. *Mystici Corporis* 75.

286. The possession of God in the beatific vision is the core of what Scripture reveals heaven to be in texts such as 1 Corinthians 13:12, Revelation 22:4, Matthew 5:8, and as the CCC teaches in 163 and 1028. CCC 473 says Christ had "intimate and immediate knowledge . . . of his Father," and it cites St. Gregory the Great defending the idea of Christ having the beatific vision even while he walked the earth. When the *Catechism* uses the language of "intimate and immediate knowledge," it means Christ would not have to believe in God through the mediation of images as human persons do in this life; rather, he would have direct and immediate knowledge of God, which is the essence of what the beatific vision is.

this text have nothing to do with whether someone would, years after Christ, be assumed into heaven or not.

OBJECTION 2: No one other than Christ has been bodily resurrected.

> For as in Adam all die, so also in Christ shall all be made alive. But each in his own order: Christ the first fruits, then at his coming those who belong to Christ (1 Cor. 15:22–23).

> For the Lord himself will descend from heaven with a cry of command, with the archangel's call, and with the sound of the trumpet of God. And the dead in Christ will rise first (1 Thess. 4:16).

In the minds of many Protestants these texts could not be any clearer. "No one will be bodily resurrected until Christ comes again at the end of time!"[287]

This contention is reminiscent of Protestants who claim Mary could not be sinless because 1 John 1:8 and Romans 3:23 say: "If we say we have no sin, we deceive ourselves," and, "All have sinned and fall short of the glory of God." Yet just as there are exceptions to the universal norm that all have sinned, there can be exceptions to the norm that no one will be bodily resurrected until the end of time when Christ comes again. There are four key points to consider with regard to exceptions:

1. There are exceptions to other general theological norms in Scripture. Consider Matthew 3:5–6: "Then went out to [St. John the Baptist] Jerusalem and all Judea and all the region about the Jordan, and they were baptized by him." John the Baptist did not literally baptize everyone in those areas. This text was never intended to be taken in such a strict, literal sense; it simply means he baptized a lot of folks. I think we

---

287. Geisler and MacKenzie, *Roman Catholics and Evangelicals*, 311, 314.

could all agree that *at least* Herod, Herodias, and her daughter, who conspired to put John to death, were exceptions.[288]

2. Hebrews 9:27 declares, "It is appointed for men to die *once*, and after that comes judgment." Yet in many places in Scripture we see exceptions to this norm by way of resurrections from the dead. Not only do we see Elijah, Elisha, Jesus, St. Peter, and St. Paul raising the dead in Scripture, but after Jesus' death, "the tombs also were opened, and many bodies of the saints who had fallen asleep were raised, and [came] out of the tombs" (Matt. 27:52–53). These people presumably died at least twice! We also have the examples of those who will be alive when Jesus comes again and so will never die at all.[289]

3. We have examples of other "assumptions" in Scripture. Enoch and Elijah were taken up bodily into heaven in a manner out of the ordinary.[290] The "two witnesses" of Revelation 11:12 will also be bodily assumed into heaven quite dramatically before the Second Coming of Christ.[291] If we already have all of these exceptions to the norm, God could certainly do something out of the ordinary regarding his mother without contradicting Scripture.

4. We know Mary *is* such an exception because, among other reasons, she is depicted as having been assumed into heaven in Revelation 12:1–2, 5:

---

288. Cf. Matt. 14:1–11. See also Luke 7:30.
289. Cf. 1 Thess. 4:16
290. Cf. Gen. 5:24; Heb. 11:5; 2 Kgs 2:11.
291. Some believe these two witnesses were Enoch and Elijah. Most likely, these two represent *Moses* and Elijah. According to the apocryphal book, *The Assumption of Moses*, Moses was also assumed into heaven after having died. This book is actually quoted in Jude, verse 9. One thing is clear in the text: Whoever these two witnesses will be, they seem destined to be bodily assumed into heaven as exceptions to the above-mentioned texts.

And a great sign appeared *in heaven*, a woman clothed with the sun, with the moon under her feet, and on her head a crown of twelve stars; she was with child and she cried out in her pangs of birth, in anguish for delivery . . . she brought forth a male child, one who is to rule all the nations with a rod of iron, but her child was caught up to God and to his throne.

OBJECTION 3: History doesn't support it.

When we examine the biblical objections to the Assumption of Mary, we find them to be both few and anemic. None of the biblical texts used actually deny the dogma. Perhaps this is why, even from "Bible-believing Christians," the most often heard objection to the Assumption today is an argument from history. Because there is no *written* evidence for the Assumption until many centuries after the fact, they claim, the Assumption must be a fictional story unworthy of credence. Lorraine Boettner makes the claim:

> All that the Roman Church pretends to have from an early date supporting this doctrine is an apocalyptic legend, contained in a book, *De Gloria Martyrum,* written by Gregory of Tours, southern France, in the sixth century. On the face of it it is a mere fairy tale.[292]

John Ankerberg and John Weldon make the further claim that the Assumption of Mary was practically forced upon the Church in 1950, with the dogma being contested by scholars even up to and during Vatican II.[293]

---

292. Boettner, *Roman Catholicism*, p. 163.
293. Cf. Ankerberg and Weldon, *Catholics and Protestants—Do They Now Agree?*, 258–260. The authors present a list of dates when various "unbiblical doctrines and practices" were either "1) first introduced, 2) formulated, 3) adopted by council, or 4) proclaimed by a pope." The list contains many errors, but among the items on the list is: "1950—The bodily assumption and personal corporeal presence of the Virgin in heaven was proclaimed by Pope Pius XII." This is true enough. And even though the authors do assert, "The first observance of the Feast of the Assumption began"

The more serious and informed Protestant will say this doctrine was "invented" in the fifth or sixth century.[294] But the argument is essentially this: There is nothing in history to suggest that Christians of the first four centuries (at least) believed in the Assumption. How is a Catholic to respond?

The Evidence That Demands a Verdict

The doctrine of the Assumption of Mary began with an historical event that is alluded to in Scripture and has been believed in the Church for 2,000 years. It was passed down in the oral Tradition of the Church and developed over the centuries, but it was always believed by the Catholic faithful.

It must be kept in mind that from a Catholic *and biblical* perspective, we simply do not need everything we believe to be proven by written evidence alone. It would be over 300 years before anything about the life of Abraham even began to be written down, yet we accept what was written as true.[295] The Church existed for decades before the Gospels were written, but that did not mean the Christians of these early years did not have the Faith. In what scholars believe to be the first book of the New Testament, written about twenty years after the Resurrection, Paul wrote:

> And we also thank God constantly for this, that when you received the word of God which you heard from us, you accepted it not as the word of men but as what it really is, the word of God, which is at work in you believers (1 Thess. 2:13).

A few months later, Paul would pen a second letter to these same Thessalonians, and write:

in 819 (though it was actually earlier—see below), they go on to state, "At Vatican II the bodily assumption of Mary was contested." The authors make it seem as if the Assumption of Mary was never *really* believed by the Church until 1950, and even after that it was disputed.

294. Cf. White, *Mary—Another Redeemer?*, 53.

295. Cf. Sutcliffe, *A Catholic Commentary on Sacred Scripture*, 164.

So, then, brethren, stand firm and hold to the traditions which you were taught by us, either by word of mouth or by letter.

So Scripture itself instructs us clearly not to insist on the written word alone. But if we are going to consider the written evidence for the Assumption of Mary, let us examine the facts:

1. Archaeology reveals two tombs of Mary that still exist today, one in Jerusalem and one in Ephesus. The two tombs are explained by the fact that Mary had lived in both places. But what is inexplicable apart from the Assumption of Mary is the fact that there is no body in either tomb. And there are no relics. Anyone who would peruse early Church history knows that Christian belief in the communion of saints and the sanctity of the body—in radical contrast to the Gnostic disdain for "the flesh"—led early Christians to seek out with the greatest fervor relics from the bodies of great saints. Cities, and later, religious orders, would fight over the bones of great saints. This is one reason why we have relics of the apostles and so many of the greatest saints and martyrs in history. Yet never was there a single relic of Mary's body? As revered as Mary was, this would be very strange, except for the fact of the Assumption of her body.[296]

2. To get a true sense of the antiquity of this dogma, we must travel back more than 1,400 years to the writing of St. Gregory of Tours mentioned by Boettner above. In his *Eight Books of Miracles*, in 590, he recorded:

   The course of this life having been completed by Blessed Mary, when now she would be called from the world, all the Apostles came together from their various regions to her house. And when they had heard that she was about to be taken from the world, they kept watch together with

---

296. Cf. Keating, *Catholicism and Fundamentalism*, 273–274.

her. And behold, the Lord Jesus came with His angels, and taking her soul, He gave it over to the Angel Michael and withdrew. At daybreak, however, the Apostles took up her body on a bier and placed it in a tomb; and they guarded it, expecting the Lord to come. And behold, again the Lord stood by them; and the holy body having been received, He commanded that it be taken in a cloud into paradise; where now, rejoined to the soul, [Mary] rejoices with the Lord's chosen ones and is in the enjoyment of the good of an eternity that will never end.[297]

So much for the theory that this teaching was invented in 1950! But what about Boettner's claim—which, along with similar myths, has become widespread today among Protestant apologists[298]—that it was unknown until the sixth century when Gregory wrote the passage above? Fr. Michael O'Carroll helps us present a Catholic response:

We have known for some time that there were wide-spread "Transitus Stories" that date from the sixth century that teach Mary's glorious Assumption. It was the promulgation of the dogma of the Assumption by Pope Pius XII that re-kindled interest in these stories of the end of Mary's life. In 1955, Fr. A. A. Wenger published *L'Assomption*.[299]

Fr. O'Carroll goes on to document the fact that Fr. Wenger found a Greek manuscript that verified what scholars had previously believed to be true. Because there were whole families of manuscripts from different areas of the world in the sixth century that

297. Jurgens, vol. 3, 306.
298. Geisler and MacKenzie, *Roman Catholics and Evangelicals*, 316. These two authors continue along the same lines as Boettner, claiming "the idea of the bodily assumption of Mary is first expressed in certain transitus-narratives of the fifth and sixth centuries," citing Ott's *Fundamentals of Catholic Dogma*, 209–210. Both Boettner and Ott were writing before some of the newer discoveries concerning the written evidence for the antiquity of the Assumption of Mary.
299. O'Carroll, *Theotokos*, 59.

told a similar story of Mary's Assumption, there had to be previous manuscripts from which everyone received their data. Fr. Wenger discovered one of these earlier manuscripts, believed to be the source later used by John of Thessalonica in the sixth century in his teaching on the Assumption. Fr. O'Carroll continues:

> Some years later, M. Haibach-Reinisch added to the dossier an early version of Pseudo-Melito, the most influential text in use in the Latin Church. This could now, it was clear, be dated earlier than the sixth century . . .V. Arras claimed to have found an Ethiopian version of it which he published in 1973; its similarity to the Irish text gave the latter new status. In the same year M. Van Esbroeck brought out a Gregorian version, which he had located in Tiflis, and another, a Pseudo-Basil, in the following year, found in Mount Athos.
>
> Much still remains to be explored. The Syriac fragments have increased importance, being put as far back as the third century by one commentator. The whole story will eventually be placed earlier, probably in the second century.[300]

This is significant. Recently discovered Syriac fragments of stories about the Assumption of Mary have been dated as early as the third century. And there are undoubtedly more manuscripts to be found. It must be remembered that when we are talking about these "Transitus Stories," we are not only talking about very ancient manuscripts and fragments of manuscripts, but we are talking about two different "families" of manuscripts written in nine languages.[301] They all agree on Mary's Assumption and they presuppose a story that was already widely known.

If we consider that the New Testament Gospels themselves were written some thirty to sixty years after the events they recounted, and the earliest fragments we have from the Gospels

300. Ibid.
301. Ibid.

date from about ninety years (remarkably close for ancient documents) after the fact, even the skeptical must admit that third-century fragments about the Assumption make the Catholic position
compelling. If fragment dating is pushed back to the second century, there simply could be no doubt that the Assumption was a
first-century tradition.[302]

Gnostic Fable or Christian Truth?

What about those who claim the Assumption of Mary is nothing
more than a Gnostic fable? Or those who claim the historical
narratives about the Assumption of Mary were condemned by
Pope Gelasius I? James White, for example, goes so far as to claim:

> Basically, the first appearance of the idea of the Bodily
> Assumption of Mary is found in a source that was condemned
> by the then-bishop of Rome, Gelasius I! The irony is striking:
> what was defined by the bishop of Rome as heresy at the end
> of the fifth century becomes dogma itself in the middle of the
> twentieth![303]

Mr. White's reasoning fails for several reasons.

1. Even if it were a papal document, *Decretum Gelasianum* would
   not be a "definition" by the bishop of Rome declaring the
   Assumption of Mary to be heresy, as White errantly asserts.
   The document does not make such a claim. It gives us
   a rather long list of titles of apocryphal books after having
   listed the accepted books of the Bible. That's all. One of these
   titles declared to be "apocryphal" is referred to as: "Liber qui
   appellatur Transitus, id est Assumptio sanctae Mariae," which

---

302. Cf. Comfort and Barret, *The Text of the Earliest New Testament Greek Manuscripts*, 23.
"The earliest known New Testament manuscript is P52, a fragment of John's Gospel.
[It] was dated by various paleographers to the first half of the second century—even
to the first quarter."

303. White, *Mary—Another Redeemer?*, 54.

translates as "A book which is called, 'Having been taken up, that is, the Assumption of Holy Mary.'" White evidently thought this document condemns as untrue the doctrine of the Assumption of Mary. But it did not. As a matter of history, this document does not condemn any doctrines in the books it lists at all; it declares the books themselves to be apocryphal and therefore not part of the canon of Scripture. This would be something akin to the Church's rejection of *The Assumption of Moses* and *The Book of Enoch* as apocryphal works. The fact that these works are apocryphal does not preclude St. Jude from quoting both of them in Sacred Scripture.[304] Because a work is declared apocryphal or even condemned does not mean that there is no truth at all to be found in it.

2. There is real question among scholars today as to whether what is popularly called the *Decretum Gelasianum* was actually written by Pope Gelasius.[305] It was probably written in the sixth century (Pope Gelasius died in the late fifth century) in Italy or Gaul and was most likely not a papal work at all. It was falsely attributed to several different popes to give it credibility and acceptance. This was a common practice in the early centuries of the Christian era.[306]

3. If the teaching of the Assumption had genuinely been condemned by the pope, great saints and defenders of orthodoxy such as Gregory and later John Damascene would not have taught it. Further, we would have found other writers condemning this teaching as it became more and more popular throughout the world. And we certainly would not see the

304. Vv. 9, 14.

305. *The Oxford Dictionary of the Christian Faith*, 462. Some of the manuscripts claim Pope Damasus (r. 366–384) as the author, some claim Pope Hormisdas (514–523). The work is "a private compilation which was composed in Italy (but not at Rome) in the early sixth century. Other scholars . . . think it originated in Gaul." See also Ernst von Dobschütz, *Das Decretum Gelasianum de libris recipiendis et non recipiendis in kritischem Text herausgegeben und untersucht von Ernst von Dobschütz*.

306. Ibid.

Assumption celebrated in the liturgy as we do as early as the fifth century in Palestine, Gaul in the sixth,[307] universally in the East in the seventh century, and in the West in the eighth century.[308] Far from supporting the idea of dissension over the Assumption, this reveals just how widespread the teaching truly was.

Why didn't the early Fathers write about the Assumption? The most obvious reason would be that since Gnostics, who were among the main enemies of the Faith in the early centuries of the Christian era, *agreed with the Church* on that belief, there would have been no need to defend it. Much of early Christian literature was apologetic in nature, dealing with problem areas in the Church that needed to be addressed. But there is simply no record of anyone disagreeing on the matter of the Assumption. Likewise we don't find works from the early Fathers on Jesus' celibacy— because there was universal agreement on this topic, too.

Even so, it is not as though there was no written evidence to support the Assumption either. We now have what some believe to be a fourth-century homily on the prophet Simeon and the Blessed Virgin Mary by Timothy, a priest of Jerusalem, which asserts Mary is "immortal to the present time through him who had his abode in her and who assumed and raised her above the higher regions."[309] Evidently, there was disagreement in the circulating stories of the Assumption of Mary as to whether she was taken up alive or after having died. But whether or not she was assumed was not in question. Indeed, the Church even to this day has not decided *definitively* whether Mary died or not.[310]

---

307. *The Catholic Encyclopedia*, vol. 2, 6.
308. *The Oxford Dictionary of the Christian Church*, 117.
309. Quoted in O'Carroll, *Theotokos*, 388. The author states that there is disagreement among scholars as to the dating of this homily. "Fr. M. Jugie, A.A. opting for the fourth century against Dom Bernard Capelle, O.S.B., an eminent liturgical historian, who defends the sixth or seventh centuries as the probable time."
310. The teaching of the ordinary magisterium of the Church is that Mary died and so we give religious assent to this teaching. Pope Pius XII mentions Mary's death nine times in *Munificentissimus Deus* alone (17, 20, 21, 29, 35, 39, and 40). For centuries, the

The Witness of St. Epiphanius

The work of St. Epiphanius, great fourth-century bishop and defender of orthodoxy, gives us more insights into the antiquity of
the Assumption. In his classic *Panarion* ("Bread Box") or *Refutation
of All Heresies*, he offers a point-blank endorsement of the dogma:

> Like the bodies of the saints, however, [Mary] has been held in
> honor for her character and understanding. And if I should say
> anything more in her praise, she is like Elijah, who was virgin
> from his mother's womb, always remained so, and was taken up,
> but has not seen death.[311]

By comparing her to Elijah, Epiphanius indicates that Mary *was
taken up* bodily, just as the Church continues to teach 1,600 years
later.

Epiphanius was not entirely sure whether Mary actually died.
James White quotes him as writing "For her end no one knows,"[312]
suggesting that this argues against popular belief in her Assumption. But White does not give the full context:

> The holy virgin may have died and been buried—her falling
> asleep was with honor, her death in purity, her crown in
> virginity. Or she may have been put to death—as the Scripture

Church celebrated "the Feast of the Dormition" of our Lady before it was called the
Assumption. And it certainly seems fitting that Mary would be fully conformed to the
death of her son through her own experience of death. However, if one holds to the
more ancient date of the homily of Timothy of Jerusalem, and if we add the fourth-
century evidence from Epiphanius we will see below, we also have ancient evidence
for belief among Christians that Mary never died. Theologically, one could argue that
Mary was already *spiritually* fully conformed to the death of her son without dying
herself. Further, the fact that believers who are alive when Jesus comes again will never
die, according to 1 Thessalonians 4:16, does not mean that they too could not be "fully
conformed to the death of the Son of God." Moreover, one must consider that if, as
Hebrews 11:5 records, Enoch could have been assumed "so that he did not experience
death," it could be argued as fitting that Mary should be assumed without dying as
well. Thanks be to God for the Church that separates the wheat from the chaff!

311. *Panarion* 79, 5,1.
312. White, *Mary—Another Redeemer?*, 51

says, "And a sword shall pierce through her soul"—her fame
is among the martyrs and her holy body, by which light rose
on the world, [rests] amid blessings. Or she may have remained
alive, for God is not incapable of doing whatever he wills. No
one knows her end.[313]

The fact that Epiphanius says Mary may have "died and been
buried" says nothing of the Assumption. We say in the creed that
Christ was "crucified, died, and was buried"—this does not mean
he was not resurrected. That Epiphanius holds out the possibility
of her physical martyrdom does not exclude the Assumption either. Epiphanius is simply speculating about whether or not Mary
died. But whether she did or not, he insists, she would have been
subsequently *taken up*. It would also seem strange that he would
say her body is "amid blessings" if he did not believe it was taken
up into heaven.

The Most Important Thing

What is absolutely crucial for us to consider here is that among
all of this *documentary* (written) evidence of the Assumption being
taught as early as the third century—and it may well yet be moved
back further—we find not a single condemnation of this teaching
by any Christian writer.[314] And when one considers that the oral
tradition always precedes the written, this ancient written evidence becomes all the more important. Gnosticism is condemned
in volume upon volume of Christian polemics, but never the Assumption of Mary. When Helvidius, Jovinian, and others denied
the Perpetual Virginity of Mary in the fourth century, for example, they were quickly and decisively denounced. Why is it that we
find absolute silence when it comes to anyone condemning the
Assumption? The only attempt by modern Protestant polemicists

313. *Panarion* 78, 23, 8.
314. Pope St. John Paul II, "The Church Believes in Mary's Assumption," General Audience,
      July 2, 1997. John Paul says the *Transitus Mariae* accounts may have their origin in "the
      second and third centuries."

to claim a condemnation comes from the *Decretum Gelasianum*—one which, even if it were authentic (it is most likely *not*), does not condemn the Assumption of Mary as a doctrine in the first place.

Perhaps the Anglican writer H.S. Box sums up our thoughts best when it comes to the history of the dogma of the Assumption:

> It is indeed true that apocryphal legends were in early times associated with Mary's death, burial and resurrection, but as Thomas Mozley pointed out in his *Reminiscences of Oriel College and the Oxford Movement* (1882), the belief was never founded on the story of the Assumption. "The story was founded on the belief, and testifies to the fact of that belief."

> Although the apocryphal stories do not form the basis for belief in the Assumption, and provide no certain argument for the truth of the doctrine, their antiquity is an indication of an early tradition that the end of our Lady's life on earth was unusual, and that her body was saved from corruption. Of the early stories of the Assumption it may be said that all sought to supply the known fact with unknown details. The faithful believed that Mary is body and soul in glory. Writers set to work to guess the rest of the story.[315]

OBJECTION 4: Who cares?

The final objection to the Assumption of Mary, which is actually another category of objections, is one we saw before when we considered the Perpetual Virginity of Mary. This objection doesn't involve scriptural or historical arguments but rather just a claim that it really doesn't matter.

Well, in fact, it does matter, for four crucial reasons.

---

315. Mascall and Box, *The Blessed Virgin Mary*, 89–95.

1. It bears repeating that the Assumption of Mary is a dogma of our Catholic faith that if anyone knowingly rejects, then as with the rejection of any other infallible teaching of the Church, he imperils his soul. Recall CCC 89:

> There is an organic connection between our spiritual life and the dogmas. Dogmas are lights along the path of faith; they illuminate it and make it secure. Conversely, if our life is upright, our intellect and heart will be open to welcome the light shed by the dogmas of faith.

All of the dogmas of the Faith affect our spiritual lives and our spiritual lives will either help or hinder us with regard to our openness to receive the dogmas. This dogma is no different.

"Okay, fine," says a Protestant, "You're Catholic. But I'm not. Is that all you have? Why should the Assumption matter to *me*?"

2. In the Assumption we see, in a particular way, Mary revealed as "our hope," as Catholics call her in the "Hail, Holy Queen" prayer. Mary is our "hope" inasmuch as we see in her all of God's promises about our final salvation, resurrection, and glorification fulfilled in a real human person. She serves as a certain sign of hope for God's faithful.

Mary is also rightly viewed as "hope of all humanity" because in her we see the glory of the Church. As Mary is the bride of the Holy Spirit, the Church is the bride of Christ. In the life of the Mother of God we see the faithfulness of God to his bride. God truly preserved his bride from "all spot and wrinkle" and brought her home to him in heaven.[316] Like Mary, the Church is Virgin and Mother, free at her core from all "spot and wrinkle."[317] She is being prepared for her own

---

316. Cf. Eph. 5:25–27; John 14:1–6.
317. We make a distinction here between individuals in the Church who sin and the

glorious assumption, if you will, at the end of time.[318] In Mary, we see fully realized what awaits the bride of Christ. In Mary, our mother, the virtue of hope is both birthed and nurtured.

"Wait just a minute," say Protestants. "Mary isn't our hope; *Jesus* is. Scripture says, 'Christ in you, the hope of glory' (Col. 1:27).[319] All you have said is meaningless."

The Catholic response is to agree, at least in part: Yes, Jesus is our hope. Nothing and no one can add to the hope that is ultimately in Christ alone. But this does not exclude the biblical notion that members of the body of Christ (not just Mary) can serve as models of hope for each other. The hope they communicate is only communicated because they are *in Christ* as members of *his body*, but that in no way minimizes the importance of that communicated gift.[320]

Another way to look at this is to say Jesus is our hope because he made salvation possible for us; Mary is our hope in the

spotless Bride of Christ. This is why the CCC 827 says the Church is "at once holy and always in need of purification."

318. 1 Thessalonians 4:16 depicts an "assumption" of sorts for the Church on earth. Revelation 21:1–2 tells us the Church glorious will also "descend" from heaven. Of course, both of these texts describe the Second Coming of Christ, which is beyond words. "Eye has not seen, ear has not heard, nor has it entered into the hearts of men, what God has for those who love him" (1 Cor. 2:9).

319. Cf. Hunt, *A Woman Rides the Beast*, 440.

320. There is no contradiction here. Christ as our "one teacher" of Matthew 23:8 does not exclude the possibility that we can have other "teachers" (see James 3:1; Eph. 4:11) who cooperate with and participate in Christ's mission. The same can be said for Christ as our "pastor," "bishop," "intercessor," and "mediator" (see 1 Pet. 2:25; 1 Tim. 2:5). There are many who are called to participate in the "pastorate" and "bishopric" of Christ (see Eph. 4:11; 1 Tim. 3:1). And all Christians are called to participate in the intercession and mediation of Christ because the Church is "his body, the fullness of [Christ] who fills all in all" (Eph. 1:23). We can "intercede" or "mediate" grace through prayer for one another because of Christ who is in us (see Gal. 2:20). Nothing and no one *adds* to Christ as our unique teacher, pastor, bishop, or intercessor. However, Christ has chosen to include his faithful in his mission through various gifts and ministries.

sense that she demonstrates to us in her life and person that salvation is not only possible, but has been made actual in a human being.

As we mentioned at the outset of this book, at the most sacred moment in all of salvation history, while he was accomplishing the Redemption of the world on the cross, Jesus exhorted John and all of us to behold his mother (John 19:27). If Jesus could command us to look to Mary at *that* moment, then obviously looking to Mary does not mean looking away from Christ. Indeed, in looking to Mary (and all the saints) we see Christ at work. On the cross our Lord and savior gifted us with two things that he knew he could never be for us: *a perfect mother* and *a perfect disciple of Christ*, in whom we can find and experience the hope that is necessary for salvation.

3. In the abstract, we can have hope without Mary. We don't strictly need anyone but God in Christ for salvation. God could save us all by himself, no doubt. But the truth is: God has freely chosen to save us through the instruments of one another. Paul refutes the notion that "all we need is God" in 1 Corinthians 12:21: "The eye cannot say to the hand, 'I have no need of you,' nor again the head to the feet, 'I have no need of you.'" And why? Because we are called to be instruments to bring faith and salvation to others:

> What then is Apollos? What is Paul? Servants through whom you believed, as the Lord assigned to each (1 Cor. 3:5).

> Take heed to yourself and to your teaching; hold to that, for by so doing you will save both yourself and your hearers (1 Tim. 4:16).

How does this apply to Mary's Assumption? It is one thing to know the dogmas of the faith in the abstract; it is another to actually see them fulfilled in a disciple of Jesus Christ who has gone before us. That enlivens hope within us. And according to

Scripture, the virtue of hope serves as "the anchor of our souls" and "saves us."[321] It empowers us to "hold fast to our profession" and keeps us from despair and the bitterness through which many are "defiled."[322] It is critical for our spiritual lives.

4. The Blessed Mother, and in particular her Assumption, shows us that sanctity is something attainable in *this* life. When Jesus commands us to "be perfect as your heavenly Father is perfect" in Matthew 5:48, we can not only have the *faith* to believe this is true—Jesus commanded it—but in Mary we have the virtue of *hope* enlivened. We have the assurance of faith that God's promise has already been fulfilled in her, which at the same time gives birth to a confident assurance rooted in hope that his promise will be fulfilled in us as well if we are "faithful unto death" (Rev. 2:10).

Sanctity in this life is not only possible, but is *actual* in the life of our Blessed Mother.

With all of God's holy angels and saints we can declare "thanks be to God!" for the definition of the Assumption given by our Holy Father Pope Pius XII. But even more importantly, we can together exclaim "thanks be to God!" for the Assumption of the Blessed Virgin itself—the hope of all humanity.

---

321. Cf. Heb. 11:19; Rom. 8:24.
322. Cf. Heb. 3:6, 12:15.

PART V

MEDIATRIX AND CO-REDEMPTRIX

12

OTHER REDEEMERS?

UNDERSTANDING

GOD'S PLAN OF SALVATION

Lumen Gentium, Vatican II's Dogmatic Constitution on the Church, gives us the most in-depth and developed Mariology of any ecumenical council in the history of the Church, especially when it comes to Mary's role in God's plan of salvation. And its most prevalent image—absolutely essential to understanding Mary's salvific role—is the image of Mary as *mother*—Mother of God and Mother of the Church, the people of God.

As we've already considered, John's Gospel especially, taken in tandem with the Book of Revelation—both most likely authored by the same apostle—reveals Mary to be not only the mother of Jesus but also mother of "all those who keep the commandments of God and have the testimony of Jesus Christ" (see John 19:27 and Rev. 12:17). In these verses of Scripture we find summed up the essence of Mary's role. As only a mother can, Mary gives birth to and nurtures both Christ and his body, the Church.[323]

Lumen Gentium 61 expounds on this idea, explaining that it is only in light of her calling to be "a mother to us in the order of grace" that we can say, "In a wholly singular way [Mary] cooperated by her obedience, faith, hope, and burning charity in the

---

323. Mary's maternity of Christ is different from her maternity of the Church just as each member of Christ's body has an essentially different relationship with Christ than he does with other members of Christ. Mary's motherhood did not contribute to Christ's salvation because Christ did not need to be saved. He saved Mary, not the other way around. However, in relation to the Church, Mary plays a salvific role in being an instrument of grace to all of her sons and daughters, the body of Christ.

Savior's work of restoring supernatural life to souls."

Notice, the Church is not saying Mary is another redeemer, or that Mary can do anything of eternal value apart from Christ; rather, she was called to "cooperate . . . in the savior's work." In a strict sense, salvation is Christ's work alone. There is no other person qualified to reconcile men to God, objectively speaking, than Jesus Christ.[324] Man is only involved secondarily and instrumentally in God's plan of salvation, and only because God willed it to be so.

It is not as though God had to do it this way. He could have done it more efficiently all by himself! But it was Christ himself who said of his Church, "[H]e who hears you hears me" (Luke 10:16). In fact, he went so far as to say that his Church would "do the works that [he did]; and greater works than these" by his power at work in it (John 14:12). The truth is, as an integral part of his eternal plan of salvation God both *willed* and *empowered* his Church to save souls.[325] Mary is simply the preeminent example of this truth. Like all Christians, she was and is called to cooperate in Christ's salvific work freely and actively in accordance with her particular gifts, thus becoming a secondary cause of the salvation of souls.[326] *Un*like any other Christian, Mary is called to bring the whole Christ, head and body, to the whole world. Thus, again, she participates in a singular way in God's plan of salvation in that she alone, outside of the godhead, participates in the salvation *of all*.

Lumen Gentium 62 sums it up nicely:

> This motherhood of Mary in the order of grace continues uninterruptedly from the consent which she loyally gave at the Annunciation and which she sustained without wavering beneath the cross, until the eternal fulfillment of all the elect. Taken up to heaven she did not lay aside this saving office but by her manifold intercession continues to bring us the gifts of

324. Cf. 1 Tim. 2:5.
325. Cf. 1 Cor. 7:16, 9:22; 1 Tim. 4:16; James 5:19–20; Romans 11:14, etc.
326. Cf. Luke 1:38, 2:34–35; John 2:1–5, 11, 19:26; Rev. 12:5, 17; 1 Cor. 9:22; 1 Tim. 4:16; Jas 5:19–20. For a fuller explication, see Chapter 13.

eternal salvation . . . Therefore the Blessed Virgin is invoked in the Church under the titles of Advocate, Helper, Benefactress, and Mediatrix.

In his great encyclical *Salvifici Dolores*, Pope St. John Paul II adds a crucial detail to our portrait of Mary's role in salvation, explaining the intricate role *suffering* had to play in Mary's salvific calling.

It is especially consoling to note—and also accurate in accordance with the Gospel and history—that at the side of Christ, in the first and most exalted place, there is always his Mother through the exemplary testimony that she bears *by her whole life* to this particular Gospel of suffering. In her, the many and intense sufferings were amassed in such an interconnected way that they were not only a proof of her unshakeable faith but also a contribution to the redemption of all (25).[327]

Revelation 12:2 alludes to this suffering of Mary via the image of her "pangs of labor" in giving birth to Christ. Simeon had prophesied it in Luke 2:34–35 when he foretold "the sword" that would "pierce [Mary's] soul that the thoughts of many hearts may be revealed."

327. In recent years, we have seen a considerable movement in the Church petitioning the Holy See for the definition of a fifth Marian dogma, Mary as *Co-Redemptrix and Mediatrix of All Grace*. Cardinal Ratzinger (later Pope Benedict XVI), specifically with regard to the term Co-Redemptrix, explained why he believed this would not happen "for the foreseeable future" in his book, *God and the World*. He claimed it to be "the position of the Congregation of the Doctrine of the Faith" that *the theology* of Co-Redemptrix is entirely orthodox, but *the term* is problematic because it often leads to confusion as to the *first cause* of salvation being Christ. This is why, Ratzinger said, other Marian titles are better able to communicate Mary's role in salvation. We argue that *Mother of the Church, Mother of the Eucharist*, or *Mother in the Order of Grace*, as we've seen from *Lumen Gentium,* express Mary's role adequately while also emphasizing the fact that she is not the first cause of grace. *Mediatrix of All Grace* does not seem to bring with it quite the same level of confusion, though it has not been defined infallibly either. Both terms can be used by Catholics as they have been used by the ordinary magisterium of the Church, but both need to be clearly explained in order to avoid misunderstanding.

Where the Confusion Lies

This all sounds well and good to Catholics; but if we run down just a few of the phrases used in these above-cited documents— for example, that Mary has a "saving office," that her suffering represents "a contribution to the redemption of all," or, by her "manifold intercession [she] continues to bring to us the gifts of salvation"—to say these statements are controversial to our Protestant friends would be a gross understatement. As one who used to be on the outside looking in, I understand just how unhinged this sounds to folks who have been raised on a steady (and un-biblical) diet of *sola fidei*—believing that there is nothing at all we can contribute to our own salvation, much less to the salvation of others—so is there any wonder these words from the council and the holy father would sound outlandish?

And yet these statements are deeply rooted in a biblical under-standing of salvation. The first step, then, to understanding Mary's proper role in God's plan of salvation is to understand what the Bible says about that plan.

The Seven Essentials

There are seven essential biblical ideas that must be considered in order to understand God's plan of salvation.

1. Christ's sacrifice is sufficient.

Catholics and most Protestants generally agree on this point. Christ's sacrifice is infinitely efficacious for the forgiveness of sins. In fact, in the course of the recent and ongoing dialogues between representatives of the Lutheran World Federation and theologians representing the Catholic Church on the doctrine of justification, the Lutherans and Catholics involved could declare together:

> In faith we together hold the conviction that justification is the work of the triune God. The Father sent his Son into

the world to save sinners. The foundation and presupposition of justification is the incarnation, death, and resurrection of Christ. Justification thus means that Christ himself is our righteousness, in which we share through the Holy Spirit in accord with the will of the Father. Together we confess: By grace alone, in faith in Christ's saving work and not because of any merit on our part, we are accepted by God and receive the Holy Spirit, who renews our hearts while equipping and calling us to good works.[328]

1 John 2:1–2 tells us Christ's sacrifice is "the propitiation for our sins, and not only our sins, but the sins of the whole world."

2. God's salvific will is universal.

Scripture is clear that God both positively "wills all to be saved and come to the knowledge of the truth" (1 Tim. 2:4) and negatively is "not willing that any perish, but that all should come to repentance" (2 Pet. 3:9). And yet, Jesus was unequivocal when he said "[these] shall depart into eternal punishment, but the righteous into eternal life" (Matt. 25:46). Not everyone will be saved. These two truths lead us to point three.

3. Man has free will.

Catholics believe man was constituted by God as *naturally* and *essentially* free, and that this freedom is not destroyed when a man comes to God through Christ. We say that grace never destroys nature; rather, it heals and perfects it. And this freedom is precisely what we see in Scripture. From God's commandment to Adam in Genesis 2:17 not to eat "of the tree of the knowledge of good and evil" lest he die, to God's word to Israel in Deuteronomy 30:19 to choose between life and death, to our Lord telling us in Revela-

---

328. *Joint Declaration on the Doctrine of Justification by the Lutheran World Federation and the Catholic Church* 15. Cf. 1 John 2:1–2; CCC 1992.

tion 3:20, "Behold, I stand at the door and knock; if anyone hears my voice and opens the door, I will come in to him," the Bible is clear: Man is free either to accept or reject God's call to follow him.

Our Lord himself removed all doubt concerning man's freedom when he revealed that as God from all eternity he willed to gather "Jerusalem" as his own, but they refused him:

> Jerusalem, Jerusalem, killing the prophets and stoning those who are sent to you! How often I would have gathered your children together as a hen gathers her brood under her wings, and you would not! (Matt. 23:37).

4. We cooperate with God in our salvation.

Justification, or salvation, is the work of God first and foremost, but it's also the work of man exercising his free will, aided by grace, in an ongoing cooperation with God's initiative. As Augustine said, "Indeed we also work, but we are only collaborating with God who works."[329] Philippians 2:12 says it like this: "Work out your own salvation with fear and trembling; for God is at work in you, both to will and to work for his good pleasure."[330]

Though man cannot merit anything before he actually enters into Christ, as we will see in more detail in number 6 below, he is called by God to cooperate with grace both before and after entering into Christ. The former is what the Church has termed man's necessary "preparation" to receive grace. And even that must be aided by grace. Then, after entering into Christ, he is called to continue to respond freely to the promptings of grace as he walks with the Lord and can then begin to merit reward from God.

In the final moments of his life on earth, St. Stephen spoke powerful words to the very men who were about to martyr him—words to which any preacher of the Gospel must remain

---

329. *On Grace and Free Will*, 31.
330. Revelation 2:10 makes clear the Christian must "be faithful unto death" and only then will Christ "give [him] the crown of life." Matthew 10:22 says, "[Y]ou will be hated by all for my name's sake. But he who endures to the end will be saved."

faithful no matter the cost. But for our purpose now he also made very clear that man has an essential role in preparing himself to receive grace when in Acts 7:51 he spoke of the "stiff-necked" and "uncircumcised in heart and ears" who "resist the Holy Spirit"—those who were about to stone him.

Thus, says Stephen, the unregenerate can either resist, or by implication receive, the grace of the Holy Spirit offered by God.[331]

Upon entering into Christ through faith and baptism, Christians are then called to cooperate with grace and, because they have now entered into Christ, merit eternal life. Scripture reveals this essential cooperation both through clear statements such as 2 Corinthians 6:1–2—"Working together with [Christ], then, we entreat you not to accept the grace of God in vain"—and in more subtle texts in which Scripture reveals man's cooperation as so intimate with God's working in him that the effect of that cooperation can be and is attributed to the man himself:

> "Since we have these promises, beloved, let us cleanse ourselves from every defilement of body and spirit, and make holiness perfect in the fear of God" (2 Cor. 7:1–2).

> "Having purified your souls by your obedience to the truth . . . love one another earnestly from the heart" (1 Pet. 1:22).

> "If anyone purifies himself from what is ignoble, then he will be a vessel for noble use . . . ready for any good work" (2 Tim. 2:21).

> "And [Jesus] said to the woman, 'Your faith has saved you; go in peace'" (Luke 7:50).

---

331. See also 2 Corinthians 6:1–2. We are speaking here of adult converts who retain the use of reason, of course, because babies or the severely mentally handicapped do not have the ability to proffer obstacles to grace.

"Take heed to yourself and to your teaching; hold to that, for by so doing you will save both yourself and your hearers" (1 Tim. 4:16).

In our next point we will consider in more detail the Lutheran notion (which unfortunately infects much of the Protestant world) that says man is entirely passive when it comes to salvation. But for now we note that these texts say just the opposite. They present the Christian as fully and actively engaged in his own salvation (and that of others). These texts do not say "God has cleansed you . . . purified you . . . saved you," etc. It would be entirely true to say just that, but instead these texts say that Christians cleanse, purify, and save themselves, precisely because they are integrally and causally involved in the process. That sounds like free human cooperation.

5. God rewards good works.

It is no secret that Martin Luther eliminated all works as having anything to do with our justification/salvation. And by that Luther meant that *man himself* has absolutely nothing to do with his own salvation. His will is entirely passive in the process. In fact, that is the entire thesis of what most call his greatest written work, *The Bondage of the Will*. Commenting on Paul's Letter to the Romans, Luther wrote:

> The assertion that justification is free to all that are justified leaves none to work, merit or prepare themselves . . . For if we are justified without works, all works are condemned, whether small or great; Paul exempts none, but thunders impartially against all.[332]

Paul's point in saying justification is a free gift was not to eliminate works, or man's free cooperation, as necessary for salvation *in all*

---

332. Luther, *The Bondage of the Will*, 294.

categories. Men must, for example, choose to open the free gift (see Rev. 3:20; 2 Cor. 6:1, etc.). Paul was answering "Judaizers"—believers in Christ who were attempting to reestablish the law of the Old Covenant as necessary for salvation in the New. This was tantamount to forfeiting Christ, or rejecting the free gift, because it represented an attempt to be justified *apart from Christ.* Paul says in Galatians that those Christians who were being led astray in this way had fallen from grace precisely because they were attempting to "build up again" the law that had been "torn down" through the cross of Christ (2:18). Then he adds:

> You are severed from Christ, you who would be justified by the law; you have fallen away from grace. For through the Spirit, by faith, we wait for the hope of righteousness. For in Christ Jesus neither circumcision nor uncircumcision is of any avail, but faith working through love. You were running well; who hindered you from obeying the truth? (Gal. 5:4–7).

In Paul's writings, any works done either *before* entering into Christ or *apart* from Christ profit nothing for salvation. These are the "works" texts used by Luther and many Protestants today.[333] But works accomplished *in* Christ—*faith working through love*—represent an entirely different category. Before Christ, unregenerate men are "dead in trespasses and sins," and "by nature children of wrath," as Paul writes in Ephesians 2:1–3. But after entering into Christ, says Philippians 4:13, "I can do all things in [Christ] who strengthens me." And according to Romans 2:6–7, "all things" includes meriting eternal life by doing good works.

> For he [God] will render to every man according to his works: to those who by patience in well-doing seek for glory and honor and immortality, he will give eternal life.

---

333. Romans 3:28 and 4:5, and Galatians 2:16, speak of "works" done *apart* from Christ being unable to contribute to salvation. Ephesians 2:8–9 speak of works done *before* entering into Christ being unable to save.

6. Salvation is merited.

When the Catholic Church speaks of "merit," it means nothing more than the reward God guarantees to those who—while first in a state of grace—cooperate with grace via a faith formed by charity.

> *The charity of Christ is the source in us of all our merits* before God. Grace, by uniting us to Christ in active love, ensures the supernatural quality of our acts and consequently their merit before God (CCC 2011).

In Pauline terms, we saw it above:

> For in Christ Jesus neither circumcision nor uncircumcision is of any avail, but faith working through love (Gal. 5:6).

Even works that appear to be righteous externally profit nothing if they are not accomplished in the love of Christ.

> If I give away all I have, and if I deliver my body to be burned, but have not love, I gain nothing (1 Cor. 13:3).

The Church emphasizes in complete harmony with the biblical text that man can only merit after he has entered into Christ through faith and baptism. Or, as Paul says it: "It is not I, but Christ in me and the life that I now live I live by the faith of the Son of God" (Gal. 2:20). So, if a man is not in Christ, he cannot merit.

> Since the initiative belongs to God in the order of grace, *no one can merit the initial grace* of forgiveness and justification, at the beginning of conversion. Moved by the Holy Spirit and by charity, *we can merit* for ourselves and for others the graces needed for our sanctification, for the increase of grace and charity, and for the attainment of eternal life . . . (CCC 2010).

Scripture gives us manifold examples of how what man does—*his works*—will be rewarded with either salvation or damnation.[334] This could be a dictionary definition of "merit." But for brevity's sake, we will only cite one text here. In Galatians, Paul uses the image of "continuing to sow" the seed of good or wicked works in order to merit either heaven or hell:

> Do not be deceived; God is not mocked, for whatever a man sows, that he will also reap. For he who sows to his own flesh will from the flesh reap corruption; but he who sows to the Spirit will from the Spirit reap eternal life. And let us not grow weary in well-doing, for in due season we shall reap, if we do not lose heart (6:7–9).

7. Christians save souls through Christ.

Once we understand the biblical truth that all Christians really can and must merit eternal reward in and through Christ, we can then proceed to considering his role in meriting the grace of salvation for others. Concerning Christians in general, the *Catechism* teaches:

> With regard to God, there is no strict right to any merit on the part of man. Between God and us there is an immeasurable inequality, for we have received everything from him, our Creator. The merit of man before God in the Christian life arises from the fact that *God has freely chosen to associate man with the work of his grace.* The fatherly action of God is first on his own initiative, and then follows man's free acting through collaboration, so that the merit of good works is to be attributed in the first place to the grace of God, then to the faithful. Man's merit, moreover, itself is due to God, for his good actions proceed in Christ, from the predispositions and assistance given

---

334. See Matt. 5:44–45, 10:22, 32–33, 12:36–37, 24:44–51, 25:31–46; Eph. 5:3–6; 1 Cor. 6:9–11; 2 Cor. 7:10; Rom. 2:13–16, 6:16, 10:9–10; Heb. 10:26–38, 12:10–16, etc.

by the Holy Spirit . . . Moved by the Holy Spirit, *we can then merit* for ourselves and for others the graces needed for our sanctification, for the increase of grace and charity, and for the attainment of eternal life (2007–2008, 2010).

Concerning Mary's role in salvation, the *Catechism* elsewhere says:

"But the Blessed Virgin's salutary influence on men . . . flows forth from the superabundance of the merits of Christ, rests on his mediation, depends entirely upon it, and draws all power from it."

"No creature could ever be counted along with the Incarnate Word and Redeemer; but just as the priesthood of Christ is shared in various ways both by his ministers and the faithful, and as the one goodness of God is radiated in different ways among his creatures, so also the unique mediation of the Redeemer does not exclude but rather gives rise to a manifold cooperation which is but a sharing in this one source" (CCC 970; cf. *Lumen Gentium* 60,62).

Among Protestants we tend to find vehement responses to texts such as these. Consider Dave Hunt's response to this prayer composed by John Paul II—"Sustain us, O Virgin Mary, on our journey of faith and obtain for us the grace of eternal salvation":

To suggest that Mary must or even can in any way "obtain for us the grace of eternal salvation" is a denial of the sufficiency of Christ's sacrifice upon the cross for our sins and a rejection of the grace and love of God and Christ."[335]

Well, if you deny man has any role to play in his own salvation, then you would have to agree with Hunt, and with Luther, that he could have no role in anyone else's salvation either. But one has to won-

---

335. Hunt, *A Woman Rides the Beast,* 446.

der why then Paul would bother to "[pray] to God for [the Jews] that they may be saved," if his prayers could not "obtain for [them] the grace of salvation?"[336] For Catholics who believe, as James 5:16 says, "The prayer of a righteous man has great power," there is no problem with saying *any* Christian can "obtain for us the grace of eternal salvation." And Mary is certainly a Christian. This is what intercession is all about. We pray that God grant the graces of salvation, healing, and more. Christians can "obtain" for another— through Christ working in them—the "grace of eternal salvation."

Ultimately, the problem boils down here to something we've seen before: Luther's (and Hunt's . . . and Protestantism's) errors run smack into plain texts of Scripture. They begin with the unbiblical presupposition that "man can have nothing to do with his salvation or the salvation of others causally," and they end in denying the very Bible they hold dear.

As we've seen, Scripture makes very clear that man has a secondary causal role to play in his own salvation. The same can be said for his role in the salvation of others. By cooperating with God's grace, Christians not only participate in their own salvation, but contribute to the salvation of the souls of others. Here are just a few examples:

"And convince some, who doubt; save some, by snatching them out of the fire; on some have mercy with fear, hating even the garment spotted by the flesh" (Jude 22–23).

"To the weak I became weak, that I might win the weak. I have become all things to all men that I might by all means save some" (1 Cor. 9:22).

"Inasmuch then as I am an apostle to the Gentiles, I magnify my ministry in order to make my fellow Jews jealous, and thus save some of them" (Rom. 11:13–14).

336. Cf. Rom. 10:1.

"Wife, how do you know whether you will save your husband? Husband, how do you know whether you will save your wife?" (1 Cor. 7:16).

"Take heed to yourself and to your teaching: hold to that, for by so doing you will save both yourself and your hearers" (1 Tim. 4:16).

"My brethren, if any one among you wanders from the truth and someone brings him back, let him know that whoever brings back a sinner from the error of his way will save his soul from death and will cover a multitude of sins" (James 5:19–20).

"Let us rejoice and exult and give him the glory, for the marriage of the Lamb has come, and his Bride has made herself ready; it was granted her to be clothed with fine linen, bright and pure—for the fine linen is the righteous deeds of the saints" (Rev. 19:7–8).

"Now I rejoice in my sufferings for your sake, and in my flesh I complete what is lacking in Christ's afflictions for the sake of his body, that is, the Church" (Col. 1:24).

"If we are afflicted, it is for your comfort and salvation; and if we are comforted, it is for your comfort, which you experience when you patiently endure the same sufferings that we suffer" (2 Cor. 1:6).

Breaking It Down

To make this even clearer, we need to distinguish between what members of the body of Christ (including Mary, of course) are empowered to do and what Christ alone can do by his own power when it comes to salvation.

Paul describes the difference in 1 Corinthians 3:5–9, using a farming metaphor:

What then is Apollos? What is Paul? Servants through whom you believed, as the Lord assigned to each. I planted, Apollos watered, but God gave the growth . . . For we are God's fellow workers; you are God's field.

Christians are empowered by grace to "plant the seeds" of the gospel, and/or to "water the soil," while God alone "brings the increase" in the process of salvation. The essential truth communicated here is that Christ's role in "bringing the increase" is qualitatively different from that of the members of the Church whom he empowers to "plant seeds" and "water the soil," yet all three are essential to the process—even to the point that Paul can refer to Christians as God's *sunergoi*, or "co-laborers" in bringing people to the Faith. In that sense, all Christians are "co-redeemers" with Christ.

"Planting seeds" and "watering the soil" can take many forms. Prayer (James 5:16; Phil. 1:19), sacrifice (Phil. 4:18; Heb. 13:15–16), sharing the gospel (1 Tim. 4:16; James 5:19–20), suffering in union with Christ (Rom. 8:17; Col. 1:24), or any good work done in Christ (Rom. 2:6–7, Matt. 10:42), as long as it is done freely, knowingly, and in union with Christ, can contribute to the salvation of souls. This is the essence of the Catholic and biblical understanding of God's plan of salvation as it relates to man's cooperation with the finished work of Christ on the cross.

Jesus Is the Savior

At this point we should emphasize the Catholic position concerning Christ's singular role in "giving the growth" in salvation. In 1 Timothy 2:5, Paul describes Christ as the "one mediator between God and men." Hebrews 7:23–25 uses the term "intercessor" as a synonym for mediator. In fact, we argue that if 1 Timothy lays out the theology of who Christ is by nature—our one intercessor who alone mediates for us at the right hand of God the Father, in heaven—Hebrews reveals that intercession/mediation in action:

For there is one God, and there is one mediator between God and men, the man Christ Jesus (1 Tim. 2:5).

The former priests were many in number, because they were prevented by death from continuing in office; but [Christ] holds his priesthood permanently, because he continues forever. Consequently, he is able for all time to save those who draw near to God through him, since he always lives to make intercession for them (Heb. 7:24–25).

Christ is our unique intercessor, saving our souls in the process. And yet Paul clearly calls all Christians to be "intercessors" in Christ as well. The verses immediately leading up to 1 Timothy 2:5 are telling:

First of all, then, I urge that supplications, prayers, intercessions, and thanksgivings be made for all men . . . This is good, and it is acceptable in the sight of God our Savior, who desires all men to be saved and to come to the knowledge of the truth (1 Tim. 2:1–3).[337]

Thus, the Church does what Christ does: it intercedes for and brings salvation to the world. To use Paul's image from 1 Corinthians 3 once again, members of the Church do the "planting" and the "watering," God alone can "bring the increase," but any farmer knows you do cannot have a crop without all three. So it is with our salvation.

The Body Beautiful

Another way of understanding this very biblical notion of the people of God interceding/mediating salvation in Christ is to consider the Church as the body of Christ, as Paul describes it in

---

337. In 1 Peter 2:5–9, Scripture reveals all of the baptized to be members of "a royal priesthood" in our one true priest, Jesus Christ. A priest, by definition, is "a mediator between God and men." Thus, all Christians are mediators in Christ, the one mediator.

1 Corinthians 12:12–27. So intimate is the relationship between Christ and his Church that he could say to Paul before his conversion, "Saul, Saul, why are you persecuting *me*" (Acts 22:7). In Ephesians 1:22–23, Paul tells us that the Church *is* Christ, extended in this world:

> [A]nd [God] has put all things under [Christ's] feet and has made him the head over all things for the Church, which is his body, the fullness of him who fills all in all.

Thus, to claim it is a contradiction to say that Christians can efficaciously intercede for salvation because Christ is our one intercessor would be like claiming it is a contradiction to say Tim Staples's fingers and hands had anything to do with the writing of *Behold Your Mother* because it was Tim Staples who wrote it. The simple truth is: Tim Staples used his fingers and hands to do the work.

A Final Question

"So then," one might ask, "if all Christians are called to be co-redeemers and mediators in Christ, and if all Christians are called to participate in God's plan of salvation, why all the fuss about *Mary*?"

From a Catholic and biblical perspective, there certainly ought to be a fuss about Mary, because although all Christians are called to "save souls," as we have seen, no other Christian other than the Mother of God has ever been called to cooperate with God in *saving the entire world* and in *bringing the grace of God to the entire world*. Individual Christians participate in various ways in bringing others to Christ and building up other members of the body of Christ. In so doing, they "save souls." However, Mary uniquely participates as both *Mother of God* and *Mother of the Church* in the salvation *of all,* as we will examine in our next chapter.

13
MARY'S SAVING OFFICE

Whenever the topic of Mary's role in salvation comes up, many Protestants respond that the notion is nothing less than blasphemy. And yet, when we actually get down to sharing with our Protestant friends those Scripture texts that deal with the mother of our Redeemer, the results are often remarkable. Not long ago I was sitting in a restaurant discussing Mary with an Evangelical minister when, unexpectedly, he leaned forward, placed his face into his hands, paused, and then looked up at me with tears in his eyes saying, "Oh, my Lord, Tim, this stuff is true! What am I going to do?" (He has since become Catholic.)

In this chapter we will discuss some of what I shared with this minister and thousands of others over the years about Mary's role in salvation from a biblical perspective.

Mary Has Nothing to Do With it . . . Except Everything

Protestant apologist Ron Rhodes, in his book, *Reasoning from the Scriptures with Catholics*, writes:

> My point is that *Mary has no role whatsoever* [in salvation], other than being the divinely chosen human instrument through whom the divine Messiah and Redeemer would be born into the world. Once that was accomplished, the biblical record assigns no further role to Mary, and she is hence *not even mentioned* in the Epistles.[338]

---

338. Rhodes, *Reasoning from the Scriptures with Catholics*, 286. It should be noted that Mary is clearly mentioned in Galatians 4:4: "But when the time has fully come, God sent

254   BEHOLD YOUR MOTHER

"Other than being the divinely chosen human instrument" is reminiscent of the old saying, "Other than that, Mrs. Lincoln, how was the play?" Mr. Rhodes, in essence, says, "Mary has no role whatsoever to play in salvation . . . except the most important role of all." All Christians are called to contribute to the salvation of some; Mary brought the whole Christ to the whole world. But other than that . . .

Unfortunately Ron Rhodes is not alone when it comes to this sentiment. Among many Protestants, especially of the Evangelical and Fundamentalist traditions, Mary seems to be viewed as a mere receptacle that was used for nine months—and that was the end of her contribution. And even that contribution is minimized.

Form-fitted blinders seem to come free of charge along with this tendency to minimize Mary's role in Scripture. But I can hardly put down Rhodes or anyone else in this, because I once wore my own pair with pride.

In this chapter we will respond to Rhodes's claims by examining Mary's saving role in each of five pivotal events in salvation history. We will see that Mary alone, among human persons, is present and involved in each:[339]

- The Incarnation in Luke 1:37–38.
- The birth of Jesus' ministry at the wedding feast of Cana in John 2.
- The prophecy of Simeon in Luke 2:34–35.
- The Crucifixion of our Lord in John 19:25–27.
- The entire text of Revelation 12, in which we see a cosmic overview of the spiritual battle that encapsulates salvation history.

---

forth his Son, born of woman, born under the law, to redeem those who were under the law." Perhaps Rhodes meant to say Mary was not mentioned *by name,* but the truth is, the woman is Mary.

339. This is not intended to be an exhaustive list. We could add the preparation for the coming of the Holy Spirit at Pentecost (Acts 1), the finding of the child Jesus (Acts 2), the many prophecies from the Old Testament, and more, that speak of Mary in her role in God's plan of salvation.

The Incarnation

Luke 1:31–45:

> And behold, you will conceive in your womb and bear a son, and you shall call his name Jesus . . . And Mary said to the angel, "How can this be . . . And the angel said to [Mary], "The Holy Spirit will come upon you, and the power of the Most High will overshadow you; therefore the child to be born will be called holy, the Son of God . . . For with God nothing will be impossible." And Mary said, "Behold, I am the handmaid of the Lord; let it be to me according to your word." And the angel departed from her . . . And blessed is she who believed that there would be a fulfillment of what was spoken to her from the Lord.

To quote Ron Rhodes, Mary is here revealed to be "the divinely chosen human instrument through whom the divine Messiah and Redeemer would be born into the world." And because there was no human father in the process, we can say that Mary was a *singular* instrument. The Incarnation was a unique event, and Mary was the only human person involved. No other human but Mary contributed to Jesus' human nature.

Despite Calvinist claims to the contrary, it does not take intellectual rigor to understand that Mary's *fiat* (Latin for "let it be done") signals that she was free in her response to the angel. The implications of this are staggering: when Mary said "let it be," she gave God free rein to come into the world and save us. This is a textbook definition of Mary as *Co-Redemptrix*. She cooperated with God's grace in the Redemption of the whole world.

As we examine it more deeply, we notice that the text—especially verses 37–38—emphasizes that God willed the fulfillment of messianic prophecy to be dependent upon the response of Mary. This is revealed by more than just her *fiat*. The words leading up to Mary's fiat are even more decisive in revealing the truth that until Mary said yes to God, the eternal plan of God for our salvation would remain only in the realm of the "possible."[340] After she said yes, the entire universe would be forever changed!

The Importance of the Word

When I was in the seminary studying Greek and we were translating this text in class, I recall my professor telling us that though there are multiple ways this text could be translated (as there are with many New Testament texts), many modern translations fall short of really doing it justice.

Consider verse 37. The Greek reads:

hoti (because) *ouk* (not) *adunateisei* (will be impossible) *para* (with) *tou* (the) *theou* (God) *pan* (every) *rhema* (word).

A literal translation would be: "because with God, every word shall not be impossible." But modern translators typically render it something like, "For with God nothing will be impossible," as we see in the RSV:CE.[341] The problem with this translation is

---

340. It is worth repeating that whenever we say the plan of God was "dependent upon" Mary's response, there is no natural necessity implied. God freely chose to associate the free response of Mary with the plan of salvation. As such, we can say there is a causal relationship because God willed it to be so. And this is true when it comes to the people of God in general. This is precisely why the prophet Ezekiel could say of the personal choices and action of a prophet, or by allusion, anyone among the people of God: "If I say to the wicked, 'You shall surely die,' and you give him no warning nor speak to warn the wicked from his wicked way, in order to save his life, that wicked man shall die in his iniquity; but his blood I will require at your hand" (Ezek. 3:18). Not only do all of the faithful merit reward from God by "sav[ing] a soul" as James 5:20 says, but we are also responsible if we do not "warn the wicked." It is not that there is no other way the "wicked" one could be saved—another avenue may or may not be offered to him—but it is simply a fact that God has chosen to use the people of God to bring his truth to the world. This great gift and calling brings with it great responsibility. Mary is the preeminent example of this profound truth.

341. We are not saying this translation is errant; but it is weak. Evidently, the translators took the word for *not* (*ouk*) and placed it in apposition with *every word* (*pan rhema*), giving them "not every word shall be impossible." Then they translated *word* as *thing*, leading to *not everything*, which leads to *nothing*. Thus we arrive at "with God nothing will be impossible."

it ends up losing the word *word* (*rhema*, in Greek) in verse 37, and then missing what appears to be an important play on *rhema* between verses 37 and 38.[342] When the angel declares that "with God, every word (*rhema*) shall not be impossible," Mary responds, "Behold, I am the handmaid of the Lord, let it be to me according to your *word*" (*rhema*).

Yes, there seems to be a play on *words* here. Pun intended! A more literal translation helps us to see more clearly why the Fathers and the Church down through the ages placed such emphasis on Mary when exegeting this text. Mary's yes is essential to "every word" of God being moved from potency to act—from that which is merely potential to the manger in Bethlehem.

We also need to consider the Greek word for "shall be impossible"—*adunateisei*—a compound composed of a verb form of *possible* (*dunatos*) and *not* (*a*). If you place *ouk* (another word for *not* also in this verse) in apposition with the "not possible," you have two negatives—*not* be *not* possible—which can be translated as a positive.[343] In simple terms, this text can be translated, "Every word (*rhema*) with God is possible."[344]

Now, there are two words for *word* in the Greek New Testa-

---

342. We believe the Douay-Rheims gets closest to the Greek here when it translates the text, "Because no word shall be impossible with God." The problem with that translation is it loses the word *pan*, which translates as *every* or *all*, that seems to be in apposition with *word*. *Every word* becomes *no word*.

343. This is *not* a classic case of a Greek double negative, which can be used in some contexts to emphasize a positive. However, whether you translate it as "shall not be impossible" or as "shall be possible," the meaning is the same. The text seems to be indicating that the word of the Lord is possible to be fulfilled, but is dependent upon Mary's response in order for the *word* to be fulfilled.

344. The text can be translated several ways. The RSV translates it as: "For with God nothing will be impossible." The Douay-Rheims translates it as, "No word shall be impossible with God." The NAB has it "For nothing will be impossible for God." In all of these translations, we can see the fact that Mary's response is essential for the fulfillment of God's word. However, as Joseph Thayer points out (in agreement with the DRV), the text is really trying to get across the idea that "from God no word shall be without power" (*Greek-English Lexicon,* 12). In other words, God's word is "living and active" (Heb. 4:12) and will accomplish what it says if we will submit to the Lord. Mary does just that so that God's word becomes fruitful for her and for the entire world.

ment—*logos* and *rhema*—that are basically synonyms, used interchangeably in both the New Testament and the LXX.[345] *Rhema* means a "matter of speech, thing . . . command" that carries with it a substantial reality.[346] Many scholars believe the sense of *word* in the New Testament is informed by the Hebrew concept of *dabar*, which to the ancient mind was a richer concept than the modern *word*. It had substantial being. The *dabar Yahweh* or "word of God" was generally understood to be a creative power from God more real than my fingers here on my hand.[347]

This makes this text all the more intriguing. To the Hebrew mind, God's word was more real than the heavens and the earth.[348] When God speaks, all of nature must give way to the power of his word.

We can see many examples of *word* being used like this in Scripture. Genesis 1:3: "And God said, 'Let there be light'; and there was light." By the time the inspired author gets finished with saying, "God said, let there be light," he has to put the next verse in the past tense! When God spoke, his word brought forth its material reality concurrently. Or Psalm 33:6: "By the word of the Lord the heavens were made, and all their host by the breath of his mouth." God's *dabar* is creative and powerful. It does what God says it will do! We see the same in the New Testament, for

345. There has been much said and written about the distinction between *logos* and *rhema*, especially in the "Word Faith" movement. The *rhema* is said to be the spoken word, while the *logos* is the written. This is not true. 1 Peter 1:23–25 uses the words synonymously, as does Ephesians 6:17, Hebrews 4:12, and other texts. Both are generally used for "word." More important for our purpose is the influence that the Hebrew *dabar* has on both: they both carry the connotation of a thing or a substantial reality.

346. Barclay Newman gives as the meaning of *rhema*: "what is said, word, saying; thing, matter, event, happening," in *A Concise Greek-English Dictionary of the New Testament*, 159. Thayer comments on this particular text that "thing" here actually means, "The subject matter of speech, thing; and that . . . in so far as it is a matter of command," in *Greek-English Lexicon*, 562–563. To translate *rhema* as *thing* is acceptable as long as one can see that the thing referenced is the commandment of God, or the *word* of God.

347. Kittel, *Theological Dictionary of the New Testament*, vol. 4, 93, 99–100.

348. Jesus' words in Matthew 24:35 come to mind: "Heaven and earth will pass away, but my words will not pass away." He is equating *his word* with *God's word*. He is revealing himself to be God.

example, Hebrews 11:3: "By faith we understand that the world was created by the word of God (Gr., *rhemati theou*) so that what is seen was made out of things which do not appear."

I remember my Greek professor making the point that for many if not most of the first-century Jews hearing the text of Luke 1, the response would have been, "What do you mean, every word with God is *possible*? The word of God is more real than the heavens and the earth! What is going on here?" Well, in the next verse, we see just what is going on. Mary responds to the angel:

> Behold, I am the handmaid of the Lord; let it be done unto me according to your *word*.

When we connect the two instances of *word* here, we get a powerful sense of why Elizabeth would a short time later (v. 45) say, "Blessed is she who believed that there would be a fulfillment of what was spoken to her from the Lord." Mary is *blessed* indeed. According to the text, the fulfillment of the word of God was contingent upon the free response of a girl around fourteen. Indeed, "God chose what is foolish in the world to shame the wise" (1 Cor. 1:27).

And precisely what word is the angel referring to as being fulfilled? It's not just one word. According to the text it's *every* word (Gr., *pan rhema*) of God. Everything spoken or written concerning the coming of the Messiah—all of the prophecies down through the centuries—was dependent upon the response of this chosen girl. As a result of her *fiat*, the Word of God was made flesh and dwelt among us and humanity could be saved.

History Brings Perspective

Throughout the history of the Church—especially in the writings of the great Fathers and Doctors—this text of Luke 1 has been key in fleshing out Mary's role in God's plan of salvation. In a great majority of these writings, the reference is used in the context of explaining Mary's role in bringing salvation to the world. St. Irenaeus is one of the earliest (only "Matheiteis" and St. Justin Martyr being older), writing in the second century, and reveals that there was a remarkable depth in understanding Mary as Co-Redemptrix from the very earliest days of the Christian era. He sounds like any Catholic would today when he writes using this same text:

> Mary the Virgin is found obedient, saying, "Behold the handmaid of the Lord; be it unto me according to thy word." But Eve was disobedient; for she did not obey when as yet she was a virgin. And even as she, having indeed a husband, Adam, but being nevertheless yet a virgin . . . having become disobedient, was made the cause of death, both to herself and to the entire human race; so also did Mary, having a man betrothed [to her], and being nevertheless a virgin, by yielding obedience, became the cause of salvation, both to herself and the whole human race . . . And thus also it was that the knot of Eve's disobedience was loosed by the obedience of Mary. For what the virgin Eve had bound fast through unbelief, this did the Virgin Mary set free through faith.[349]

For nearly 2,000 years, our text of Luke 1 was also foundational to the Christian understanding of Mary as "the New Eve." Just as Eve had a (secondarily) causal role in the fall, Mary has an analogously causal role to play in the redemption.

St. Bernard of Clairvaux, a Doctor of the Church writing in the twelfth century, sums up the Christian understanding of this text down through the centuries in poetic fashion in a famous homily entitled "In Praise of the Virgin Mother":

> You have heard, O Virgin, that you will conceive and bear a son; you have heard that it will not be by man but by the Holy Spirit. The angel awaits an answer; it is time for him to return to God who sent him. We too are waiting, O Lady, for your

---

349. *Against Heresies* III, 22, 4

word of compassion; the sentence of condemnation weighs heavily upon us.

The price of our salvation is offered to you. We shall be set free at once if you consent. In the eternal Word of God we all came to be, and behold, we die. In your brief response we are to be remade in order to be recalled to life.

Tearful Adam with his sorrowing family begs this of you, O loving Virgin, in their exile from Paradise. Abraham begs it, David begs it. All the other holy patriarchs, your ancestors, ask it of you, as they dwell in the country of the shadow of death. This is what the whole earth waits for, prostrate at your feet. It is right in the doing so, for on your word depends comfort for the wretched, ransom for the captive, freedom for the condemned, indeed, salvation for all the sons of Adam, the whole of your race.

Answer quickly, O Virgin. Reply in haste to the angel, or rather through the angel to the Lord. Answer with a word, receive the Word of God. Speak your own word, conceive the divine Word. Breathe a passing word, embrace the eternal Word . . . See, the desired of all nations is at your door, knocking to enter . . . *Behold, the handmaid of the Lord*, she says, *be it done to me according to your word*.[350]

It is precisely because Mary was entirely free in her response to the angel that she became what Irenaeus called "the cause of salvation, both to herself and the entire human race."[351]

---

350. *In Praise of the Virgin Mother*, quoted in Office of Readings, December 20.

351. In Mary's *fiat* we also see the importance of our own. In a sense, not only the angels and saints but God himself awaits our *yes* to the promptings of his grace. It will never equal Mary's, but our *yes* will contribute to saving both ourselves and those in our smaller or larger circles of influence (cf. 1 Tim. 4:16). In Mary we see our own dignity and lofty calling as members of Christ.

The Wedding Feast of Cana

John 2:1–11:

> On the third day there was a marriage at Cana in Galilee, and
> the mother of Jesus was there . . . Jesus also was invited to the
> marriage, with his disciples. When the wine failed, the mother
> of Jesus said to him, "They have no wine." And Jesus said to
> her, "O woman, what have you to do with me? My hour has
> not yet come." His mother said to the servants, "Do whatever
> he tells you." Now six stone jars were standing there, for the
> Jewish rites of purification . . . Jesus said to them, "Fill the jars
> with water." . . . He said to them, "Now draw some out and take
> it to the steward of the feast." So they took it. When the steward
> of the feast tasted the water now become wine, and did not
> know where it came from . . . [he] said . . . "Every man serves
> the good wine first; and when men have drunk freely, then the
> poor wine; but you have kept the good wine until now." This,
> the first of his signs, Jesus did at Cana in Galilee, and manifested
> his glory; and his disciples believed in him.

There is much more to this text than we have space here to consider, but we want to achieve two main goals here. First, to consider the scriptural references revealing that, as the New Adam and
the New Eve, Jesus and Mary recapitulate all that was lost in the
Garden of Eden. And then, to focus on the Marian emphases that
are specific to salvation.

The New Eve

1. St. John begins his Gospel with words that anyone familiar
   with the Old Testament would connect with Genesis 1: "*In the
   beginning was* the Word."

2. It is no coincidence that John sets the wedding feast on "day
   seven" of seven conspicuous "days" he lays out in Chapters 1

and 2. Hearkening back to the seven days of the first creation, day one goes from 1:6–28. Day two runs from 29–34. Day three from 35–42. Day four from 43 through 51. And then, day seven begins in 2:1 as "the third day" after the fourth day, wherein Jesus would begin his ministry that would "make all things new," or bring about "a new heaven and a new earth" (Rev. 21:1, 5).

3. Jesus uses the term *woman* for his mother, which is a reference to Mary as the prophetic woman of Genesis 3:15 and Jeremiah 31:22.

4. Through Mary's intercession, Jesus performs his first sign, and manifests his glory as the Messiah, the anointed one of God. The New Eve is integral to the mission of the New Adam.

Marian emphases specific to salvation:

1. Because of the work done through Mary's intercession, the text says, the disciples believed in Jesus. Thus, Mary is not only instrumental in "giving birth" to Christ's ministry in which he would "make all things new" (Rev. 21:5), but also in "giving birth" to the disciples' faith—a faith apart from which it is "impossible to please God" (Heb. 11:6).

2. Mary intercedes for the people at the wedding feast, the members of which symbolize the entire people of God— who, elsewhere in John's writing, are invited to a much greater "marriage supper of the Lamb" (Rev. 19:7–9).

3. Jesus' first sign, or miracle, as a result of Mary's intercession, is the transformation of "six stone jars" of purification waters— these would be the *baptismoi*, or baptismal waters of the Old Covenant—into wine, a prophetic symbol of New Covenant

perfection.[352] There is no separating Mary from the ministry of her Son inaugurating the New Covenant from its beginning to the very end, as we will see when we get to the Crucifixion in John 19.

A Reformed Objection

James White unsurprisingly disagrees with our interpretation of John 2:

> The fact that Mary approaches the Lord to meet the need of the people gathered at the feast shows that she is desirous that he in some way manifest his true nature and mission. Jesus rebukes her understandable impatience, reminding her that they are both bound by the Father's divine timetable, and they cannot alter what he has determined.[353]

As a Protestant apologist, White predictably attempts to downplay Mary's role in this text, but does he succeed? In response, there are two crucial points to be made:

1. White is not getting the full impact of what Mary is saying to Jesus in this text. Jesus simply *does not* enter into his ministry, perform his first miracle, and bring his disciples to faith (or perhaps a deeper level of faith), *until Mary intervenes.* "My hour is not yet come," he says. And yet he responds to Mary's intercession and *performs his inaugural miracle anyway.* Mary truly gives birth to Jesus' ministry.

2. It's true that Mary was indeed "desirous that he in some way manifest his true nature and mission." White is also correct in

---

352. In Mark 7:4, we find these purification waters referred to as "baptismous" in Greek. And in Isaiah 25:6; Jeremiah 31:12; Joel 2:19, 24; Luke 5:37–39, etc. we find "wine" to be a symbol of the New Covenant. And this is not to mention the importance of the symbol of wine used in our New Covenant eucharistic sacrifice.

353. White, *Mary—Another Redeemer?*, 26.

saying that Jesus "rebukes" Mary according to the wording of the text. But he is wrong when he says Jesus rebukes Mary for her "impatience." There is nothing in the text that says or implies anything about "impatience," or any defect in Mary for that matter.

But what of the rebuke? There has been a whole lot of ink spilled over the language of John 2:5: "O woman, what have you to do with me? My hour has not yet come." There can be no doubt that this is the language of rebuke. On the surface it is almost scandalous. So what is going on here?

This idiomatic Greek expression, *ti emoi kai soi*—"what have you to do with me"—is the same expression used by the demons possessing the demoniacs of Gadara in Matthew 8:28–29:

> And when he came to the other side, to the country of the Gadarenes, two demoniacs met him, coming out of the tombs, so fierce that no one could pass that way. And behold, they cried out, "What have you to do with us, O Son of God? Have you come here to torment us before the time?"

Scripture scholar Fr. William Leonard says somewhat euphemistically that the language indicates "a divergence of viewpoints between the two parties concerned." He shows how this phrase is a *Hebraism*—a Hebrew phrase that was being transliterated into Greek—used in multiple texts in the Old Testament, always portending a similar meaning of rebuke (see Judg. 11:12; 2 Sam. 16:10, 19:22; 2 Kings 3:13; 2 Chron. 35:21).

However, here is the crucial point: Fr. Leonard explains that what *seems* to be a refusal on the surface is actually "a refusal *ad mentem*"—a refusal "to a purpose," or "with a purpose in mind."[354] We have another well-known "refusal ad mentem" in Matthew

---

354. Leonard, *A Catholic Commentary on Sacred Scripture*, 984.

15:22–28, where Jesus rebuked a Canaanite woman three times as she came to ask him to heal her demonized daughter. Jesus' initial refusals to that woman and to his mother serve to underscore the importance of intercession. The Canaanite woman's daughter was eventually healed, but not until she had persisted in her intercession for her daughter. Mary's divine Son eventually performed his first miracle, brought the apostles to faith, and launched the ministry that would bring all of God's—and Mary's—children eternal life. But just as with the Canaanite woman, it would not happen without Mary's determined intercession, even in the face of an apparent rebuke. Both of these great women are icons for all and teach by example the perennial truth: it has pleased God to involve our cooperation in his work of salvation. "God has freely chosen to associate [all Christians] with the work of his grace" (CCC 2008), and to associate Mary with that work to a singular and preeminent degree.

The Redemption: From Prophecy to the Cross to Heaven

Luke 2:34–35:

Simeon blessed them and said to Mary his mother, "Behold, this child is set for the fall and rising of many in Israel, and for a sign that is spoken against (and a sword will pierce through your own soul also), that thoughts out of many hearts may be revealed."

John 19:25–27:

But standing by the cross of Jesus were his mother, and his mother's sister, Mary the wife of Clopas, and Mary Magdalene. When Jesus saw his mother, and the disciple whom he loved standing near, he said to his mother, "Woman, behold, your son!" Then he said to the disciple, "Behold, your mother!" And from that hour the disciple took her to his own home.

Revelation 12:1–2, 4–5, 17:

> And a great sign appeared in heaven, a woman clothed with the sun, with the moon under her feet, and on her head a crown of twelve stars; she was with child . . . And the dragon stood before the woman . . . that he might devour her child . . . but her child was caught up to God and to his throne . . . Then the dragon was angry with the woman, and went off to make war on the rest of her offspring, on those who keep the commandments of God and bear testimony to Jesus.

For just a brief review, as we have already covered some of this ground, we note the parallels between the first Eve of the Old Covenant and the New Eve of the New Covenant.

Eve is referred to as *woman* ten times in Genesis 2–3 before she is named "Eve."	Jesus calls Mary *woman* in John 2:4, and again from the cross in John 19:26, and she is called woman eight times in Revelation 12.
The woman is then specifically named Eve because she is "mother of the living" in that all of humanity are her "seed" (Gen. 3:20).	Mary is Mother of all "who keep the commandments of God and bear testimony to Jesus"—her "offspring" (Gr., *spermatos*; Rev. 12:17, cf. John. 19:26).
Eve reaches out in disobedience to the fruit from the "tree of the knowledge of good and evil" and brings death to herself and all of her children (Gen. 3:3, 12–13).	Mary reaches out in faith to the New Covenant cross, or "tree," bringing life to herself and all of her children (1 Pet. 2:24; Luke 2:34–35; John 19:26; Rev. 12:17).

By their disobedience Adam and Eve each contribute to the death of their progeny and are each rebuked by God (Gen. 3:16, 17).	Jesus and Mary are each prophesied to obey God and suffer so that their progeny would have eternal life in God (Luke 2:34–35; John 19:26–27).
Eve, "the woman," is overcome by the dragon, "the serpent" as he is called in Genesis 3:1–6, and brings death to her children.	Mary, "the woman," is pursued by the dragon, "that ancient serpent," referencing Genesis 3, but he cannot overtake her. As a result she is depicted as giving birth to all Christians in Revelation 12:17.

With this review in mind, now we want to emphasize Mary's role specific to salvation at the foot of the cross and into eternity.

The prophet Simeon tells us that "the sign of contradiction," the cross, was set to be the sign of salvation for "many" (or "all") in Israel.[355] But in the same breath he reveals a sword will pierce Mary's soul as well. Why? So that the *thoughts* of *many hearts* would be revealed.[356] Jesus and Mary would suffer so that the same "many" would be saved!

In John 19 we see the fulfillment of this prophecy. On a natural level we know that no one suffers as a mother does when her child suffers. But given the gift of grace and the resulting knowledge of Christ that she surely had, Mary must have suffered more

---

355. *Many* and *all* are, at times, used synonymously in the New Testament, e.g., Romans 5:18–19.

356. The Greek text here reads *ek pollon kardion dialogismoi*—"the thoughts out of many hearts" may be revealed. The Greek word for *thoughts* is where we get the word *dialogue.* The suffering of Christ on the cross pierces the soul of every man and reveals the innermost dialogue of the heart. It is in that "dialogue of the heart" where souls are purified and transformed by grace. Mary's suffering with Christ uniquely participates in both the suffering of Christ and the resulting redemption.

than any human person has ever or will ever suffer. Though her pains were not bodily, they were more intense than any of us are capable of feeling because none of us could ever love as she loved. Ecclesiastes 1:18 says it so well: "For in much wisdom is much vexation, and he who increases in knowledge increases in sorrow." Thus, we see "Our Lady of Sorrows" here at the foot of the cross.

It was at the foot of the cross, in that holy hour of her immeasurable suffering, that Jesus gave Mary to be the spiritual mother of St. John, thus connecting her suffering even more clearly to the redemption of souls. We know from Matthew 27:56 that John's birth mother was present at the Crucifixion too, so it would be strange for Jesus to refer to Mary as John's mother unless there was something much deeper going on; and indeed there was. *Lumen Gentium* 57–58 explains:

> This union of the mother with the Son in the work of salvation is made manifest from the time of Christ's virginal conception up to his death . . . when . . . she heard Simeon foretelling at the same time [of her presenting Christ in the temple] that her Son would be a sign of contradiction and that a sword would pierce the mother's soul, that out of many hearts thoughts might be revealed (cf. Luke 2:34–35 . . . [58] Thus, the Blessed Virgin advanced in her pilgrimage of faith, and faithfully persevered in her union with her Son unto the cross where she stood, in keeping with the divine plan, grieving exceedingly with her only begotten Son, uniting herself with a maternal heart with His sacrifice, and lovingly consenting to the immolation of this Victim which she herself had brought forth. Finally, she was given by the same Christ Jesus dying on the cross as a mother to His disciple with these words: "Woman, behold thy son."

Through her suffering Mary gives birth to her spiritual son, and—since "the beloved disciple" stands in for all Christians—to the whole Church. John confirms this for us at the "back of the book," affirming in Revelation that Mary is not only his own mother and the mother of Jesus, but the mother of all "who keep the commandments of God and bear testimony to Jesus" (12:17).

This biblical data indicates to us, just as the fathers of Vatican II declared:

> This maternity of Mary in the order of grace began with the consent which she gave in faith at the Annunciation and which she sustained without wavering beneath the cross, and lasts until the eternal fulfillment of all the elect. Taken up to heaven she did not lay aside this salvific duty, but by her constant intercession continued to bring us the gifts of eternal salvation ... This, however, is to be so understood that it neither takes away from nor adds anything to the dignity and efficaciousness of Christ the one Mediator.

> For no creature could ever be counted as equal with the Incarnate Word and Redeemer. Just as the priesthood of Christ is shared in various ways both by the ministers and by the faithful, and as the one goodness of God is really communicated in different ways to His creatures, so also the unique mediation of the Redeemer does not exclude but rather gives rise to a manifold cooperation which is but a sharing in this one source.[357]

All About Eve

As we wind down our thoughts concerning Mary's role in God's plan of salvation, perhaps it would be helpful to consider one final time her antecedent in *Eve*. In the Old Testament, the power and dignity of "the woman" is revealed in the fact that Eve did not have just a role, but a *primacy* in bringing death to all of her children. Any reading of the fall that assigns Eve anything less than an essential role does violence to the text.

---

357. *Lumen Gentium* 62.

In the New Testament, in fact, St. Paul so emphasizes Eve's role in the fall that some wrongly accuse him of misogyny.[358]

> I permit no woman to teach or to have authority over men; she is to keep silent. For Adam was formed first, then Eve; and Adam was not deceived, but the woman was deceived and became a transgressor (1 Tim. 2:12–14).

Yet this is not misogyny. In fact, those convicting Paul of misogyny here should also call him guilty of misandry in Romans 5:12–18:

> Therefore as sin came into the world through one man and death through sin . . . death reigned from Adam . . . even over those whose sins were not like the transgression of Adam . . . many died through one man's trespass . . . the effect of that one man's sin . . . death reigned through that one man . . . as one man's trespass led to condemnation for all men.

Paul was not a hater of women or men. He acknowledged both Adam and Eve's essential roles in original sin. Adam had ultimate responsibility as the "head" of the woman (see 1 Cor. 11:3), but Paul also asserts definitively that Eve's role was not superfluous. We could even say that Eve had a certain *primacy* between our two original parents, for she was first mover who brought about the fall through her intercession with Adam. 1 Timothy 2 is a powerful revelation of the power of woman that can be used for evil or good.

There is no doubt that it is the new Adam, Jesus Christ, who has the ultimate responsibility, as well as the ultimate power, for the restoration and salvation of the world. But it would be just as much an error to diminish the essential role of the new Eve in salvation as it would be to diminish the role of the first Eve in the fall. According to Scripture, it was through Eve's intercession that

---

358. O'Connor, *The New Jerome Biblical Commentary*, 811–812. Unfortunately, Fr. O'Connor claims, "The injunctions reflect the misogyny of 1 Timothy 2:11-14 . . . "

death came into the world. And, according to Scripture, it was through Mary's intercessory role that new life is brought into the world.

That's what calling Mary *Co-Redemptrix* is all about.

CONCLUSION

QUEEN OF QUEENS: MARY'S REGAL ROLE IN THE KINGDOM OF GOD

Pope Pius XII pithily summarized the core reasons Christians ought to honor Mary with the title of Queen of Heaven and Earth:

> According to ancient tradition and the sacred liturgy the main principle on which the royal dignity of Mary rests is without doubt her divine motherhood. In holy writ, concerning the son whom Mary will conceive, we read this sentence: "He shall be called the son of the most high, and the Lord God shall give unto him the throne of David his father, and he shall reign in the house of Jacob forever, and of his kingdom there will be no end," and in addition Mary is called "Mother of the Lord," from this it is easily concluded that she is a queen, since she bore a son who, at the very moment of his conception, because of the hypostatic union of the human nature with the Word, was also as man, king and lord of all things. So with complete justice St. John Damascene could write: "When she became mother of the creator, she truly became queen of every creature." Likewise, it can be said that the heavenly voice of the Archangel Gabriel was the first to proclaim Mary's royal office.[359]

If we understand that Jesus is the king of Israel, then we know who Mary is: the *queen mother*. It really is that simple.

We could add Revelation 12 to the mix in demonstrating Mary's queenship:

---

359. *Ad Caeli Reginam* 34.

And a great sign appeared in heaven, a woman clothed with the sun, with the moon under her feet, and on her head a crown of twelve stars; she was with child . . . she brought forth a male child, one who is to rule all the nations with a rod of iron, but her child was caught up to God and to his throne . . . Then the dragon was angry with the woman, and went off to make war on the rest of her offspring, on those who keep the commandments of God and bear testimony to Jesus (Rev. 12:1–2, 5, 17).

Here Mary is clearly depicted as a cosmic queen giving birth to both Christ and all Christians, all the while wearing her royal crown. She rules and reigns with her divine Son at the center of the perennial battle between the kingdom of God and the kingdoms of this world in union with "the serpent" of old. These texts alone demonstrate Mary to be queen of the kingdom of Christ.

But here's the problem. Although Pope Pius XII says "it is easily concluded that [Mary] is a queen," it is not so easy for millions outside of the Catholic Church to conclude. For the skeptic, then, we are going to show in this chapter how a fuller understanding of Old Testament typology can be the key to illuminating the truth of Mary's queenship.

Hidden in the Old and Revealed in the New

The "kingdom of David"—which Christ came to (in a sense) reconstitute, in accord with prophecy—is the most prominent type of "the kingdom of Christ" in the New Covenant, and it also reveals Mary's role as queen of that New Covenant kingdom.[360]

I will raise up your [King David's] offspring after you, who shall come forth from your body, and I will establish his kingdom.

360. The kingdom of Christ is not a *strict* reconstitution of the kingdom of David because Christ fulfills and transcends the old kingdom as well. Christ's kingdom is "not of this world" and "everlasting," whereas the kingdom of David was not (cf. John 18:36; Luke 1:33).

He shall build a house for my name, and I will establish the throne of his kingdom forever. I will be his father, and he shall be my son (2 Sam. 7:12–14).

For to us a child is born, to us a son is given; and the government will be upon his shoulder, and his name will be called Wonderful Counselor, Mighty God, Everlasting Father, Prince of Peace. Of the increase of his government and of peace there will be no end, upon the throne of David, and over his kingdom, to establish it, and to uphold it with justice and with righteousness from this time forth and for evermore. The zeal of the Lord of hosts will do this (Isa. 9:6–7).

From the very first verse of the New Testament through the book of Revelation, we find Jesus referred to as this prophetic "son of David," or "the holy one, the true one, who has the key of David."[361] There can be no doubt that Christ is revealed as the king. But what is revealed to us about a queen?

Scott Hahn provides the answer in the remarkable ancient office and Old Testament type of the *gebirah* (Heb., *great lady*):

In the ancient Near East, most nations were monarchies ruled by a king. In addition, most cultures practiced polygamy; so a given king often had several wives. This posed problems. First, whom should the people honor as queen? But more important, whose son should receive the right of succession to the throne? In most Near Eastern cultures, these twin problems were resolved by a single custom. The woman ordinarily honored as queen was not the wife of the king, but the mother of the king.[362]

It can be difficult for us in the modern Western world to understand ancient monarchical concepts. But first-century Jews un-

361. E.g., Matthew 1:1; Revelation 3:7.
362. Hahn, *Hail, Holy Queen*, 78.

derstood the notion of the *kingdom* that Jesus preached because *they lived it*. They knew that a kingdom meant that there was a king. And, in ancient Israel as in many nearby cultures, if there was a king there was a *queen mother*.

2 Kings 11:1–4:

> Now when Athaliah the mother of Ahaziah saw that her son was dead, she arose and destroyed all the royal family. But Jehosheba, the daughter of King Joram, sister of Ahaziah, took Joash the son of Ahaziah, and stole him away from among the king's sons who were about to be slain, and she put him and his nurse in a bedchamber. Thus she hid him from Athaliah, so that he was not slain; and he remained with her six years, hid in the house of the Lord, while Athaliah reigned over the land.

Queen Athaliah ruled in Israel for six years after her son, King Ahaziah, died. She was a wicked woman and so may not seem to be the greatest type of the Blessed Mother. But then there were many wicked kings in ancient Israel, too, who were nonetheless types of Christ. (Even the great King David himself is quite well-known for his moral failings.) Leaving aside Athaliah's wickedness, we see in this text a scriptural example of the importance and the authority of the queen mother.

2 Chronicles 15:16:

> Even Maacah, his mother, King Asa removed from being queen mother because she had made an abominable image for Asherah. Asa cut down her image, crushed it, and burned it at the brook Kidron.

Queen Mother Maacah was not exactly a picture of holiness, either. But her office was a powerful one in ancient Israel. Maacha held royal authority and was only deposed from it because she made an idol.

Jeremiah 13:18:

Say to the king and the queen mother: "Take a lowly seat, for your beautiful crown has come down from your head."

Both the king and the queen mother wore royal crowns, just as Mary is depicted wearing in Revelation 12:1.

Perhaps the best example of the power and authority of the queen mother in the Old Testament is found personified in Bathsheba in 1 Kings.

1 Kings 1:11–16, 22:

Then Nathan said to Bathsheba the mother of Solomon, "Have you not heard that Adonijah the son of Haggith has become king and David our lord does not know it? Now therefore come, let me give you counsel, that you may save your own life and the life of your son Solomon. Go in at once to King David, and say to him, 'Did you not, my lord the king, swear to your maidservant, saying, "Solomon your son shall reign after me, and he shall sit upon my throne"? Why then is Adonijah king?' Then while you are still speaking with the king, I will come in after you and confirm your words." So Bathsheba went to the king in to his chamber (now the king was very old, and Abishag the Shunamite was ministering to the king). Bathsheba bowed and did obeisance to the king, and the king said, "What do you desire?" . . . While she was still speaking with the king, Nathan the prophet came in.

While King David was still alive, Bathsheba was merely one among many of his wives. As such, she had to bow before her husband the king when making a request of him. In this case, in order to ensure that her request would be granted by the king, she also needed the aid of Nathan the prophet. However, after David's death, Bathsheba received a crown and a drastic change in authority. Bathsheba became the queen mother.

1 Kings 2:13–23:

Then Adonijah the son of Haggith came to Bathsheba the mother of Solomon. And she said, "Do you come peaceably?" He said, "Peaceably." Then he said, "I have something to say to you." She said, "Say on." He said, "You know that the kingdom was mine, and that all Israel fully expected me to reign; however the kingdom has turned about and become my brother's, for it was his from the Lord. And now I have one request to make of you; do not refuse me." She said to him, "Say on." And he said, "Pray ask King Solomon—he will not refuse you—to give me Abishag the Shunammite as my wife." Bathsheba said, "Very well; I will speak for you to the king."

So Bathsheba went to King Solomon, to speak to him on behalf of Adonijah. And the king rose to meet her, and bowed down to her; then he sat on his throne and had a seat brought for the king's mother; and she sat on his right. Then she said, "I have one small request to make of you; do not refuse me." And the king said to her, "Make your request, my mother; for I will not refuse you." She said, "Let Abishag the Shunammite be given to Adonijah your brother as his wife." King Solomon answered his mother, "And why do you ask Abishag the Shunammite for Adonijah? Ask for him the kingdom also; for he is my elder brother, and on his side are Abiathar the priest and Joab the son of Zeruiah." Then King Solomon swore by the Lord, saying, "God do so to me and more also if this word does not cost Adonijah his life!"

What a change! Once, Bathsheba bowed to the king. Now the new king—Solomon—bowed to *her*. (At that time the king of Israel bowed to *no one* except God . . . and evidently the queen mother.) As wife of the king, Bathsheba had to beg her husband David for a favor with the assistance of Nathan. As queen mother, Bathsheba needed no assistance and would be refused nothing.

A Power Play, Ancient Israel Style

If we read these verses from 1 Kings too quickly, we could miss one of the Old Testament's most telling examples of the power of the queen mother. The context of 1 Kings 2 depicts Adonijah, the elder brother, attempting to usurp the throne from his brother Solomon. He tried to use the power of the queen mother to manipulate his way to the top, cleverly asking Bathsheba to intercede with her son King Solomon to give him one of David's former wives, Abishag. It seems strange to us, but in ancient Israel, this power play was a nearly flawless plan. Adonijah already had Joab, David's general, many military leaders, and the high priest on his side. If he could acquire one of David's wives, it would be the last thing he needed to complete the coup d'état. Adonijah knew the king could refuse his mother nothing. So he made his request of Bathsheba.

Bathsheba seemed not to know that what she was asking of her royal son could cost him his kingdom. She may not have been the sharpest knife in the kitchen. And Adonijah *almost* succeeded in his plan—but he made a fatal mistake. He did not reckon that he was dealing with the wisest man who had ever walked the planet. When Solomon heard of the request Adonijah had made of the queen mother, he saw through his brother's plans and had him immediately killed. Because of the power of the intercession of the queen mother, he knew he couldn't refuse his mother's request—but now he didn't have to! Adonijah didn't seem to have considered that outcome.

The high degree of power and authority wielded by the queen mother in the kingdom of Israel gives us a context to appreciate in a deeper way the intercessory power of Mary as exemplified at the wedding feast of Cana in John 2. Are we saying that *whatever* Mary asks will be brought to pass by her divine Son? Yes, we are. If it was so for the Old Covenant type, how could it be anything less for the New Covenant fulfillment? We should always keep in mind, however, that Mary will never ask her Son to do anything that is contrary to his will. Her perfectly obedient will is only to do his will.[363] Mary never places her divine Son in the predicament that Bathsheba posed to her royal son.

Queen and Mother Prophesied

Psalm 45 is a text we have seen before. Verses 1–9 prophesy in some detail about Christ the king:

> My heart overflows with a goodly theme; I address my verses to the king . . . In your majesty ride forth victoriously for the cause of truth and to defend the right . . . Your divine throne endures forever and ever. Your royal scepter is a scepter of equity; you love righteousness and hate wickedness. Therefore God, your God, has anointed you with the oil of gladness above your fellows; your robes are all fragrant . . . From ivory palaces stringed instruments make you glad; daughters of kings are among your ladies of honor.

In the New Testament, the inspired author of Hebrews 1:8–9 quotes verses 6–7 of this very text as referring to Christ, his divinity, and his kingship. Immediately following those verses is another, lesser-known, prophecy that speaks of Mary:

> [A]t your right hand stands the queen in gold of Ophir. Hear, O daughter, consider, and incline your ear; forget your people and your father's house; and the king will desire your beauty. Since he is your lord, bow to him; the people of Tyre will sue your favor with gifts, the richest of the people with all kinds of wealth. The daughter of the king is decked in her chamber with gold-woven robes; in many-colored robes she is led to the king, with her virgin companions, her escort, in her train. With joy and gladness they are led along as they enter the palace of the king. Instead of your fathers shall be your sons; you will

---

363. 1 John 5:14 tells us that we will receive whatever we ask of God, "if it is in accord with [God's] will." Mary always prays thus; we strive to do so as best we can.

make them princes in all the earth. I will cause your name to be celebrated in all generations; therefore the peoples will praise you forever and ever (Ps. 45:9b–17).

Set in the context of a royal wedding, on the literal level this psalm referred to the king of Israel, likely Solomon, receiving a new bride, with his mother standing at his right to symbolize her power and authority. But on the spiritual level it refers to Christ and Mary. T.E. Bird says of this text:

> But although the poem may have been written in honor of a royal wedding (probably Solomon's), the inspired writer's thoughts reach beyond the actual event; he sees a king fairer than an ordinary man (3), one whom he addresses as "God" (7, 8), one whose throne is to remain forever (7), whose rule is to extend over the world . . . It is not surprising, therefore, that Jews and Christians have seen here the espousals between the Messiah and his people. The Targum treats the Psalm as strictly Messianic; St. John Chrysostom could say that on this point Jews and Christians were agreed (PG 55, 183); St. Thomas Aquinas gives the Catholic interpretation: "The subject-matter of this psalm is the espousals between Christ and the Church." On feasts of the Blessed Virgin, the Psalm is recited as Matins; (10–16) are applied to her as the Spouse of the Holy Ghost and the Queen of Heaven.[364]

Who is this woman of whom the Lord said, "I will cause your name to be celebrated in all generations; therefore the peoples will praise you forever and ever"? Not one of Solomon's wives fit the prophetic description.

Most every Christian—indeed most of the world beyond Christendom—knows the name of the Mother of God—*Mary*—

---

364. Bird, *A Catholic Commentary on Sacred Scripture*, 456.

who in fulfillment of this prophetic text said, "All generations shall call me blessed."[365]

Adoring the Queen of Heaven?

Many Protestants will concede that the evidence here presented is at least interesting, maybe even compelling. But they often cannot get past one biblical text from the Old Testament that casts a shadow over all that we've said so far. Norman Geisler and Ralph MacKenzie present that text—Jeremiah 7:18—along with commentary that represents the misguided faith of millions:

> Do you not see what they are doing in the streets of Judah and in the streets of Jerusalem? The children gather wood, the fathers kindle fire, and the women knead dough, to make cakes for the queen of heaven; and they pour out drink offerings to other gods, to provoke me to anger.

Geisler and MacKenzie comment:

> To call Mary "Queen of Heaven," knowing that this very phrase comes from an old pagan idolatrous cult condemned in the Bible (cf. Jer. 7:18), only invites the charge of Mariolatry. And Mariolatry is idolatry.[366]

I can certainly sympathize with their thinking here. I once thought the same. But the truth is, this text has absolutely nothing

---

365. Mary is most obviously the mother of the king—Jesus. But she is also a member of the Church, as are all Christians, and as such can be viewed as a bride of Christ as well. It must always be emphasized that just as we say with regard to all members of the Body of Christ in relation to Christ, this union is *not* sexual. It is *nuptial*, but this term is used by analogy. It is in this analogical context that some mystical writers will refer to Mary as having a *nuptial* relationship with Christ inasmuch as Christ is God. The great fourth-century Father and mystic, St. Ephrem of Syria, described Mary as if from her own lips: "I am a mother because of your conception, and bride am I because of your chastity" (*Hymns on the Nativity*, 16, 10).

366. Geisler and MacKenzie, *Roman Catholics and Evangelicals*, 322.

to do with the Blessed Mother as Queen of Heaven for at least three reasons:

1. Jeremiah here condemns the adoration of the Mesopotamian goddess Astarte.[367] She is in no way related to Mary. In fact, "she" did not and does not exist in reality. Mary, on the other hand, was a real historical person who was—and is—a queen by virtue of the fact that her Son was—and is—the king.

2. Jeremiah condemned *offering sacrifice* to "the queen of heaven." In Scripture, we have many examples of the proper way we should honor great members of the kingdom of God. We give "double honor" to "elders who rule well" in the Church (1 Tim. 5:17). Paul tells us we should "esteem very highly" those who are "over [us] in the Lord" (1 Thess. 5:12–13). We sing praises to great members of the family of God who have gone before us (Ps. 45:17). We bow down to them with reverence (1 Kings 2:19). We carry out the work of the Lord in their names (Matt. 10:40–42),[368] and more.

But there is one thing we ought never to do: *offer sacrifice* to them. Offering sacrifice is tantamount to the adoration that is due God alone. And this is precisely what Jeremiah was condemning. The Catholic Church does not teach—*and has never taught*—that we should adore Mary.[369] Catholics offer sacrifice exclusively to God.[370]

---

367. Cf. Brown, Fitzmeyer, Murphy, *The Jerome Biblical Commentary,* 310.

368. The Douay-Rheims and King James Versions of Scripture translate Matthew 10:42 best: "Whoever shall give to one of these little ones even a cup of water *in the name of a disciple,* verily I say to you he shall not lose his reward." This is not to be confused with the condemnation of sectarianism in 1 Corinthians 1:11–13. There Paul condemns dividing the body of Christ [by misusing the name of a disciple in dividing from other Christians, not doing good works in the name of a disciple] as Jesus says is proper to do in Matthew 10:40–42.

369. CCC 2110–2114. Cf. *Lumen Gentium* 66–67; CCC 971.

370. In every generation, Holy Mother Church is careful in liturgical prayer to use language of veneration for the saints as opposed to the language of adoration due to God alone.

3. To the Evangelical and Fundamentalist, the mere fact that worshipping someone called "queen of heaven" is condemned in Jeremiah 7 eliminates the *possibility* of Mary being the true Queen of Heaven and Earth. This simply does not follow. That there is a counterfeit queen does not mean there can't be an authentic one. This reasoning followed to its logical end would lead to abandoning the entire Christian faith! We could not have a Bible because Hinduism, Islam, and many other false religions have "holy books." We could not call Jesus *Son of God* because Zeus and Hera had Apollo, Isis and Osiris had Horus, etc. The fact that there was a false "queen of heaven" worshipped in ancient Mesopotamia does not negate the reality of the true queen who is honored as such in the kingdom of God.

Some Protestant apologists make a different objection: If Mary was truly a queen, why didn't she wear a crown? Why wasn't she driven in chariots and catered to in her every want? Those who ask this question seem to require worldly accolades as proof of Mary's queenship.

But we must remember that Christ's kingdom is "not of this world" (John 18:36). No Protestant would deny that Christ was king even while he walked the earth, yet he was hardly treated in accordance with his royal dignity. His crown was made of thorns. Why should we expect something different of Mary, whose road to glory (revealed in Revelation 12) passed through the suffering and ignominy of the cross; whose own soul, according to Simeon's prophecy, was pierced by a sword (Luke 2:34–35)?

Phillipians 2:5–9 tells us that Christ is the ultimate example of the way of humility:

> Have this mind among yourselves, which was in Christ Jesus, who, though he was in the form of God, did not count equality with God a thing to be grasped, but emptied himself, taking the nature of a servant . . . he humbled himself, and became

obedient unto death, even death on a cross. Therefore God has highly exalted him . . .

The Greek word here *servant* is *doulos,* which can also be translated as *bond-slave.* This is a word that was packed with meaning for the ancient Jewish people. In the Old Covenant, a Hebrew *doulos* could only be held as such for six years. By the seventh year, he must go free. However, if the slave had grown to love his master and wanted to become his servant in perpetuity, the Bible gives this prescription to the master:

[Y]ou shall take an awl and thrust it through his ear into the door, and he shall be your bondman forever (Deut. 15:17).

In the image of the *doulos,* Jesus freely chose to become a slave, offering not his ear but his entire body to be nailed to the wood of a cross. Yet even during his Passion he did not pause from being king. On the contrary, this was the essence of his true kingship: He was called to suffer and die in obscurity so that his subjects might have life. In similar fashion, Mary—who declared herself the "*doulei* [feminine of *doulos,* usually translated *handmaid*] of the Lord" in Luke 1:38—was called to suffer at the foot of the cross in this same obscurity.

Honor to Whom Honor Is Due

Elizabeth's response to the salutation of Mary in Luke 1:43— "And why is this granted me, that the mother of my Lord should come to me?"—also reveals Mary's queenship. In ancient Middle-Eastern culture, the younger honored the elder,[371] yet here it is the elder Elizabeth who honors her younger kinswoman Mary.

Why did Elizabeth revere Mary so? Elizabeth herself gave us the answer: Because Mary was mother of the Lord—because of

---

371. Consider Jacob/Esau in Genesis 33:3, or Joseph/Jacob in Genesis 48:12, just to name two examples.

her *relation to Jesus the king*. Most Christians today understand Jesus' royal position in the kingdom, but unfortunately not as many
understand the biblical fact, which Elizabeth demonstrates, that
the king's mother is owed honor and respect as well.

In the fourth century, St. Athanasius pointed out that not only
humans but angels honor Mary. This is perhaps even more significant, because generally speaking when we examine examples
of angels appearing to men in Scripture, there is never a doubt as
to who is the superior. When John saw an angel, for example, he
wanted to worship him and had to be corrected:

> And the angel said to me, "Write this: Blessed are those who
> are invited to the marriage supper of the Lamb." And he said
> to me, "These are true words of God." Then I fell down at his
> feet to worship him, but he said to me, "You must not do that!
> I am a fellow servant with you and your brethren who hold the
> testimony of Jesus. Worship God" (Rev. 19:9–10).

You would think John would have learned from this admoni-
tion[372] to knock off the worshipping of angels, but a little later we
see a repeat:

> I John am he who heard and saw these things. And when I
> heard and saw them, I fell down to worship at the feet of the
> angel who showed them to me; but he said to me, "You must
> not do that! I am a fellow servant with you and your brethren

---

372. Haydock, *The Douay-Rheims New Testament,* 1652; 1656. Fr. Haydock shows there
are various ways to view this text. One interpretation would say John "wishes to
adore the angel, but not with the supreme worship of *latria* . . . but the angel, through
respect for St. John, still refuses the proffered honor, and to show the holy society
that was hereafter to exist between angels and men, who were to compose but one
and the same family." That is the minority opinion. Of the more probable opinion,
Haydock writes: "St. Athanasius and St. Augustine think St. John took the angel to
be Jesus Christ, and as such was desirous of paying him the supreme homage, *latria*."
(Augustine, *On the Gospel of John,* Tract. 13, 2; Athanasius, *Four Discourses Against the
Arians,* Discourse 2, 16, 23.)

the prophets, and with those who keep the words of this book. Worship God" (Rev. 22:8–9).

We may be tempted to criticize John, but let us recall that this man was "the beloved disciple" of Jesus who knew our Lord more intimately than any of us. The truth is, no man by his natural powers could discern whether an angel was in fact God, a good angel, or a demon. The angelic nature is so far superior to the human that a particular grace would be required for discernment.[373]

Given this knowledge of the angelic nature's superiority, we discover a remarkable difference comparing John's response to the presence of an angel with the familiarity with which Mary converses with the archangel Gabriel. Athanasius wrote:

If I say that the angels and archangels are great—but you are greater than them all, for the angels and archangels serve with trembling the One who dwells in your womb, and they dare not speak in his presence, while you speak to him freely.[374]

Because of Mary's calling to be Mother of God and Queen of Heaven and Earth, the plenitude of grace she received rendered her superior to the angels in the order of grace—*even in this life.*[375]

---

373. Even the Archangel Michael "did not presume to pronounce a reviling judgment upon [Lucifer], but said, 'The Lord rebuke you'" (Jude 9). St. Thomas argues in the *Summa* (I, Q. 63, Art. 7, Repl. Obj. 1) that Lucifer is a fallen cherub. This comes from the Vulgate translation of Ezekiel 28:14, which says of the devil, "Thou a cherub stretched out." The NAB says, "With the cherub I placed you." The RSV:CE says, "With an anointed guardian cherub I placed you"— bringing out the image of Lucifer's being associated with the two guardian cherubim over the Ark of the Covenant. Some argue Lucifer to be an archangel; if that were the case St. Michael would still rely upon God's power to battle with his equal. But if Lucifer were a fallen cherub, he would have been above an archangel in the choir of angels according to nature. Hence the idea he would not "presume" in battling with Lucifer, but appealed directly to God to deal with the devil. How much more would we, mere humans—need grace in order to combat, or even to discern the presence of, the devil who so often comes to us "disguis[ing] himself as an angel of light" (2 Cor. 11:14)?

374. *Homily of the Papyrus on Turin*, quoted in Gambero, *Mary and the Fathers of the Church*, 106.

375. Though Mary was unique among human persons in that she was already superior to

As St. Ephrem said, as Christ's queen mother, Mary is queen of the entire universe.[376] Her dominion far exceeds that of even the greatest of the angels.

We in the modern Western world—in particular in the United States—have for the most part lost all sense of the honor that is due in justice to kings and potentates. Perhaps this is one reason why a Protestant view, void of that sense, works well in America. But one thing is certain: That was not the view of the authors of Scripture. They understood the honor due to kings and queens, and they lived it. And the Church understands it too, even unto this day, for it knows that the nature of the kingdom of God does not change with the politics of the modern world.

In the end, the truth about Mary as Queen of Heaven and Earth brings us back to where we started on this journey through Scripture and history considering the truth about the Marian doctrines. All of the Marian doctrines are first and foremost Christocentric. Everything about Mary's queenship is entirely dependent upon and points to Mary's divine and royal Son. But it also reveals something about humanity.

The road to the book of Revelation and the triumph of Mary gloriously crowned as Queen of Heaven and Earth had to pass by the foot of the cross, and even more, through her own mystical

---

the angels even before she was glorified, in her we see our future. If we endure until the end and are finally saved, *we* may well be superior to the angels like she is, because of our union with Christ. The Son of God did not become an angel, he became a man! Ephesians 1:20–21 tells us that God "raised [Christ] from the dead and made him sit at his right hand in the heavenly places, far above all rule and authority and power and dominion." Ephesians 2:6 says God has "raised *us* up with him, and made *us* sit with him in the heavenly places in Christ Jesus." This seems to indicate that in Christ, Christians too will be exalted above "all rule authority and power and dominion" (a reference to angels). According to Francisco Suarez (*De Angelis*, 7, 13), it was Lucifer's envy of man's exultation over the angelic nature (cf. Wis. 2:24) that became "the occasion of the pride of Lucifer" and was the source of both his "fall from grace" and his hatred for each and every human being. Cf. *The Catholic Encyclopedia*, 765.

376. *Hymni de B Mana*, ed. Th. J. Lamy, t. II, Mechliniae, 1886, hymn. XIX, 624. Quoted in Pope Pius XII, *Ad Caeli Reginam*, 10.

death with Christ on the cross. Thus, the royal calling of *all* Christians is echoed in the life and person of Mary:[377]

> He who conquers, I will grant him to sit with me on my throne, as I myself conquered and sat down with my Father on his throne (Rev. 3:21).

We all love to ponder our royal calling and the glory that awaits Christians in heaven, but Mary reminds us in stark terms that there is no bypassing Calvary before reaching the triumph and glory of heaven. If the Queen of Heaven and Earth was called to the suffering of the cross—to share in Christ's crown of thorns before she could receive her own crown of stars—how could any Christian not acknowledge his own calling, according to Romans 8:17, to "suffer with him in order that [he] may be glorified together with him"?

---

377. Cf. *Lumen Gentium* 65.

AFTERWORD
MARY'S ONGOING PLACE IN OUR LIVES

Having finished the writing of this book, I reflected upon how many things I might have included but did not. This work can be just a beginning—perhaps a foundation—for a lifetime of reflection upon "our tainted nature's solitary boast," as the poet Wordsworth so beautifully described our Blessed Mother.

Not long ago I was introduced to some beautiful "brides of Christ" from a religious order called the Sisters of Mary, Mother of the Eucharist. That is a relatively new title for Mary that connects Mary as Mother of God with her role in God's plan of salvation in a most powerful way. On one level, we can see its fittingness in light of the Real Presence. If the Eucharist is truly Jesus present, body, blood, soul, and divinity, then of course Mary is the Mother of the Eucharist. Simple enough. But its significance goes deeper still.

When we think of Mary as Mother of the Church we often think of her involvement in every Christian's being "born" into the family of God in baptism. As Scripture says, Mary is the mother of all those "who keep the commandments of God and bear testimony to Jesus" (Rev. 12:17). *Mother of the Eucharist* gives us deeper insight into Mary's ongoing role in bringing us the gifts of salvation, as *Lumen Gentium* says. This is not something we can view in a test tube; it is a matter of faith. But if in the Holy Sacrifice of the Mass we are truly present with Mary at the foot of the cross, suffering with her son "that thoughts out of many hearts may be revealed" (Luke 2:35), then in some sense, every time we receive the Eucharist Mary is present to us mystically and we are receiving the fruit of her prayer and suffering into our everyday lives, for our salvation. This one title of our Lady alone could be the subject of years of meditation without ever fully plumbing its depths.

It is my hope and prayer that this book, which for me has been a labor of love, will for you be a source of help in defending the honor of our Lord, our Lady, and Holy Mother Church. But I also hope it will be a catalyst for every reader to dive deeper into Mariology and thereby dive deeper into our Faith. As with all Catholic theology, though we are speaking of a deposit of faith that is unchangeable, "once for all delivered to the saints" (Jude 3), this deposit is by no means static. It grows and develops while never changing in substance. I pray that each of us will truly take to heart the words of Jesus and truly *behold our mother* in the context of the deposit of faith. In beholding her beauty and her truth, we behold truth himself—Jesus Christ.

APPENDIX I
PATRISTIC EVIDENCE FOR
THEOTOKOS

Many Protestants allege that the dogma of Mary, Mother of God, was invented in the fourth or fifth century. Jimmy Swaggart, for example, claims, "the use of the term 'Mother of God' originated about A.D. 381."[378] He doesn't bother to give a citation or justification for his contention, but at any rate, the assertion is demonstrably false. We have already seen Mary as *Theotokos* revealed to us in Sacred Scripture. But we also find this teaching in some of the very earliest Christian writings and in the teachings of some of the greatest defenders of orthodoxy in the Patristic period. An exhaustive study of this topic is beyond the scope of this book, but we will briefly examine some of the earliest examples.

St. Ignatius of Antioch

In what is one of the most ancient among all of the writings of the Fathers, we discover a remarkably clear statement from the beloved bishop and martyr, St. Ignatius of Antioch, writing ca. A.D. 107:

> For our God, Jesus Christ, was, according to the appointment of God, conceived in the womb by Mary, of the seed of David, but by the Holy Ghost. He was born and baptized, that by his passion he might purify the water.[379]

Ignatius is one of very few "apostolic Fathers," meaning he was a contemporary of the apostles themselves. He is quoted or alluded

378. Swaggart, *Catholicism and Christianity*, 102.
379. *Letter to the Ephesians*, 18:2.

to by multiple Fathers and early Christian writers including St. Polycarp and St. Irenaeus in the second century, Origen in the third century, and many more in years and centuries following. He penned these particular words in his Letter to the Ephesians as he journeyed toward Rome, where he would be martyred for confessing his Christian faith before Emperor Trajan.

The casualness with which this great saint refers to God being conceived in Mary's womb is striking. Evidently, the belief that Mary was the Mother of God was already common teaching at the very beginning of the second century. Even though the actual title of *Theotokos* is not mentioned, the theology is unequivocal: *God was born.*

St. Irenaeus of Lyons

In the latter half of the second century, St. Irenaeus, the bishop of Lyons and defender of the Catholic faith, teaches the theology of *Theotokos* very clearly. In fact, his greatest work, *Against Heresies* (ca. A.D. 177), was prophetic in its condemnation of anyone who would "divide" Christ into "parts." This is exactly what Nestorians would end up doing 250 years later when they would deny Mary to be Mother of God—as would Walter Martin, Eric Svendsen, Jimmy Swaggart, and multitudes of Protestants today.

> Although they certainly do with their tongue confess one Jesus Christ, they make fools of themselves, thinking one thing and saying another . . . alleging [as they do,] that one Being suffered and was born, and that this was Jesus; but that there was another who descended upon Him, and this was Christ, who ascended again . . . whom they assert to be incomprehensible, invisible, and impassible.[380]

Though the Gnostics Irenaeus was dealing with "divided Christ" in a more radical way than the later Nestorians, or some of the

---

380. *Against Heresies* III, 16, 6.

much-later Protestants would, the principles this ancient Bishop of Lyons uses to combat them can be applied to all three situations.[381] Irenaeus teaches the same *being* (we would say person) who suffered and died was also the being who is the *invisible God*. In this next passage, Irenaeus is very clear in saying the Eternal Word of God and Son of God becomes the Son of man while remaining the same being, or subject, who is Lord and Almighty God. For Irenaeus, there is only one *he* with regard to the Son of God. *He* is both God and man because "he took up man into himself," but he remains the divine Son of God/Word of God.

> There is therefore ... one Christ Jesus, who came by means of the whole dispensational arrangements [connected with him], and gathered together all things in himself. But in every respect, too, he is man, the formation of God; and thus he took up man into himself, the invisible becoming visible, the incomprehensible being made comprehensible, the impassible becoming capable of suffering, and the Word being made man, thus summing up all things in himself: so that as in super-celestial, spiritual, and invisible things, the Word of God is supreme, so also in things visible and corporeal He might possess the supremacy, and, taking to himself the pre-eminence, as well as constituting himself head of the Church ...

> [I]nasmuch as he is himself the Savior of those who are saved, and the Lord of those who are under authority, and the God of all those things which have been formed, the only-begotten of the Father ... the Word of God, who became incarnate when the fullness of time had come, at which the Son of God had to become the Son of man.[382]

---

381. Nestorians who historically denied the theology of *Theotokos,* along with Protestants, do not claim there are "two beings"—one representing "Jesus" and the other "the Christ"—at least as overtly as the Gnostics did; however, they do, in effect, divide Christ. Thus, Irenaeus's teaching is useful for the discussion.

382. Ibid., 6–7.

Irenaeus goes on to say those who would "divide up Christ" into the man Jesus and a divine Christ have a "doctrine that is homicidal . . . lowering and dividing the Son of God in many ways."[383] Moreover, and most precisely to our point, anyone attempting to teach that Mary was the mother of Jesus while denying her to be the Mother of God would raise the ire of this great saint and apologist precisely because Irenaeus believed, as Catholics have for 2,000 years, that Mary gave birth to that one being (or person) who is the divine Word of God:

> He declares in the plainest manner, that the same Being who was laid hold of, and underwent suffering, and shed his blood for us, was both Christ and the Son of God . . . the Son of God, is one and the same, who did by suffering reconcile us to God, and rose from the dead; who is at the right hand of the Father, and perfect in all things; "who, when he was buffeted, struck not in return; who, when he suffered, threatened not;" and when he underwent tyranny, he prayed his Father that he would forgive those who had crucified him. For he did himself truly bring in salvation: since he is himself the Word of God, himself the only-begotten of the Father, Christ Jesus our Lord.[384]

> For I have shown from the scriptures that no one of the sons of Adam is as to everything, and absolutely, called God, or named Lord. But that he is himself in his own right, beyond all men who ever lived, God, and Lord, and king eternal, and the incarnate Word, proclaimed by all the prophets, the apostles, and by the Spirit himself . . . Now, the scriptures would not have testified these things of him, if, like others, he had been a mere man. But that he had, beyond all others, in himself that pre-eminent birth which is from the most high Father, and also

---

383. Ibid., 8.
384. Ibid., 9.

experienced that pre-eminent birth which is from the Virgin, the divine scriptures do in both respects testify of him.[385]

There can be no doubt that the *he* who was "[begotten] from the most high Father" in eternity, and born of Mary, or who "also experienced that pre-eminent birth which is from the Virgin," according to Irenaeus, was God. Thus:

> The Word himself, born of Mary, who was still a virgin, rightly received in birth the recapitulation of Adam, thereby recapitulating Adam in himself.[386]

Or, later in this same work:

> The Virgin Mary . . . being obedient to his word, received from an angel the glad tidings that she was to bear God.[387]

The theology of *Theotokos* could hardly be clearer. The eternal Word Himself, almighty God, was born of Mary so that Mary could be said to have carried God in her womb. That sounds a lot like "ascribing birth to deity"!

The *Sub Tuum* (ca. 250)

From the third century we have an ancient Coptic Catholic prayer called the *Sub Tuum*—a prayer sung as a hymn—that gives us an early example of the specific title *Mother of God*. It is doubtful that the third-century fragment containing this ancient hymn is the original document, though—it was likely a copy of a hymn already in use in Alexandria, Egypt—so the title was most likely used even earlier. The Greek text uses the term *Theotokos* about 200 years before the Council of Ephesus:

---

385. Ibid., 19, 2.
386. Ibid., 21, 10, cited in Jurgens, *The Faith of the Early Fathers*, vol. 1, 93.
387. Ibid., V, 19, 1, cited in Jurgens, 101.

> Under your mercy, we take refuge, Mother of God, do not reject our supplications in necessity. But deliver us from danger, [O you] alone pure and alone blessed.[388]

ORIGEN (246)

While rebuffing Nestorius and his spiritual advisor (the presbyter Anastatius), the fifth-century historian Socrates gives us insight into the belief of the great third-century Christian writer, Origen, by mentioning a then-extant commentary on Romans he wrote in 246:

> Origen also in the first volume of his *Commentaries* on the apostle's epistle to the Romans, gives an ample exposition of the sense in which the term *Theotokos* is used. It is therefore obvious that Nestorius had very little acquaintance with the treatises of the ancients.[389]

The same can be said of moderns who deny Mary as the Mother of God and claim this understanding is a novelty of the fourth or fifth century.

Beginning in the early fourth century, *Theotokos* becomes much more commonplace in the writings of the Fathers as well as in popular devotion, most likely due to Arius's denial of the divinity of Christ. "Mother of God" represented an ancient antidote to the novel heresy. Fr. Valentine Long explains:

> The dated salutation [*the Sub Tuum*] refutes the assumption that St. Athanasius, who deserves high praise for so much else, invented the term *Theotokos*. His predecessor in the Alexandrian see, Patriarch Alexander, had used it with force in the official deposition of Arius before the Council of Nicaea. St. Cyril of Jerusalem, with a casualness that indicates a general

---

388. Cited in Gambero, *Mary and the Fathers of the Church* , 69–70, 79.
389. *Ecclesiastical History* 32, citing Origen, *Commentary on Romans*, I, 1, 5.

acceptance of the term, refers in his catechism to "the Virgin Mother of God" in her blessed childbirth. Then Eusebius in his *Life of Constantine* relates that the emperor's saintly mother had the Cave of Bethlehem elaborately decorated out of love and reverence for "the Mother of God."[390]

ALEXANDER OF ALEXANDRIA (324)

Alexander was the bishop of Alexandria, where one of his priests, Arius, originated the heresy that bears his name. Arius denied that Mary was Mother of God because he denied Jesus was God. Thus that title became an important spiritual weapon and tool for apologetics in the war against the Arians before, during, and after the Council of Nicaea in 325. Alexander, in a letter written to another bishop also named Alexander, in 324, gives us a pre-Nicene example:

> After this, we acknowledge the resurrection of the dead, of which Jesus Christ our Lord became the firstling; who bore a body not in appearance but in truth, derived from Mary the Mother of God.[391]

ST. CYRIL OF JERUSALEM (350)

> Many, my beloved, are the true testimonies concerning Christ. The Father bears witness . . . the Holy Ghost bears witness . . . the Archangel Gabriel bears witness . . . the Virgin Mother of God bears witness.[392]

---

390. Long, *The Mother of God*, 23.
391. *Letter to Another Bishop Alexander and to All Non-Egyptian Bishops*, 12.
392. *Catecheses*, 10, 19.

St. Athanasius of Alexandria (365)

The Word begotten of the Father from on high, inexpressibly, inexplicably, incomprehensibly, and eternally, is He that is born in time here below of the Virgin Mary, the Mother of God.[393]

St. Epiphanius (374)

For this is the Holy Savior who came down from heaven, who deigned to fashion our salvation in a virginal workshop ... who did not change His nature when he took on humanity along with His divinity . . . who took on the human flesh and soul; being perfect at the side of the Father and incarnate among us, not in appearance, but in truth . . . from Mary, the Mother of God through the Holy Spirit.[394]

St. Gregory Nazianzen (382)

If anyone does not accept the holy Mary as *Theotokos*, he is without the Godhead.[395]

In addition to these examples are affirmations of the *Theotokos* from other fourth-century Fathers, such as St. Gregory of Nyssa, as well as St. Jerome, St. Augustine, St. John Cassian, and others in the fifth century and beyond. One thing is certain from our research: when you consider Mary as Mother of God, you are truly considering the *faith of our fathers.*

---

393. *On the Incarnation of the Word of God,* 8.
394. *The Man Well-Anchored,* 75.
395. *Letter* 101.

APPENDIX II

PATRISTIC EVIDENCE FOR MARY'S PERPETUAL VIRGINITY

During the first 250 years of Christian history, the Fathers of the Church were more certain of the truth of the Perpetual Virginity of Mary than they were of the canon of Scripture. There was some disagreement about which books belonged in the Bible, but there was no disagreement when it came to Mary ever-virgin.

Tertullian was the only Christian writer we know of in these early centuries even to posit the possibility that Mary had other children. And he did so only after he had been infected with the rebellion of the Montanists and lost credibility among the Catholic faithful of his day. In fact, a century and a half later, when the fourth-century heretic Helvidius attempted to use Tertullian as an authority on this issue, Jerome dismissed the idea in a sentence: "Of Tertullian I say no more than that he did not belong to the Church."[396]

Tertullian is not recognized by many to be a true Father of the Church because, as far as we know, he died a heretic. The true Fathers were *unanimous* on the Perpetual Virginity of Mary.[397] It would not be until the fourth century that a few challenges to the dogma arose; but the swift and decisive condemnations that were issued against them—from Jerome, Athanasius, Augustine, Ambrose, Epiphanius and many more—only confirm how universal the teaching was. As a matter of history, these few who denied the doctrine were fighting against the whole Christian world!

We will not attempt to exhaust the examples of the Fathers on

---

396. *On the Perpetual Virginity of Blessed Mary*, 19.

397. This is an open question. Unlike the Doctors of the Church, of whom we have a formal list approved by the Church, there is no official list of Church Fathers. Some hold Tertullian to be a Father, some don't.

this topic, but we will respond to claims like this one from Eric Svendsen, who asserts:

> The Bible nowhere teaches [the Perpetual Virginity of Mary]— nor did the earliest church Fathers.[398]

He says this without any historical justification, of course. But in order to demonstrate both the antiquity and universality of this teaching among the Fathers, we will begin with some of the very earliest Christian writings we have and move forward through the first five centuries of the Christian era, sampling some of the works of the greatest Christians of the period.

THE PROTOEVANGELIUM OF JAMES (CA. A.D. 140)

This is one of the oldest extrabiblical writings extant and it is extremely significant to note that one of its central themes was the Perpetual Virginity of Mary. In fact, according to the renowned Patristics scholar Johannes Quasten, "The principal aim of the whole writing is to prove the perpetual and inviolate virginity of Mary before, in, and after the birth of Christ."[399]

This second-century author records Mary's presentation in the temple at the age of three, very much in the tradition of Samuel, who had been similarly presented to the service of the Lord by his mother, Hannah, in 1 Samuel 1:11, 22. After her dedication to the Lord, Mary would have served in the temple much as did Anna the prophetess—who is mentioned in Luke 2:37—and many other women through the centuries (see 1 Samuel 2:22). According to this ancient document, a vow of perpetual virginity was included in her life of consecrated service.

The *Protoevangelium* also records that by the age of twelve, due to her maturation as a young woman, it was necessary for Mary to have a guardian who would respect her vow of virginity. St.

---

398. Svendson, *Evangelical Answers*, 137.
399. Quasten, *Patrology*, vol. 1, 120–121.

Joseph, who was reported to be an elderly widower who already had children by an earlier marriage, was chosen through a miraculous sign to be the guardian and protector of Mary's virginity: "Thou hast been chosen by lot to take into thy keeping the virgin of the Lord."[400]

St. Clement of Alexandria (ca. a.d. 200)

It appears that even today many hold that Mary, after the birth of her son, was found to be in the state of a woman who has given birth, while in fact she was not so. For some say that, after giving birth, she was examined by a midwife, who found her to be a virgin.[401] These things are attested to by the scriptures of the Lord, which also give birth to the truth and remain virginal . . . "She gave birth and did not give birth,"[402] Scripture says, since she conceived by herself, not as a result of union with a man.[403]

St. Clement presents Mary as a sort of archetype of the Scriptures, which also *give birth* ("to the truth") yet *remain virginal*. He similarly viewed Mary as the archetype of the Church, the ever-virginal bride of Christ. Both were virgins who give birth yet remain virgins: "She (the Church) is virgin and Mother simultaneously; a virgin undefiled and a mother full of love."[404]

Origen (ca. 230)

Because of his errors in certain matters, most famously his beliefs in universal salvation and the preexistence of human souls, like Tertullian, Origen is not regarded by some to be a Father of the

---

400. *Protoevangelium of James*, 9.
401. Clement here references the *Protoevangelium of James*, 19–20.
402. Clement here references the apocryphal *Pseudo-Ezekiel*, which other Christian writers cite as "Scripture" as well, e.g., Tertullian, *De Carne Christi* 23, PL 2, 790.
403. *Stromata*, 7, 16.
404. *The Instructor*, I, 6.

Church. A better argument could be made in favor of Origen, though, because his errors concerned matters not settled in the Church at the time of his writing. Origen was also probably the most influential Christian writer of the third century and certainly a faithful Catholic until his death in 254. He declared of Mary's perpetual virginity:

> For if Mary, as those declare who with sound mind extol her, had no other son but Jesus, and yet Jesus says to His mother, Woman, behold your son, and not Behold you have this son also, then He virtually said to her, Lo, this is Jesus, whom you bore. Is it not the case that everyone who is perfect lives himself no longer, but Christ lives in him; and if Christ lives in him, then it is said of him to Mary, Behold your son, Christ.[405]

EUSEBIUS OF CAESAREA (CA. 350)

In his classic *Ecclesiastical History*, Eusebius gives us insight into the two prevailing beliefs of the early Church concerning the *brothers of the Lord*. One belief was that they were the offspring of Joseph's prior marriage, before his first wife died and before he was espoused to Mary. This belief would be in agreement with the *Protoevangelium of James*, as we saw above. The other belief was that the *brothers of the Lord* were cousins or some other extended relation. The one opinion Eusebius never even mentions as a possibility was that Mary had other children with Joseph. In fact, no orthodox Christian thought that to be an option. The silence is truly deafening when we consider the work of the Fathers in general.

> Then James, whom the ancients surnamed the Just on account of the excellence of his virtue, is recorded to have been the first to be made bishop of the church of Jerusalem. This James was called the brother of the Lord because he was known as

405. *Commentary on John* I, ch. 6.

a son of Joseph, and Joseph was supposed to be the father of Christ, because the Virgin, being betrothed to him, "was found with child by the Holy Ghost before they came together," as the account of the holy Gospels shows. But Clement [of Alexandria] in the sixth book of his Hypotyposes writes thus:

For they say that Peter and James and John after the ascension of our savior, as if also preferred by our Lord, strove not after honor, but chose James the Just bishop of Jerusalem.

But the same writer, in the seventh book of this same work, also says:

The Lord after his Resurrection imparted knowledge to James the Just and to John and Peter, and they imparted it to the rest of the apostles, and the rest of the apostles to the seventy, of whom Barnabas was one. But there were two Jameses: one called the Just, who was thrown from the pinnacle of the temple and was beaten to death with a club by a fuller, and another who was beheaded.

Paul also makes mention of the same James the Just, when he writes: "Other apostles saw I none, save James the Lord's brother" [quoting Gal. 1:19].[406]

It is noteworthy that Eusebius seems to be content as a historian to report both acceptable opinions in this matter. He reports the theory that St. James was the half-brother of Jesus, yet he also records the ancient belief that James was the second of the "two Jameses" in the list of the apostles. This would, of course, make him the "son of Alphaeus" of Luke 6:15, rather than a "son of Joseph." This would lend credence to the belief that James was Jesus' cousin.

As a Catholic, one is permitted to believe either that the

---

406. *Ecclesiastical History* II, 1, 2–5.

"brothers of the Lord" are cousins or that they are half-brothers of Jesus, though the *sensus ecclesiae* is that the *brothers of the Lord* were his cousins. The half-brother theory is problematic, as Fr. S. Shearer points out:

> In the same way [as Helvidius's heresy of Jesus having uterine brothers was silenced in the fourth century], little more was heard until recent times of the theory of Origen, Clement of Alexandria, St. Epiphanius and some other early writers who, in defending the doctrine of the perpetual virginity of our Lady, had maintained that the "brethren of the Lord" were our Lord's half-brothers, sons of Joseph by a former marriage. St. Jerome condemned the holders of such a view as "following the ravings of the apocryphal writings." One can hardly imagine him speaking thus if the theory were widely held or supported by a well-defined tradition.

> Mary, the mother of James and Joseph, was alive at the time of the Passion (cf. Matt. 27:56, Luke 24:10). But if James and Joseph are the sons of St. Joseph (of which St. Jerome pointed out, there is no indication in Scripture), we should have to conclude that this Mary was his divorced wife. This, in view of the character of St. Joseph as portrayed in the Gospels ("a right-minded man," Matt. 1:19, etc.) is quite unthinkable. It is not surprising, then, that the *sensus Ecclesia* is certainly that St. Joseph preserved virginity and had no wife except Mary.[407]

Fr. Shearer wrote the above before the publication of the *Catechism of the Catholic Church*, which seems to confirm his thesis:

> Against this doctrine the objection is sometimes raised that the Bible mentions brothers and sisters of Jesus. The Church has always understood these passages as not referring to other children of the Virgin Mary. In fact James and Joseph, "brothers

407. Shearer, *A Catholic Commentary on Sacred Scripture*, 845.

of Jesus," are the sons of another Mary, a disciple of Christ, whom St. Matthew significantly calls "the other Mary." They are close relations of Jesus, according to an Old Testament expression.[408]

If this "other Mary" was a relative of Mary, as the *Catechism* teaches, and we wanted to say she was the former wife of St. Joseph, we would have to conclude that Joseph divorced Mary's sister (or relative) and married Mary while his first wife was still alive. This would seem to fall short of the lofty status at which the Church has placed Joseph and is therefore an unlikely scenario.

Further, in order for Jesus to be the rightful heir to the throne in Israel, it would have been fitting for him to be Joseph's firstborn son. He would most likely not have had older brothers who were sons of Joseph by an earlier marriage.

Most importantly, whether you agree that James was Jesus' half-brother or some cousin or other relative, the one thing you cannot conclude from the historical record is that Mary had other children. That option was not considered viable in the early Church.

St. Athanasius (356)

Let those, therefore, who deny that the Son is by nature from the Father and proper to his essence deny also that he took true human flesh from the ever-virgin Mary.[409]

St. Epiphanius (ca. 360)

In his greatest work, *Panarion* ("Bread Box"), Epiphanius dismantles an enormous number of errors and heresies known in his day. Here he refutes the sect he refers to as the *antidicomarianites*, who were known for *opposing Mary* and the Marian doctrines. One

---

408. CCC 500.
409. *Discourses Against the Arians*, 2, 70.

can't help but notice the passion in Epiphanius when he confronts the matter of the Perpetual Virginity. He is incensed at the thought that anyone would dare deny it!

> Whether [Mary] died, I don't know; and [even] if she was buried, she never had carnal relations perish the thought! Who will choose, from self-inflicted insanity, to cast a blasphemous suspicion [on her], raise his voice, give free rein to his tongue, flap his mouth with evil intent, invent insults *instead of hymns and glory*, hurl abuse at the holy Virgin, and deny honor to the precious vessel?[410]

POPE ST. SIRICIUS (392)

> Surely, we cannot deny that regarding the sons of Mary the statement is justly censured, and your holiness rightly abhors it, that from the same virginal womb from which Christ was born, another offspring was brought forth. For neither would the Lord Jesus have chosen to be born of a virgin if he had judged she would be so incontinent, that with the seed of human copulation she would pollute the generative chamber of the Lord's body, the palace of the eternal king.[411]

ST. AMBROSE (396)

> Imitate [Mary], holy mothers, who in her only dearly beloved Son set forth so great an example of maternal virtue; for neither have you sweeter children, nor did the Virgin seek the consolation of being able to bear another son.[412]

410. *Panarion*, 11, 5.
411. *Letter to Bishop Anysius.*
412. *Letters*, 63, 111.

St. Augustine (401)

Thus Christ by being born of a virgin who, before she knew who was to be born of her, had determined to continue a virgin, chose to approve, rather than to command, holy virginity. And thus, even in the female herself, in whom he took the form of a servant, he willed that virginity should be free.[413]

St. Cyril of Alexandria (431)

[T]he Word himself, coming into the Blessed Virgin herself, assumed for himself his own temple from the substance of the Virgin and came forth from her a man in all that could be externally discerned, while interiorly he was true God. Therefore he kept his mother a virgin even after her childbearing.[414]

Pope St. Leo the Great (450)

[N]ot by intercourse with man but by the power of God was [the Incarnation] brought about: for a virgin conceived, a virgin bore, and a virgin she remained.[415]

St. Jerome (383)

We departed from chronological sequence and saved Jerome for last here because in him you really get a sense of the indignation the Fathers held (you saw it in Epiphanius and Pope Siricius as well) for the claim that the mother of Jesus had other children.

And could the just man dare . . . to think of approaching her, when he heard that the Son of God was in her womb . . . We

413. *On Holy Virginity*, 4, 4.
414. *Against Those Who Do Not Wish to Confess That the Holy Virgin Is the Mother of God*, 4.
415. *Sermons*, 22, 2.

are to believe then that the same man who gave so much credit to a dream that he did not dare to touch his wife, yet afterwards, when he had learned from the shepherds that the angel of the Lord had come from heaven and said to them, "Be not afraid: for behold I bring you good tidings of great joy which shall be to all people, for there is born to you this day in the city of David a savior, which is Christ the Lord;" and when the heavenly host had joined with him in the chorus, "Glory to God in the highest, and on earth peace among men of good will;" and when he had seen just Simeon embrace the infant and exclaim, "Now let your servant depart, O Lord, according to your word in peace: for my eyes have seen your salvation;" and when he had seen Anna the prophetess, the Magi, the star, Herod, the angels; Helvidius, I say, would have us believe that Joseph, though well acquainted with such surprising wonders, dared to touch the temple of God, the abode of the Holy Ghost, the mother of his Lord?

Mary at all events kept all these sayings in her heart. You cannot for shame say Joseph did not know of them, for Luke tells us, "His father and mother were marveling at the things which were spoken concerning him."[416]

---

416. *On the Perpetual Virginity of Mary—Against Helvidius*, 8.

APPENDIX III
MARY'S VIRGINITY IN PARTU

In Chapter 7 we defended the Church's infallible teaching that presents Mary as virgin before (*ante partum*), during (*in partu*), and after (*post partem*) the birth of our Lord. But doesn't it seem redundant to say Mary remained virginal *during* Jesus' birth? If she was a virgin before and after, wouldn't that include the during part? Yes, it would, if the meaning of virginity *in partu* referred only to the absence of conjugal relations, but it doesn't. Among the Fathers, as well as in magisterial teaching of the Catholic Church, *in partu* denotes a particular meaning that renders its inclusion necessary. It means Mary's physical virginal integrity was maintained when she gave birth to Christ.[417]

The Biblical Texts

EZEKIEL 44:1–3

> Then he brought me back the way of the gate of the outward sanctuary which looketh toward the east; and it was shut. Then said the LORD unto me, "This gate shall be shut, it shall not be opened, and no man shall enter in by it; because the LORD, the God of Israel, hath entered in by it, therefore it shall be shut."

As we will see below, this was a common text used among the Fathers, and by the Church, to indicate Mary remained an intact virgin in giving birth to Christ. Mary is the "gate" that remains shut even while the Lord passes through it miraculously.

---

417. This virginal integrity means that Mary's womb and hymen would remain uninjured and intact even after giving birth to Christ.

SONG OF SOLOMON 4:12

> A garden locked is my sister, my bride, a garden locked, a
> fountain sealed.

To many in the early Church, this text signified that Mary's womb
was shut and "sealed" by God. Christ himself used divine power to
pass through her womb without breaking that "seal," just as he would
later pass through a "sealed" tomb at his Resurrection and through
a "door being shut where the disciples were" in John 20:19.[418]

ISAIAH 7:14

> Therefore, the Lord himself shall give you a sign; Behold, a
> virgin shall conceive, and bear a son, and shall call his name
> Immanuel.

That this prophetic *sign* or miracle would involve a virgin both
conceiving and *bearing* a child, many of the Fathers of the Church
have argued, means the miracle involved both the conception *and*
the birthing of Jesus.[419] Thus, Mary would remain a virgin, inviolate, in both conceiving and in bearing Jesus Christ.

The Historical Record

This belief is found remarkably early and widely disseminated
among the Fathers. To get a sense of its antiquity, we will go back
to two familiar sources we've seen before: the *Protoevangelium of
James* (ca. A.D. 140), and St. Clement of Alexandria's Stromata (ca.
A.D. 200). First from Clement:

---

418. As early as St. Jerome's *Letter 48—To Pammachius*, 21, we find Mary referred to as
     "the enclosed garden" of Song of Solomon 4:12. Fra Angelico's famous *Annunciation*
     masterpiece is one among many works of art depicting the Blessed Mother in this
     context as well. It was painted ca. 1430–32.
419. For example, St. Ambrose, *The Synod of Milan*, 390. We will cite the text below.

It appears that even today many hold that Mary, after the birth of her son, was found to be in the state of a woman who has given birth, while in fact she was not so. For some say that, after giving birth, she was examined by a midwife, who found her to be a virgin.[420] These things are attested to by the scriptures of the Lord, which also give birth to the truth and remain virginal . . . "She gave birth and did not give birth,"[421] Scripture says, since she conceived by herself, not as a result of union with a man.[422]

When Clement says "she was examined by a midwife, who found her to be a virgin," he is referencing the *Protoevangelium of James,* which gives very graphic details of how the midwife arrived just as the miraculous birth of our Lord was occurring, and found Mary to be an intact virgin with no signs of having undergone labor. Another woman, Salome, then examines Mary and confirms the miracle.

St. Ephrem the Syrian (ca. 350)

Who loves you is amazed and who would understand is silent and confused, because he cannot probe the mother who gave birth in her virginity. If it is too great to be clarified with words the disputants ought not on that account cross swords with your Son.[423]

St. Gregory Nazianzen (ca. 380)

Believe in the Son of God, the Word before all the ages, who was . . . in these last days, for your sake, made Son of Man, born

---

420. Clement here references the *Protoevangelium of James*, 19–20.
421. Clement here references the apocryphal *Pseudo-Ezekiel*, which other Christian writers cite as "Scripture" as well, e.g., Tertullian, *De Carne Christi* 23, PL 2, 790.
422. *Stromata*, 7, 16.
423. *Songs of Praise*, 1, 2.

of the Virgin Mary in an indescribable and stainless way, for there is no stain where God is and whence salvation comes.[424]

St. Ambrose of Milan (ca. 390)

Who is this gate, if not Mary [referring to Ezekiel 44:1–2]? Is it not closed because she is a virgin? Mary is the gate through which Christ entered this world, when he was brought forth in the virginal birth and the manner of his birth did not break the seals of virginity. . . . There is a gate of the womb, although it is not always closed; indeed only one was able to remain closed, that through which the one born of the virgin came forth without the loss of genital intactness.[425]

St. Augustine of Hippo (ca. 400)

That day, then, the Word of God, the day which shines upon the angels, the day which brightens the homeland from whence we came, was born clothed in flesh of the Virgin Mary, was wondrously brought forth, for what is more wondrous than the child-bearing of a virgin? She conceives and is still a virgin; she brings forth her child and remains a virgin. He was formed in her whom he himself formed; he gave her fertility but he did not mar her integrity.[426]

St. Proclus of Constantinople (ca. 430)

O Virgin, unmarried maid, mother without the corruption of birth . . . [427]

---

424. *Oration on Holy Baptism,* 40:45.
425. *The Consecration of a Virgin and the Perpetual Virginity of Mary,* 8, 52.
426. Sermon 189, 2.
427. *Homily* 4, 2.

Venantius Fortunatus (ca. 580)

Observe: He wanted to be born from a maiden's womb; See from whose flesh the High Lord's flesh comes forth. The venerable Spirit, wishing to dwell in a virginal house, leaves her womb intact.[428]

St. Gregory the Great (ca. 600)

What is so remarkable about the fact that, after his Resurrection, the eternal Conqueror entered through closed doors? After all ... did he not come forth without opening the Virgin's womb?[429]

St. John Damascene (ca. 730)

But just as he who was conceived kept her who conceived still virgin, in like manner also he who was born preserved her virginity intact, only passing through her and keeping her closed (Ezek. 44:2).[430]

St. Jerome (ca. 400)

We left our chronological ordering of quotes here once again in order to present St. Jerome, who, as we've said before, opposed using "apocryphal rantings" like the *Protoevangelium of James*, and yet he clearly taught the miraculous nature of Mary's virginity *in partu*. This shows Jerome's belief was rooted in a tradition that has roots before the *Protoevangelium*. In this passage from his *Homily on John*, he answers the question of how Mary could have remained a virgin *in partu*:

---

428. *Carmina Miscellanea* 8, 6.
429. *Homilae in Evangelium* 26, 1.
430. *On the Orthodox Faith* IV, 14.

Do you want to know how he was born of a virgin and how, after his birth, his mother remained a virgin? The doors were locked, yet Jesus entered. There is no doubt that the doors were locked. He who entered through the locked doors was not a phantom or a ghost but a true body. For what did he say? "Look at me and see that a ghost does not have flesh and bones as I do" (Luke. 24:39).[431]

Magisterial Statements

POPE ST. LEO THE GREAT

This is taken from the famous and dogmatic "Tome of Leo" written in 449 and read on the floor of the Council of Chalcedon, to which the fathers of the Council responded, "Peter has spoken through Leo."

Indeed he was conceived by the Holy Spirit within the womb of the virgin mother, who bore him without losing her virginity just as she conceived without losing her virginity . . .

He was generated in a new nativity, because inviolate virginity [that] did not know concupiscence furnished the material of his body. From the mother of the Lord, nature, not guilt, was assumed; and in the Lord Jesus Christ born from the womb of the Virgin, because his birth was miraculous, nature was not for that reason different from ours. For he who is true God, is likewise true man.[432]

POPE PELAGIUS I (557)

Christ Jesus true God and the same true man proceeded, that is, was born, while his mother's virginity remained intact: for

---

431. *Homily on John* I, 1–14.
432. *Lectis Delectionis Tuae*, also known as *Letter 28*, or *The Tome*, sections II and IV.

the Virgin remained such in bearing him just as she had in conceiving him.[433]

THE LATERAN COUNCIL (649), PRESIDED OVER BY POPE ST. MARTIN I

If anyone does not, following the holy Fathers, confess properly and truly that holy Mary, ever virgin and immaculate, is Mother of God . . . and that, in the latter age, she gave birth to [Christ] without corruption, her virginity remaining equally inviolate after his birth, let him be condemned.[434]

CREED OF THE COUNCIL OF TOLEDO XVI (693)

And as the Virgin acquired the modesty of virginity before conception, so also she experienced no loss of her integrity; for she conceived a virgin, gave birth a virgin, and after birth retained the uninterrupted modesty of an intact virgin.[435]

POPE PIUS IV (1555)

The Council of Trent condemns the Unitarians for a number of false teachings, among them:

[T]hat the same most blessed Virgin Mary is not the true Mother of God and did not always persist in the integrity of virginity, namely, before giving birth, in giving birth, and perpetually . . . We demand and warn on behalf of the Almighty God, Father, Son, and Holy Spirit, and by apostolic authority.[436]

Lumen Gentium, the Dogmatic Constitution on the Church, 57, declares:

---

433. *Letter to King Childebert* I.
434. Canon 3.
435. Profession of Faith, Art. 19.
436. DS 1880.

This union of the Mother with the Son in the work of salvation
is made manifest . . . at the birth of our Lord, who did not
diminish his mother's virginal integrity but sanctified it.

Significantly, the Church here footnotes Ephesians 1:18, connecting this mystery to

having the eyes of your hearts enlightened, that you may know
what is the hope to which he has called you, what are the
riches of his glorious inheritance in the saints.

The council fathers allude to the traditional understanding that
Mary's preservation of her virginal integrity even in the act of
giving birth was an example of the saving power of Christ in her
life—an example of "what are the riches of his glorious inheritance in the saints."

The *Catechism* quotes the above-cited *Lumen Gentium* 57, but
also adds:

The deepening faith in the virginal motherhood led the
Church to confess Mary's real and perpetual virginity even in
the act of giving birth to the Son of God made man. In fact,
Christ's birth "did not diminish his mother's virginal integrity
but sanctified it" (499).

The Modern Popes

Pope Pius XII, in his apostolic constitution *Munificentissimus Deus*,
refers to "the Seraphic Doctor," St. Bonaventure, who also held
this view:

Along with many others, the Seraphic Doctor held the same
views [concerning the Assumption of Mary]. He considered
it as entirely certain that, as God had preserved the most holy
Virgin Mary from the violation of her virginal purity and

integrity in conceiving and in childbirth, he would never have permitted her body to have been resolved into dust and ashes.[437]

In his encyclical *Mystici Corporis*, as well he alludes to this teaching:

> Within her virginal womb Christ our Lord already bore the exalted title of Head of the Church; in a marvelous birth she brought Him forth [*mirando partu edidit*] as the source of all supernatural life, and presented Him newly born, as Prophet, King and Priest to those who, from among Jews and Gentiles, were the first to come to adore Him.[438]

Beyond stating that *the birth* of Christ was miraculous, and not just his conception, which is itself telling, Pope Pius XII uses language—*mirando partu*—well-known in the tradition to refer to the miraculous birth of our Lord, which preserved her virginal integrity.

Pope Paul VI, in his 1967 Letter on the Blessed Virgin Mary, *Signum Magnum*, states:

> Therefore, the life of Joseph's pure spouse, who remained a virgin "during childbirth and after childbirth" as the Catholic Church has always believed and professed and as was fitting for her who was raised to the incomparable dignity of divine motherhood—was a life of such perfect union with the Son that she shared in His joys, sorrows and triumphs.

Later, in his 1974 Apostolic Exhortation, *Marialis Cultus*, he declared:

---

437. *Munificentissimus Deus* 32. Here, the Holy Father mentions this belief in passing as he is defending and explaining the Assumption.

438. Ludwig Ott quotes a better translation in his *Fundamentals of Catholic Dogma*, 206. He has *mirando partu edidit* as "she . . . gave *miraculous* birth," which we believe is more in keeping with the context of this letter. Pope Pius is not referring to a "marvelous" event; he is referring to a "miraculous" event, which is within the semantic range of *mirando* in Latin.

The Christmas season is a prolonged commemoration of the divine, virginal and salvific motherhood of her whose "inviolate virginity brought the Savior into the world."

POPE ST. JOHN PAUL II

In a general audience on January 28, 1987, Pope John Paul II references the text we cited above from the Lateran Council (649), teaching:

Mary was therefore a virgin before the birth of Jesus and she remained a virgin in giving birth and after the birth. This is the truth presented by the New Testament texts, and which was expressed both by the Fifth Ecumenical Council at Constantinople in 553, which speaks of Mary as "ever virgin," and also by the Lateran Council in 649, which teaches that "the mother of God ... Mary ... conceived [her Son] through the power of the Holy Spirit without human intervention, and in giving birth to him, her virginity remained incorrupted, and even after the birth her virginity remained intact."

On June 10, 1992, during a talk in Capua, Italy, he further declared:

It is a well-known fact that some of the Church Fathers set us a significant parallel between the begetting of Christ *ex intacta virgine* [from the inviolate Virgin] and his resurrection *ex intacto sepulcro* [from the sealed tomb]. In the parallelism relative to the begetting of Christ, some of the Fathers put the emphasis on the virginal conception, others on the virgin birth, others on the subsequent perpetual virginity of the Mother, but they all testify to the conviction that between the two saving events— the generation/birth of Christ and his resurrection from the dead—there exists an intrinsic connection which corresponds to a precise plan of God: a connection which the Church led by the Spirit, has discovered, not created.

[I]t is necessary for the theologian, in presenting the Church's doctrine on Mary's virginity to maintain the indispensable balance between stating the fact and elucidating its meaning. Both are integral parts of the mystery: the meaning, or symbolic value of the event is based on the reality of the fact, and the latter, in turn, reveals all its richness only if its symbolic meanings are unfolded.

And finally, in his *Urbi et Orbi* message of Christmas 2005, Pope Benedict XVI stated:

With the shepherds let us enter the stable of Bethlehem beneath the loving gaze of Mary, the silent witness of his miraculous birth.

A Modern Objection

Some theologians have objected to virginity *in partu*, claiming that connecting Mary's virginity to her physical "virginal integrity" is an archaic notion that needs to be abandoned.[439]

Did the Fathers and Doctors of the Church indeed think that if Mary's hymen would have been broken, she would no longer be a virgin? Perhaps some did, but if we just consider perhaps the greatest Father and perhaps the greatest Doctor of the Church—St. Augustine and St. Thomas Aquinas—we know at least with these great men this was not the case:

---

439. Albert Mitterer's famous 1952 study, *Dogma und Bioligie der Hieligen Familie*, claimed a miraculous birth of Christ was archaic and must be abandoned. And according to Alan C. Clark's 1973 paper published in *Theological Studies*, this study put the matter to rest. But as we have seen, the Church did not and does not agree, having reiterated the miraculous nature of Christ's birth again and again since then in multiple magisterial documents cited above. And this is not to mention the *monitum* the then Holy Office issued against like publications of Mitterer's that called into question this teaching of the Church.

ST. AUGUSTINE

For the sanctity of the body does not consist in the integrity of its members, nor in their exemption from all touch; for they are exposed to various accidents which do violence to and wound them, and the surgeons who administer relief often perform operations that sicken the spectator. A midwife, suppose, has (whether maliciously or accidentally, or through unskillfulness) destroyed the virginity of some girl, while endeavoring to ascertain it: I suppose no one is so foolish as to believe that, by this destruction of the integrity of one organ, the virgin has lost anything even of her bodily sanctity. And thus, so long as the soul keeps this firmness of purpose which sanctifies even the body, the violence done by another's lust makes no impression on this bodily sanctity, which is preserved intact by one's own persistent continence.[440]

ST. THOMAS AQUINAS

As stated above, the integrity of a bodily organ is accidental to virginity, in so far as a person, through purposely abstaining from venereal pleasure, retains the integrity of a bodily organ. Hence if the organ lose its integrity by chance in some other way, this is no more prejudicial to virginity than being deprived of a hand or foot.[441]

Both Augustine and Thomas understood that sanctity and virginity are not lost through the breaking of the hymen. So belief in Mary's virginity *in partu* is not meant to preserve her purity or sanctity. It goes much deeper than that—to the dignity of *Christ*. In the *Summa*, Thomas gives four central reasons for this belief:

---

440. Sermon 189, 2.
441. *Summa Theologiae* II, IIae, Q. 152, Art. 1, Reply Obj. 3.

1. Isaiah 7:14 reveals "Behold a virgin shall conceive and bear a son." Thomas held this text to indicate that her virginal integrity is revealed to remain both in conceiving *and in giving birth.*

2. He says this teaching follows because it was "in keeping with a property of him whose birth is in question, for he is the Word of God." "The word" is both conceived in the mind and proceeds out of the mind without diminishment or corruption. Therefore, it is "fitting" that the Word of God be born of an incorrupt virgin.

3. Thomas takes Augustine's position that we cited above in saying, "He came for this purpose, that He might take away our corruption. Wherefore it is unfitting that in his birth he should corrupt his mother's virginity. Thus Augustine says in a sermon on the nativity of our Lord: 'It was not right that He who came to heal corruption, should by his advent violate integrity.'"

4. It was "fitting," says Thomas, that "He who commanded us to honor our father and mother should not in his birth lessen the honor due to his mother."[442]

At first there seems to be a contradiction here. Thomas says above that the physical breaking of the hymen would not destroy virginity, but then here he says that Jesus' breaking Mary's hymen during birth would have "corrupted" her virginity. What gives?

We must understand that Thomas (and Augustine) is arguing from what is "fitting," not as a matter of natural necessity. Both Augustine and Aquinas make clear that the loss of her physical virginal integrity would not have caused Mary to lose her virginity in a moral sense. She could have remained a perpetual virgin still. Nonetheless, Thomas says it would not be "fitting" that the Son of God would destroy that which is a sign of virginity in his

442. Ibid., III, Q. 28, Art. 2.

mother. For the Fathers of the Church, as well as Thomas, that bodily integrity is important as a sign to the world of Mary's Perpetual Virginity.

Furthermore, being preserved in her virginal integrity also means she would have been preserved from the pain that would have been involved in its destruction. This leads us to our next appendix, where we will consider whether Mary was preserved from *all* of the pains of labor, not just in the preservation of her physical virginal integrity. These two concepts are distinct, but very closely related.

APPENDIX IV

MARY'S FREEDOM FROM
THE PAINS OF LABOR

In the wake of the first (human) sin of Adam and Eve, God spoke directly to our original parents and indirectly to all mankind concerning some of the far-reaching consequences of that sin: Physical death and disorder would be the lot of all mankind until the end of time.[443] Indeed, in some sense, all of creation was changed for the worse as a result of this cataclysmic sin.[444] But for our purpose we want to focus on Genesis 3:16 and one particular effect of original sin:

> To the woman [the Lord God] said, "I will greatly multiply your pain in childbearing; in pain you shall bring forth children."

Scripture teaches that as a result of original sin, God would "greatly multiply" the pains of labor not only for Eve, but for all women.[445] Many Fathers of the Church and theologians down through the centuries believed that Mary alone was exempt from such pains as a sign of her unique holiness. Thus, Mary's freedom from the pains of labor is our eighth reason for belief in the Immaculate Conception of our Lady.

The Church has taught this as well on the level of the ordinary magisterium, but not with the same degree of authority with which it has taught her virginity *in partu*. Nonetheless, that it has

---

443. Cf. Gen. 2:17.
444. Cf. CCC 396–409; Cf. Gen. 3:17, Rom. 8:22–23.
445. There are those today who posit the possibility that there would have been some sort of pain in childbearing even before the fall because the text says women's pain would "multiply." This is most likely an idiom that simply means there would be pain, not that there had already been pain and it would now be worse. Anyway, this is the general understanding of the Church, as we see in CCC 1606–1609.

been taught on the level of the ordinary magisterium and was taught by many Fathers of the Church is significant.

While there is certainly no argument from necessity here, we argue that Mary's freedom from childbirth pains was most fitting as a sign of hope for the entire body of Christ. All can see in this unique gift to Mary a sign of the ultimate deliverance from all bodily pain and suffering that awaits the Church. Mary demonstrates in a more profound way both the truth of the Immaculate Conception and the saving power of Christ in preserving her from this effect of original sin.[446]

Moreover, when we consider Mary as *the beginning of the new creation*, as we saw when we examined reasons for her Immaculate Conception, how fitting indeed is it that the "new creation" would be inaugurated without the pains of childbirth—one of the principle effects of sin in the first creation?

What evidence do we have for this belief? We will examine it from three sources: Scripture, history, and the teaching of the Catholic Church as it is communicated to the faithful through both magisterial teaching and in the liturgy. And we will then examine some of the most common objections.

Sacred Scripture

ISAIAH 66:6–8

In a chapter laden with references to the coming of the New Covenant, or "the new heavens and the new earth" as we see in Isaiah 66:22—a text referenced in Revelation 21:1—we find this startling prophecy:

---

446. Some will object here, referring to 1 Timothy 2:15: "[W]oman will be saved through bearing children, if she continues in faith and love and holiness, with modesty." But that does not mean Christian women will experience freedom from labor pains. Granted. However, Mary's "salvation" in childbearing seems to be seen in a unique sense in Catholic tradition as well as in Scripture. If she did experience freedom from labor pains, it was not out of necessity; rather, she becomes a unique salvific and eschatological sign. More on this below.

Listen, an uproar from the city! A voice from the temple! The voice of the Lord, rendering recompense to his enemies! Before she was in labor she gave birth; before her pain came upon her she was delivered of a son. Who has heard such a thing? Who has seen such things?

Not only do we find the Fathers of the Church referencing this text as referring to the miraculous birthing of Christ,[447] but we find it difficult to apply this text in its fullest sense to anything else.

LUKE 2:7

And she brought forth her firstborn son, and wrapped him in swaddling clothes, and laid him in a manger; because there was no room for them in the inn.

According to St. Thomas Aquinas (who references St. Jerome), Mary's "wrapping" and then "laying" Christ in a manger is an indicator that she did not endure the normal pains of labor.[448] Even in our day, doctors or nurses would do this kind of work. In the first century, it would be a midwife. Yet the Bible seems to indicate Mary did this *by herself.*

The Bar of History

The Gnostics of the first centuries of the Christian era were prolific. And as a result, we find much of Christian writing during this period to be apologetic responses to Gnostic claims. Not surprisingly, Gnostic writers affirmed Mary's freedom from labor pains because they characteristically denied Christ possessed a physical body at birth. Mary would naturally be free from pain in bringing forth a phantom Christ.

What is fascinating to discover is that some of the very earliest

447. For example, St. Gregory of Nyssa, *On the Song of Songs* 13, cited below.
448. *Summa Theologiae* III, Q. 35, Art. 6, Reply to Obj. 3.

Christian writers who were engaged in writing specifically *against* Gnosticism *agreed* with the Gnostics that Mary gave birth without pain. Here are some examples to give us a sense of the antiquity of this teaching:

ODES OF SOLOMON

These are Coptic Christian hymns discovered in 1909 and dated to the late first century or early second century. Their emphasis on Christ's physical body indicates that they are not Gnostic. Note the mention of Christ "[taking] on [human] nature." These ancient hymns seem to acknowledge Mary's freedom from the effects of original sin in childbirth as a matter of history, rather than for a particular theological reason.

Ode 7:

> He became like me so I could receive him, he thought like me so I could become him and I did not tremble when I saw him for he was gracious to me.

> He took on my nature so I could learn from him, took on my form so I would not turn away.

Ode 17:

> I was crowned by God, by a crown alive. And my Lord justified me. He became my certain salvation. I was freed from myself and uncondemned. The chains fell from my wrists . . .

> They became the limbs of my body and I was their head.

Ode 19:

> The Spirit opened the Virgin's womb and she received the milk.

The Virgin became a mother of great mercy; she labored, but not in pain, and bore a son. No midwife came.

ASCENSION OF ISAIAH (APOCRYPHAL)

This book "is a composite work comprising three originally distinct writings, the *Martyrdom of Isaiah* ... which is of Jewish origin; a Christian apocalypse, known as the *Testament of Ezekiel;* and the *Vision of Isaiah*, also of Christian origin."[449]

The *Ascension of Isaiah* also dates back to the first and second centuries and the Jewish part perhaps before the first century. It is noteworthy that it may well have been alluded to in the New Testament—in Hebrews 11:37. In the midst of referencing the great and heroic virtue of men and women of the Old Covenant, the inspired author of Hebrews here mentions that "they were sawn in two" just as the *Ascension of Isaiah* recounts of Isaiah. This work shows heavy Gnostic influences, but because it was most likely alluded to in Scripture, it is worth considering.[450]

Chapter 5:

And while they were alone, Mary looked up and saw a little child, and she was frightened. And at that very moment her womb was found as it had been before she had conceived.[451]

THE PROTOEVANGELIUM OF JAMES (A.D. 140)

This text was quoted often by Fathers of the Church and is definitely Christian. It is this ancient writer who gave us our traditional names of Mary's parents, St. Anne and St. Joachim. In it,

---

449. *A Catholic Commentary on Holy Scripture*, 123–124.

450. Some may argue Hebrews 11:37 and the *Ascension of Isaiah* are both referencing a common tradition so that the inspired author of Hebrews may not have been referring to it, rather to the tradition. We find this argument weak.

451. Gambero, *Mary in the Fathers of the Church*, 33–34.

there is a very graphic depiction of the birth of the Lord. Luigi Gambero writes:

> The absence of labor pains and the sometimes crudely realistic examinations carried out by the midwife and a woman named Salome, who was then punished for her unbelief, confirm Mary's virginity in the act of giving birth. At the same time, the realism with which the Lord's birth is described leads one to think that the apocryphal gospel means to oppose the error of Gnostic Docetism, which considered Christ's body to be a mere appearance or phantasm.[452]

Because this work was anti-Gnostic in nature, it gives a strong argument for the belief of Christians to coincide with Gnostics concerning this matter of Mary's freedom from labor pains. As Gambero mentioned, the author went to great lengths to make it clear that Jesus possessed an actual body and Mary was actually pregnant, yet that she gave birth in a miraculous fashion.

Perhaps even more important is the second-century work of St. Irenaeus. No one would say he was influenced by Gnosticism. He was the second century's strongest defender of orthodoxy against Gnosticism. Yet, in his *Demonstration of the Apostolic Preaching,* we find:

> For behold, [the prophet Isaiah] saith, the virgin shall conceive and bring forth a son: and he, being God, is to be with us . . . And yet, concerning his birth the same prophet says in another place: Before the pains of travail came on, she escaped and was delivered of a man-child [referring to Isa. 66:22].[453]

St. Gregory of Nyssa, brother of St. Basil and one of the three "Cappadocian Fathers," gives us a window into what was the

---

452. Ibid., 40.
453. *The Demonstration of the Apostolic Preaching,* 54.

commonly held view of the birth of our Lord in the fourth century, writing ca. 380:

> His conception did not result from the union of two humans; his birth was not polluted in any way: *there were no labor pangs*; his bridal chamber was that of the power of the Most High, which covered virginity like a cloud; the bridal torch was the splendor of the Holy Spirit; his bed was a personal condition devoid of vices; his nuptials were incorrupt . . . his birth alone *occurred without labor pains* . . . "Before the pangs of birth arrived, a male child came forth and was born" [Isa. 66:7] . . . Just as she who introduced death into nature by her sin was condemned to bear children in suffering and travail, it was necessary that the Mother of life, after having conceived in joy, should give birth in joy as well. No wonder that the angel said to her, "Rejoice, O full of grace!" [Luke 1:28] With these words he took from her the burden of that sorrow which, from the beginning of creation, had been imposed on birth because of sin.[454]

St. Proclus of Constantinople (ca. 420)

> What, then, is the mystery celebrated in yesterday's solemnity? The unexplainable mystery of the divinity and the humanity, a birth that leaves the Mother uncorrupt, an Incarnation that gives a form to the incorporeal Divinity, while it undergoes no passion, an extraordinary birth, a beginning for a generated One who has no beginning.[455]

St. Peter Chrysologus (ca. 430)

> She conceives as a virgin, she gives birth as a virgin, and she remains a virgin. Therefore, her flesh knows the power of the

454. *On the Song of Songs,* 13.
455. *Homily 3 on the Incarnation.*

miracle but does not know pain. In giving birth, it gains in integrity and knows nothing of physical suffering.[456]

St. John of Damascus (ca. 730)

His birth was in accordance with the laws of parturition, while in that it was painless it was above the laws of generation. For, as pleasure did not precede it, pain did not follow it, according to the prophet who says, Before she travailed, she brought forth, and again, before her pain came she was delivered of a manchild [Isa. 66:7].[457]

Magisterial Teaching

Though this teaching has never been the object of a formal definition of the Church and therefore is not infallible, the *Catechism of the Council of Trent* gives perhaps the clearest example of the general understanding of the Church through centuries past:

But as the Conception itself transcends the order of nature, so also the birth of our Lord . . . just as the rays of the sun penetrate without breaking or injuring in the least the solid substance of glass, so after a like but more exalted manner did Jesus Christ come forth from his mother's womb without injury to her maternal virginity.

From Eve we are born *children of wrath*; from Mary we have received Jesus Christ . . . To Eve it was said: *In sorrow shalt thou bring forth children.*[458] Mary was exempt from this law, for preserving her virginal integrity inviolate she brought forth

---

456. Sermon 117, 3.
457. *An Exposition of the Orthodox Faith*, IV, 14.
458. In Catholic tradition, you do not find the birth of Christ to be among "the Seven Sorrows" of our Blessed Mother; rather, it is one of the "seven joys" of our Lady.

Jesus . . . without experiencing, as we have already said, any sense of pain.[459]

It seems fitting: Eve's sin is causally linked to labor pain. The New Eve was uniquely free from the sin of Eve and did not experience that pain. Indeed, we would argue it would seem contrary to our sense of Jesus and Mary as the "New Adam" and the "New Eve" and, as we have seen, together the beginning of the New Covenant, to inaugurate this great and glorious covenant by experiencing pains that were the result of failure in the Old.

POPE ALEXANDER III (1169)

[Mary] indeed conceived without shame, gave birth without pain, and went hence without corruption, according to the word of the angel, or rather (the word) of God through the angel, so that she should be proved to be full, not merely half filled, with grace and (so that) God her Son should faithfully fulfill the ancient commandment that he had formerly given, namely, to treat one's father and mother with honor.[460]

The Liturgical Tradition

The Church at prayer, both East and West, reveals a common understanding of Mary having been freed from labor pains.

In the Mass of "Mary at the Foot of the Cross II," celebrated in the Latin Rite before the 1969 reform of the liturgy, the Church prayed:

---

459. *The Catechism of the Council of Trent* 1, Art. III, 45–46. We do not attempt to define physiology behind this teaching here. The *Catechism* says this great mystery can be likened to rays of sun passing through glass, but that the case of Christ is "more exalted" than that. Even at the ordinary level, the Church has never attempted to define how God actualized the miracle of Christ's birth. The Church simply teaches consistently that it was miraculous and Mary remained "intact."

460. Letter, *Ex Litteris Tuis*, written to an Islamic Sultan instructing him on the basics of the Catholic faith.

In your divine wisdom, you planned the redemption of the human race, and decreed that the new Eve should stand by the cross of the new Adam: as she became his mother by the power of the Holy Spirit, so, by a new gift of your love, she was to be a partner in his passion, and she who had given him birth without the pains of childbirth was to endure the greatest of pains in bringing forth to new life the family of your Church.

In the Byzantine liturgy, from the Feast of the Nativity of our Lord God and Savior, Jesus Christ, and from the Synaxis of the Theotokos, Tone 2:

Behold! The Image of the Father and his unchangeable eternity has taken the form of a servant. *Without suffering* he has come forth to us from an all-pure Virgin, and yet he has remained unchanged. He is true God as he was before, and he has taken on himself what he had not been, becoming man out of his love for all. Therefore, let us raise our voices in hymns, singing: O God, born of the Virgin, have mercy on us.

The liturgy of the Church has always been an exemplary tool of catechesis and moral certitude theologically as well as the primary instrument of our spiritual nourishment in Christ. Thus, the fact that the Church asks all her children to affirm Mary's freedom from the pangs of labor in liturgical prayer at Mass is a testimony as to the authority of this teaching of the Church.

The Critics' Critiques

Critics of this teaching will generally make four arguments we would do well to consider:

1. Genesis 3:16 does not say or even imply women would not have had pains *at all* during labor before "the fall"; it merely says those pains would be "multiplied." Why would Mary have experienced no pains at all?

The idea of women having labor pains before the fall is becoming more and more commonplace in popular Catholic culture today, but it has never been the teaching of the Church. In fact, as we mentioned above, CCC 1607–1609 teach the "pain of childbirth" (1607), or "pain in childbearing" (1609) to have been caused by original sin—not just an increase in that pain. Most likely, "I will greatly *multiply* your pain in childbearing" represents an idiom for "there will be much pain."

But even if the premise were true, however unlikely that may be, Mary's freedom from labor pangs was given to the Church as a singular privilege and sign accompanying absolutely unique events—the Incarnation and the Immaculate Conception. According to Scripture, there is a profound link between labor pains and original sin no matter if you believe Eve would have experienced minor pains in labor without the fall or not. Thus, freedom from all pains of labor would be a powerful sign pointing to Mary's unique holiness and freedom from the effects of original sin in order to be a fitting vessel for our incarnate Lord.

This objection also fails to consider that Jesus Christ as the New Adam and Mary as the New Eve were not just called to restore the Eden of Genesis. Adam and Eve, the Garden of Eden, and indeed all of creation, as glorious as it was originally created, was created "in a state of journeying" (*in statu viae*) toward God's ultimate plan for glory that is beyond words.[461] Thus, Mary's freedom from all pain can be viewed as a glorious and incarnational sign of the infallibly certain eschaton that will transform all of creation to a state where "[God] will wipe away every tear from their eyes, and death shall be no more, neither shall there be mourning nor crying nor pain any more, for the former things have passed away" (Rev. 21:4).

461. CCC 302.

2. If Mary did not experience the pain of childbirth, why the birth at all? Isn't this more like a Gnostic fairy tale that denies the Incarnation?

Fr. Valentine Long responds:

> The mystery of the Virgin Birth should cause no Manichaen uneasiness in any honest presentation of the facts . . . This (the Incarnation) . . . was no natural event . . . neither was the divine pregnancy in the first place. Neither was Christ's breaking out of the tomb alive. By whose authority has it become incongruous to associate the omnipotent with miracles?"[462]

In other words, a painless childbirth would no more deny the Incarnation than a virginal conception would. Christ's miraculous conception is seen in Scripture as a prophetic "sign" that the Messiah is among us.[463] It in no way denies Christ was fully man.

Would a baby born by C-section somehow be "less human" because the mother did not experience the normal sequence of labor pains? Would a baby who is cloned, as immoral as that procedure is, be less than human? Of course not! Being born truly human is not in any sense contingent upon the labor pains of the mother.

3. If Mary did not experience the pangs of labor then she would not be able to really empathize with women down through the millennia who do experience those pains.

Mary was not free from all pain, but only this one particular kind of pain and for particular theological reasons. Mary's

---

462. Valentine Long, *The Mother of God*, 52–53.
463. Cf. Isa. 7:14, Matt. 1:23.

calling from the very beginning was to suffer with her Son in a way no other human person could ever imagine. As Our Lady of Sorrows, Mary can certainly empathize with all of our pains in this life.

Perhaps more importantly, this idea leads to logical problems. Would Mary have had to experience the most physical pain of any woman in order to be able to empathize with all women? Would she have had to experience post-partum depression, too? How about sin? Why do we call her "help of sinners" if she never experienced the reality and pain of sin?

And could we not continue this line of reasoning to include Christ himself? How could Christ really understand us sinners if he never sinned? How could Christ really understand holy matrimony if he never married? And we could go on.

APPENDIX V
ANSWERING FOUR FALSE CHARGES
ABOUT PATRISTIC MARIOLOGY

In his book, *Mary—Another Redeemer?* James White makes a truly intriguing argument against the Immaculate Conception:

> Leo I, the great bishop of Rome from 440–461, rejected the idea that anyone but Christ was sinless. He taught, "Alone therefore among the sons of men the Lord Jesus was born innocent, because alone conceived without pollution of carnal concupiscence." In fact, as Philip Schaff points out, *seven different popes taught doctrine that was contrary to what was defined as "Christian dogma" in the nineteenth century.*

How is it that even Roman bishops could teach contrary to an infallible dogma? Simply because the doctrine did not exist and was not a part of anyone's thinking for the majority of Church history! Oh yes, as Marian devotion developed, more and more people spoke of her in terms that would lead one to think of her as being without personal sin, but even this does not go so far as to say that she was conceived without original sin itself . . . The early Fathers taught that Mary had sinned. Even Roman Catholic historians and theologians admit this. Ott writes the individual Greek Fathers (Origen, Basil, John Chrysostom, Cyril of Alexandria) taught that Mary suffered from venial personal faults, such as ambition and vanity . . . He also admits, "Neither the Greek nor the Latin Fathers explicitly teach the Immaculate Conception of Mary."[464]

464. White, *Mary—Another Redeemer?*, 40–41.

In a footnote, White cites Schaff as claiming that the six popes apart from Leo the Great who rejected the Immaculate Conception were Gregory I, Innocent III, Gelasius I, Innocent V, John XXII, Clement VI (1352). A little further down, he references Ludwig Ott's statement that the Fathers did not explicitly teach the Immaculate Conception to demonstrate that "the [Immaculate Conception] did not exist and was not a part of anyone's thinking for the majority of Church history!"

I will respond to these assertions in four points.

1. The sermon of Pope Leo I referenced by Schaff, like any sermon by any pope, is not an infallible declaration of doctrine. Even if one were to find error in it, it would not affect the integrity of the teaching authority of the Church. In the fifth century, Mary's freedom from original sin was not officially defined yet, and besides, Leo was not even teaching on the topic, much less defining it.

2. Curiously, White fails to provide a citation for this allegedly damning quote from Leo I. (I have tried to find it without success.) Perhaps White was mistranslating or adding his own gloss to a passage from one of St. Leo's sermons on the nativity of Christ (we have four of them—sermons 21–24). In those sermons we find passages such as this one:

> Christ, however, was begotten in a new kind of nativity, conceived by a virgin, born of a virgin, without the concupiscence of paternal flesh, without injury to maternal integrity . . . His origin is different but his nature is the same. Human usage and custom was lacking, but by divine power it was brought about that a virgin conceived, a virgin bore, and virgin she remained . . . And if in all mothers conception does not take place without stain of sin, this mother drew purification from the source whence she conceived. For the mildew of sin did not make its entry where the transferral of paternal seed did not obtain. Inviolate virginity knew no

concupiscence when it waited upon the substance. The Lord took from his mother our nature, not our fault.[465]

We see that Leo's context is a teaching about the pollution of carnal concupiscence, which can be aroused when men and women engage in sexual intercourse. Since the birth of Jesus was from a virgin there was no sexual union involved; hence, no "pollution of carnal concupiscence."[466] Moreover, here he is preaching about the unique circumstances of Jesus' conception, not contrasting that conception with Mary's or saying anything else about the state of her soul. That is not the topic of his sermon.

Even if he were correctly quoting Pope Leo in his uncited and elusive reference, White seems to be imputing to him an idea he never held and a meaning he never meant to communicate.

3. When White claims there are "six other popes" who rejected the Immaculate Conception and "taught doctrine that was contrary to what was defined as 'Christian dogma' in the nineteenth century," he relies completely upon Schaff's scholarship. In his *The Creeds of Christendom* we read in a footnote:

> The proof is furnished by the Jansenist Launoy, *Proescriptions*, *Opera I*. pp. 17 sqq., who also shows that the early Franciscans, and even Loyola and the early Jesuits, denied the Immaculate Conception of Mary. Perrone calls him an irreligious innovator (p. 34) and an impudent liar (p. 161),

---

465. Sermon 22, 2–3.

466. Leo seems to have been following the Augustinian belief that original sin is communicated through the "paternal seed" and through concupiscence that accompanies the conjugal act. The Church has never defined original sin as such, and since humans can now be conceived without sexual intercourse it seems unlikely to be true, but it was a common theological opinion and not in any way a dogmatic teaching.

but does not refute his arguments, and evades the force of his quotations from Leo, Gelasius, and Gregory by the futile remark that they would prove too much, viz., that Mary was even born in sin, and not purified before the Incarnation, which would be impious![467]

White provides the reader with an assertion backed up with a footnote referencing another footnote in another book. When we track down that last footnote, we discover it does not give one direct quotation from any of the popes accused of denying the Immaculate Conception. Neither White nor Schaff provides *one single quotation* from any of these six popes!

Instead Schaff presumes to base his conclusions on a dialogue between a Catholic theologian, Perrone, and a *Jansenist heretic,* Launoy, that occurred hundreds of years ago. And guess what? The heretic Launoy does not provide a direct reference to any of the popes listed either. Schaff seems to place his full trust in the fact that Perrone—who considered Launoy "an impudent liar"—does not individually refute each assertion. Schaff considers this to be *conclusive evidence* that these statements of various popes must exist and must declare Mary to be a sinner.[468]

Can you imagine bringing this kind of "proof" into a court of law? Or what if a polemicist were to make a similarly bold claim about Sacred Scripture without presenting one reference to an actual chapter and verse? Would not any apologist, whether Catholic or Protestant, demand to be provided with such a citation? If the polemicist could not do so, would he be taken seriously?

467. Schaff, *The Creeds of Christendom,* 1, 123.
468. We should remember that even if one *were* to find noninfallible statements from popes containing error, those would have no impact on the integrity of definitive Catholic teaching. But White and company can't even find *one* such statement from *one* pope on this matter. Score one for the Catholics!

4. White quotes Ludwig Ott's *Fundamentals of Catholic Dogma* out of context, omitting crucial information that sheds light on Ott's true meaning.

Ott *does* say, as White quotes, that some Greek Fathers taught that Mary "suffered from venial personal faults." But personal faults are not sins, and the word *sins* is nowhere to be found. White then fails to mention Ott's next words:

> The Latin Patristic authors unanimously teach the doctrine of the sinlessness of Mary. St. Augustine teaches that every personal sin must be excluded from the Blessed Virgin Mary for the sake of the honor of God (*propter honorem Domini*) [*De natura et gratia*, 36, 42], St. Ephrem the Syrian puts Mary, in her immaculateness, on the same plane as Christ. According to the teaching of St. Thomas the fullness of grace which Mary received in the active conception (according to modern theology, in the passive conception) implied confirmation in grace and therefore sinlessness [*Summa* III, q. 27, art. 5 res. 2].[469]

Ott also indeed says that neither Latin nor Greek Fathers "explicitly teach the Immaculate Conception." However, White fails again to quote what follows:

> Still, they teach it implicitly (*implicite*), in two fundamental notions:
>
> a) Mary's most perfect purity and holiness. St. Ephrem says: Thou and thy mother are the only ones who are totally beautiful in every respect; for in thee, O Lord, there is no spot, and in thy mother no stain (*Carm Nisib.* 27). Augustine says that all men must confess themselves sinners. "Except the Holy Virgin Mary, whom I desire, for

469. Ott, *Fundmentals of Catholic Dogma*, 203.

the sake of the honor of the Lord to leave entirely out of the question, when the talk is of sin" . . . (*De natura et gratia* 36,42). According to the context, however, this must be taken as referring to freedom from personal sin.

b) The similarity and contrast between Mary and Eve. Mary is on the one hand, a replica of Eve in her purity and integrity before the Fall, on the other hand, the antitype of Eve, insofar as Eve is the cause of corruption, and Mary the cause of salvation. St. Ephrem teaches: Mary and Eve, two people without guilt, two simple people, were identical. Later, however one became the cause of our death, the other the cause of our life" (*Op. Syr.* 2, 327).[470]

The Catholic Church acknowledges that there was development in the understanding of Mary's sinlessness, just as there is development in the understanding of *all* dogma. Belief in Mary's sinlessness was there from the beginning of the Christian era, but its full implications would take time to unpack. The failure of early Fathers to mention the fully developed doctrine by name, then, does not equal disbelief in it.

---

470. Ibid., 201.

APPENDIX VI
QUEENSHIP HAS ITS PRIVILEGES

While the accumulation of examples from the Old Testament concerning the "Queen Mother" is impressive, as we saw in Chapter 14 above, if we were to seek *a single typological example* from the Old Testament that communicates the most complete image of the dignity, power, and privileges of Mary as Queen of Heaven and Earth, the best place to go would be to the example of a pagan king and his Jewish wife, Esther. Let us consider this familiar yet remarkable Old Testament story.

The Book of Esther is set during the years of the exile of Israel in Babylon, specifically during the reign of Ahasuerus, king of Persia.[471] The Persian kings were very mild in their treatment of the Jews, resulting in many Jews enjoying great favor in the kingdom. Esther was the ultimate example of this favor. Scripture tells us King Ahasuerus "loved Esther more than all the women, and she found grace and favor in his sight more than all the virgins, so that he set the royal crown on her head" (Esther 2:17). The king had a harem, as was the custom of the day, but Esther's beauty and virtue had especially pleased the king, resulting in her being exalted as his most beloved queen.

Sometime after Esther was made queen, Ahasuerus promoted a man named Haman to the rank of grand vizier in the kingdom. Haman developed an intense hatred for the Jews and was determined to eliminate them from the entire kingdom. He lied to the king, claiming the Jews were rebellious and plotting insurrection, resulting in a royal edict that every Jew in the kingdom would be put to death.

When Esther's uncle, Mordecai, who had raised her after her parents' deaths, made the decree known to Queen Esther, beg-

471. *Ahasuerus* is his Hebrew name. His Greek name is the more well-known *Artaxerxes*.

ging for her intercession with the king, Esther was faced with a
dilemma:

> All the king's provinces know that if any man or woman goes
> to the king inside the inner court without being called, there is
> but one law; all alike are to be put to death, except the one to
> whom the king hold out the golden scepter that he may live.
> And I have not been called (4:11).

After prayer and fasting as well as asking all Jews in the local area
to pray and fast on her behalf, Esther put on her royal apparel and
went before the king. When she entered the palace and throne
room with much fear and trepidation, the king "comforted her
with soothing words, and said to her, 'What is it Esther? I am your
brother. Take courage; you shall not die, for our law applies only
to the people. Come near'" (15:8–10).[472] Esther then revealed Haman's plot, and the king reversed the edict of death and instead
had Haman executed for his treachery.

Some ninety years ago, Bishop Frederick Justus Knecht ex-
pounded upon the powerful Marian typology found in the book
of Esther:

> *Esther is a type of the ever Blessed Virgin Mary.* Esther, on account
> of her beauty, was raised from her low estate to be queen: Mary,
> on account of the beauty of her pure and humble heart, was
> raised to be the Mother of the Redeemer, and afterwards,
> Queen of Heaven. Esther alone was exempted from the king's
> severe law: Mary alone is exempted from the curse of original
> sin. Esther, adorned in splendid garments, went before the
> king, prayed for her people, and was heard: Mary, the Queen of

---

472. These verses are found in the LXX and in Catholic Bibles, but not in Protestant bibles.
But even without them, one still gets the idea from the text that the law of death to
those who approach the king without invitation did not apply to Queen Esther (see
any Protestant version of Esther 4:10–5:3).

Heaven, radiant with virtues and merits, goes before the throne of God to intercede for her people.[473]

Esther's freedom from the law of death was rooted in her royal dignity. Her people, Israel, came to experience that freedom through her intercession. What a beautiful image of our blessed queen and mother. Through her intercession the penalty of death that has come upon us all through the sin of Adam and Eve is removed and we can experience the freedom of a truly royal sonship.

---

473. Knecht, *A Practical Commentary on Holy Scripture*, 356.

WORKS CITED

John Ankerberg and John Weldon, *Catholics and Protestants—Do They Now Agree?* (Eugene, Or.: Harvest House Publishers, 1995).

William Barclay, *The Daily Study Bible Series* (Philadephia: The Westminster Press, 1976), Vols. 1–17.

Lorraine Boettner, *Roman Catholicism* (Philadelphia: The Presbyterian and Reformed Publishing Company, 1962).

Raymond E. Brown, S.S., Joseph A. Fitzmeyer, S.J., Roland E. Murphy, O. Carm., eds., *The Jerome Biblical Commentary* (Englewood Cliffs, N.J.: Prentice Hall, 1968).

John Calvin, *Commentary on a Harmony of the Evangelists, Matthew, Mark, and Luke,* trans., Rev. William Pringle (Grand Rapids, Mich.: Christian Classics Ethereal Library, 2009).

Catechism of the Catholic Church, second edition (Citta del Vaticano: Libreria Editrice Vaticana, 1997).

Catechism of the Council of Trent (Rockford, Ill.: TAN Books and Publishers, 1982).

The Catholic Encyclopedia (New York: The Encyclopedia Press, 1913). Vols. 1–15.

Alan Clark, *The Virgin Birth* (London: Catholic Truth Society, 1973).

F. L. Cross, ed., *The Oxford Dictionary of the Christian Church* (Oxford: Oxford University Press, 1997).

Heinrich Denzinger, *Compendium of Creeds, Definitions, and Declarations on Matters of Faith and Morals,* ed., Robert Fastiggi and Anne England Nash, forty-third edition (San Francisco: Ignatius Press, 2012).

Austin Flannery, ed., *Vatican Council II—The Conciliar and Post Concilar Documents* (Boston, Mass.: St. Paul Editions, Daughters of St. Paul),Vols. 1–2.

Frank E. Gaebelein, ed., *The Expositor's Bible Commentary* (Grand Rapids, Mich.: Regency Reference Library, Zondervan Publishing House, 1979),Vols. 1–12.

Luigi Gambero, S.M., *Mary and the Fathers of the Church*, trans.,Thomas Buffer (San Francisco: Ignatius Press, 1999).

Norman Geisler and Ralph MacKenzie, *Roman Catholics and Evangelicals—Agreements and Differences* (Grand Rapids, Mich.: Baker Books, 1995).

Scott Hahn, *Hail, Holy Queen* (New York: Doubleday, 2001).

John Hardon, S.J., *The Catholic Catechism* (New York: Image Books, Doubleday, 1981).

George Haydock, *The Douay-Rheims New Testament of Our Lord and Savior Jesus Christ with a Comprehensive Catholic Commentary* (Monrovia, Ca.: Catholic Treasures, 1992),Vols. 1–2.

James Allen Hewett, *New Testament Greek—A Beginning and Intermediate Grammar* (Peabody, Mass.: Hendrickson Publishers, 1986).

David Hill, *Greek Words and Hebrew Meanings* (Cambridge: Cambridge University Press, 1967).

Dave Hunt, *A Woman Rides the Beast—The Roman Catholic Church and the Last Days* (Eugene, Or.: Harvest House Publishers, 1994).

E. Kautzsch, ed., *Gesenius' Hebrew Grammar* (Oxford: Clarendon Press, 1910).

Karl Keating, *Catholicism and Fundamentalism* (San Francisco: Ignatius Press, 1988).

Frederick Justus Knecht, D.D., *A Practical Commentary on Holy Scripture* (Rockford, Ill.: TAN Books and Publishers, 2003).

St. Irenaeus, *The Demonstration of the Apostolic Preaching,* trans., Armitage Robinson, D.D. (New York: The Macmillan Co., 1920).

Henry George Liddel and Robert Scott, *A Greek-English Lexicon* (Oxford: Oxford University Press, 1990).

Valentine Long, O.F.M., *The Mother of God* (Chicago: Franciscan Herald Press, 1976).

Patrick Madrid, ed., *Surprised by Truth* (San Diego, Ca.: 1994).

Walter Martin, *The Kingdom of the Cults* (Minneapolis: Bethany Fellowship, Bethany Publishing House, 1977).

James McCarthy, *The Gospel According to Rome—Comparing Catholic Tradition and the Word of God* (Eugene, Or.: Harvest House Publishers, 1995).

Fr. Mateo, *Refuting the Attack on Mary* (San Diego, Ca.: Catholic Answers, 1999).

J. Michael Miller, C.S.B., ed., *The Encyclicals of John Paul II* (Huntington, Ind.: Our Sunday Visitor, 1996).

Albert Mitterer, *Dogma und Biologie der Hieligen Familie* (Vienne: Herder Verlag, 1952).

William D. Mounce, *The Analytical Lexicon to the Greek New Testament* (Grand Rapids, Mich.: Zondervan Publishing House, 1993).

The Navarre Bible (Dublin: Four Courts Press, 1988).

Jacob Neusner, *The Babylonian Talmud—A Translation and Commentary* (Peabody, Mass.: Hendrickson Publishers, 2005), Vols. 1–22.

Barclay M. Newman, *A Concise Greek-English Dictionary of the New Testament* (London: United Bible Societies, 1971).

Dom Bernard Orchard, O.S.B., ed., *A Catholic Commentary on Sacred Scripture* (New York: Thomas Nelson & Sons, 1953).

Michael O'Carroll, C.S.S.P., *Theotokos—An Encyclopedia of the Blessed Virgin Mary* (Collegeville, Minn.: The Liturgical Press, 1982).

Ludwig Ott, *Fundamentals of Catholic Dogma* (Rockford, Ill.: TAN Books and Publishers, 1952).

Jaroslav Pelican (Vols. 1–30) and Helmut T. Lehman (Vols. 31–55), eds., *Luther's Works* (St. Louis: Concordia Publishing House, Vols. 1–30; Philadelphia: Fortress Press, Vols. 31–55; 1955).

Wayne Pipken, trans. and ed., *Selected Writings of Huldrych Zwingli* (Eugene, Or.: Pickwick Publications, 1984).

Johannes Quasten, *Patrology* (Allen, Tex.: Christian Classics, 1986).

Archibald Thomas Robertson, *Word Pictures in the New Testament*, Vols. 1–6 (Nashville, Tenn.: Broadman Press, 1930).

Philip Schaff, *The Creeds of Christendom* (Grand Rapids, Mich.: Baker Book House, 1990).

Philip Schaff and Henry Wace, eds., *Nicene and Post-Nicene Fathers*, Vols. 1–38 (Peabody, Mass., 1994).

Herbert Weir Smyth, *Greek Grammar* (Cambridge, Mass.: Harvard University Press, 1984).

Robert Charles Sproul, *The Holiness of God* (Wheaton, Ill.: Tyndale House Publishers, 1985).

Eric Svendsen, *Evangelical Answers: A Critique of Current Roman Catholic Apologists* (Lindenhurst, N.Y.: Reformation Press, 1999).

Jimmy Swaggart, *Catholicism and Christianity* (Baton Rouge, La.: Jimmy Swaggart Ministries, 1986).

Norman P. Tanner, ed., *The Decrees of the Ecumenical Councils* (Washington, D.C.: Georgetown University Press, 1990).

St. Thomas Aquinas, *Commentary on the Gospel of John*, part 1, chapters 1–7, trans., James A. Weisheipl, O.P. (Albany, N.Y.: Magi Books, 1998).

St. Thomas Aquinas, *Summa Theologica*, trans., Fathers of the English Dominican Province (Westminster, Md:. Christian Classics, 1981).

J.W. Wenham, *The Elements of New Testament Greek* (Cambridge: Cambridge University Press, 1981).

John Wesley, Joseph Benson, *The Works of the Reverend John Wesley* (London: Thomas Cordeux, 1812).

William Whiston, trans., *The Works of Josephus—Complete and Unabridged* (Peabody, Mass.: Hendrickson Publishers, 1987).

James R. White, *Mary—Another Redeemer?* (Minneapolis, Minn.: Bethany House Publishers, 1998).

C.D. Yonge, trans., *The Works of Philo—Complete and Unabridged* (Peabody, Mass.: Hendrickson Publishers, 1993).

Robert M. Zins, *Romanism—The Relentless Roman Catholic Assault on the Gospel of Jesus Christ!* (Huntsville, Ala.: White Horse Publications, 1995).